MANAGING OLDER EMPLOYEES

MANAGING OLDER EMPLOYEES

Gordon F. Shea

Jossey-Bass Publishers
San Francisco • Oxford • 1991

MANAGING OLDER EMPLOYEES
by Gordon F. Shea

Library of Congress Cataloging-in-Publication Data

Shea, Gordon F., date.
Managing Older Employees / Gordon F. Shea —1st ed.
p. cm.—(The Jossey-Bass management series)
Includes bibliographical references and index.
ISBN 1-55542-391-4
1. Aged—Employment—United States. I. Title II. Series.
HD6280.S52 1991
658.3′042—dc20 91-20922
CIP

Manufactured in the United States of America

The paper in this book meets the guidelines for permanence and durability of the Committee on Production Guidelines for Book Longevity of the Council on Library Resources.

JACKET DESIGN BY VICTOR ICHIOKA

FIRST EDITION

Code 9194

The Jossey-Bass Management Series

Consulting Editors
Human Resources

Leonard Nadler
Zeace Nadler
College Park, Maryland

To my grandchildren

Shawn Rabideau
Trevor Shea
and
Christine Shea

May their working lives be long and joyful.

While people enjoy their work they may in time slow down,
but they will find few reasons to stop.

CONTENTS

	Preface	xi
	The Author	xvii
	Part One: A Revolution in the Modern Workplace	**1**
1.	Changing Perspectives on Older Employees	3
2.	Facing the Demographic Imperatives	16
3.	Shedding Common Myths About Older Employees	28
4.	Addressing the Issues of Health and Wellness	44
	Part Two: Older Employees and Organizational Success	**59**
5.	Realizing the Potential of Older Workers	61
6.	Successful Health and Wellness Programs	71

7. Training and Education 85

8. Motivating and Building Morale 101

9. Appraising Older Employee Performance 114

Part Three: Supervision and Leadership 125

10. Ensuring Success on the Job 127

11. Developing Productive Work Teams 139

12. Overcoming Low Productivity 152

13. Leadership Techniques for Maximum Performance 169

14. Creating Alternative Work Programs 180

15. Keeping Pace with Changes in the Workforce 190

Resource: Legal Aspects of Working with Older Employees 207

References 221

Index 232

PREFACE

I will be sixty-five years old when this book is published. Each day, I look forward to my work with enthusiasm, energy, and the expectation of joy. On most days, I receive the abundant satisfaction that comes from being able to do good work. In these respects, I am like millions of other older people, both in the United States and elsewhere around the globe, who enjoy being able to stay connected with the work of society, who contribute to our economic well-being, and who reap the rewards of having friends and associates in the workplace.

While some people are happily retired, many others long for a return to some type of useful work. We need policies and methods for ensuring that those who are able to and want to work can do so. I have been fortunate. I have known the pleasures of challenging work, been treated well by supervisors, and been able to grow and develop in the workplace. I have also started and currently run my own business. Along the way, I have had a lot of fun at work, enjoyed more triumphs than failures (oh, there have been some of each), and been helped by a lot of loyal friends. These are the things that keep people in the workforce. They are what wise, considerate, and effective managers can provide. If managers do their job well, the workplace problems of older employees will largely be solved. It is to this end that this book is aimed. I just hope that I can continue to work for another sixty-five years.

In *Managing Older Employees* I provide managers at all levels with some straightforward ideas about how they might manage even more effectively a resource that we have long taken for granted—our older employees. The ideas presented here emerge from the comprehensive research that went into this book, research that often contradicts common stereotypes, misinformation, and ill-conceived biases about the abilities and problems of older employees that pervade our business world.

I hope that this book helps fill the current gap left by a lack of concentration on the whole issue of managing older employees, including how to view older people as a company resource and how to lead them effectively. It offers lessons from the companies that manage older workers productively and shows the reader how to avoid the traps encountered by organizations that squander or abuse the potential inherent in older employees. So much of our economic and social health rests on the quality of the management offered to our workforce and the productivity gains or losses that this leadership produces that I consider this to be one of the most critical issues facing our society today.

As in all situations, new problems can be the impetus to new opportunities if we react wisely. My position on our use of our older working population is simple and positive—we have an enormous human resource available that will flee the workplace if we continue to treat it badly but that can contribute mightily to our gross national product and the quality of our lives if we respond constructively, fairly, and humanely.

For the purposes of this book, I use the workplace-oriented definitions of *training, education,* and *development* popular in the human resource development field:

- *Training*—learning focused on the present job of the learner
- *Education*—learning focused on a future job for the learner
- *Development*—learning that is not job-focused

Thus, when training is offered by an employer (as is generally the case), it is intended to correct deficiencies in performance, to introduce new methods or processes, to update or refresh understanding of a policy or procedure, or to accomplish some similar purpose. From this perspective, it is usually job-related education (rather than training) that organizations fail to provide to the older worker, because some organizations (or their managers) do not see the older employee as having much of a future with them.

Audience

Among the types of readers who can benefit from this work are the following:

- Executives and top-level policy makers who determine how the organization's human resources are conserved, developed, or squandered and who are concerned about the effects of their decisions on the long-term viability of their organization's workforce and of society as a whole.
- Managers and leaders at all levels who daily interact with older employees in the workplace. These individuals have the greatest personal impact on the working lives of older workers and can benefit most from the productivity inherent in them.
- Human resource managers or personnel managers, who often recommend or determine how the people in the organization will be treated, collectively and individually. The policies and procedures that they promulgate need to take into account the effects of their actions on the workforce on which they depend.
- Trainers and consultants. This book can serve as a resource to course designers, educators, human resource specialists, and other consultants in a wide range of disciplines.
- General readers. I also believe that this work can be of interest and value to general readers ranging from lawmakers to personnel specialists and from older workers themselves to individuals interested in the future of our nation. The book also deals occasionally with other groups and populations within the workforce, such as younger employees, minorities, and unions, who

may also find it of interest, for their futures are all inseparably linked with the fate of older employees.

The management of older employees is becoming a worldwide problem. Demographics in Western Europe, Japan, and other technically advanced nations are following similar patterns. A host of other rapidly developing countries, from Korea to Singapore and from Brazil to Mexico, will have an aging workforce like that of the United States in only a few decades (if not sooner). Gradually, most Third World countries will follow similar aging patterns, which will compound their other social and economic problems. Consequently, there is much need for all people to study the experiences of more developed societies, swap ideas, and learn from each other. I have done some borrowing from abroad and used examples from the experiences of other societies to demonstrate important points. I hope that this book is useful in furthering this exchange.

Overview of the Contents

Part One provides a national perspective on the effective use of our aging workforce and frames the more detailed discussions that follow.

Chapter One offers a challenge to management and others to adapt successfully to a variety of workforce and workplace changes while conserving the productivity of older employees. It discusses older workers as a national resource, considering how old is old in today's context and demonstrating that many, if not most, retired Americans prefer some type of work to the idleness that some people experience in retirement.

In Chapter Two, I provide the facts and figures that enable the reader to appreciate the demographic and labor-force shifts that make the effective management of older people imperative and describe what the payoffs will be if we are successful.

Chapter Three deals with a number of key myths that lead employers to shed older employees and offers some counter data for reality assessment.

Chapter Four offers considerable information on the realities of the health of older employees and how it can be enhanced in the workplace.

Part Two deals with the general problems of employing older people from an organizational perspective.

Chapter Five describes the high productivity potential of older workers to contribute to organizational success. It offers powerful data to counteract the often erroneous notion that people become less able as they age, and it explains how to capitalize on the special productive assets offered by older workers.

In Chapter Six, I offer many examples of how employers have profitably contributed to the general health and wellness of their older employees.

Chapter Seven deals with training and educating our older workforce, explains how critical those efforts are becoming, and describes what some leading firms are doing with special methods to update older employees.

Chapter Eight provides a host of ideas on how supervisors and managers can increase the output of older workers and effectively overcome past demotivation. In Chapter Nine, I suggest proven methods that employers can use to fairly appraise older employee performance and achieve age-neutral human resource management.

Part Three focuses more specifically on one-to-one relationships between managers and leaders and the older employee.

With Chapter Ten, I begin a discussion of what individual supervisors can do to ensure older worker success on the job. In this chapter, I deal with fair and effective supervisory leadership, offering suggestions for providing a safe and productive workplace and addressing the possible problems of a younger supervisor who must oversee the work of older employees.

Chapter Eleven focuses on team development, addressing the problems of continued inclusion, resolving age-related work-group conflict, and the special contributions that older employees can make to work-group success.

Chapter Twelve deals in great detail with the problem of what to do when an older employee is not producing adequately or appears to be "retired on the job."

Chapter Thirteen provides a wide variety of proven techniques for maximizing employee output and gaining the best from an older person. This chapter also deals with workplace and leadership developments that will affect older employees at work.

Chapter Fourteen offers a wide variety of case studies and examples of what has been done and can be done to ensure continued productive employment of older workers. This includes alternative work arrangements, new approaches to setting organizational policies, and sources of help that managers can tap in their own efforts to offer greater work opportunities to America's aged.

Chapter Fifteen portends some dynamic developments that could greatly affect our future workforce, draws together the various threads of managing a productive older workforce, and offers a challenging opportunity for our common future as our workforce ages.

The book also provides a special resource section, which explains the Age Discrimination in Employment Act and suggests ways that managers and their organizations can avoid lawsuits and legal actions under this law.

Acknowledgments

I would like to express appreciation to Jeffrey Eicher, Miriam Schneider, Christine Shea, and Jose Silva, research assistants, for their help in assembling the research materials on which many of the conclusions in this book are based. Also thanks to Leonard Nadler, Zeace Nadler, and Steven Piersanti, who helped edit this book, for their extensive patience and great help in the manuscript, and to the person who played computer magic with the text, Mirga Massey, a truly exceptional secretary.

Beltsville, Maryland Gordon F. Shea
August 1991

THE AUTHOR

Gordon F. Shea is president of PRIME Systems Company, a training and human resource development firm headquartered in Beltsville, Maryland. He holds a B.A. degree from Syracuse University and an M.A. degree from George Washington University in geography and economic development.

Shea received extensive air force training in electronics and worked as a technical writer and production engineer for corporations such as Honeywell and Litton Industries. Before forming PRIME Systems Company, he served for twenty-five years as a supervisor, manager, and executive in government and private industry.

Shea is the author of eight previous books and numerous articles on management. His works include *The New Employee* (1981), *Creative Negotiating* (1983), and *Building Trust for Personal and Organizational Success* (1988). As a trainer and educator, he regularly conducts short courses, seminars, and workshops for corporations, government agencies, associations, and universities. He has trained for or consulted with more than 500 organizations.

Shea is a public speaker who appears regularly on the lecture circuit. In addition, he keynotes conventions, professional association meetings, and executive conferences.

Managing Older Employees

Part One

A REVOLUTION IN THE MODERN WORKPLACE

To successfully manage our aging workforce, we must substitute reality for our myths and assumptions about older people. This part provides an overview of the problems and opportunities related to the employment of older people.

First, the United States, as well as other societies, is undergoing tremendous changes related to our aging population, our global competitive position, and the social meaning of work. How we manage these several "revolutions" will determine in large measure our economic, social, and political future.

Second, we need to establish the nature, dimensions, and directions of the workforce changes that are under way in America.

Third, many common myths about older workers are demonstrably false but still widely held. Until these myths are wiped away, they will continue to cloud our judgment and perpetuate many past errors.

Fourth, we need a more general understanding of the importance of meaningful work to the mental, emotional, and physical health of older people and of how we can improve their workplace wellness.

These four primary concerns provide a general perspective on the more detailed issues related to how we manage older employees.

Chapter 1

Changing Perspectives on Older Employees

America has always been a young country—young in people, young in hope, young in ideals, young in culture, young in attitudes, and young in outlook—until recently. The unspoiled nature of the land when Europeans arrived, the experimentation with a fresh form of government, the vast opportunities for the dominant culture, rejection of old-world values, and the hard physical work required to clear the forests, work the farms, and run the factories led to a logical focus on youth, strength, and vigor, rather than on contemplation, experience, and wisdom. At the same time, slave ship captains and plantation owners paid premium prices for the young and able slaves, and the Native American tribes relied on their young warriors to stem the encroachment of the European-based civilization. For the most part, youth carried the burden and reaped many of the rewards. After all, one might never live to get old—and most did not.

This focus on the young, our hope and our future, grew naturally in the minds of the people. Until recently, old age, often starting in a person's forties, was a time of decline, of ailments and lessened abilities. With child factory labor common until the twentieth century and children seen as assets by farm families, who produced them in large numbers, the gains from youth were apparent to all. Because young adults, until recent decades, often had their intellectual growth stunted and suffered the accumulated ravages of common diseases, marginal nutrition, polluted work environments, and common plagues, growing old was seldom seen as a benefit.

Yet just as things were beginning to change—that is, as many common diseases were being conquered, the life-span was extending, the standard of living of the average person was improving, retirement for some seemed a possibility, and the health and wellness of older people were improving—Hollywood, radio, and eventually television discovered the youth market, and our economic focus came to generate a youth-oriented culture. In the 1950s and 1960s, it became fashionable to "not trust anyone over thirty," but youth's time was running short.

In the last two decades, it has become apparent to even the less alert observer that our society is undergoing substantial changes related to our age concepts and age realities. Gray-power politics, a significant and growing proportion of our population retired from productive contribution to the commonweal, and the aging of the workforce itself portend great changes in the way society deals with older people now that the post–World War II baby boom is well into middle age.

Since our society and our workforce are aging rapidly, new ways must be found to ensure a longer working life for those who wish or need it, enhanced contribution to society of the skills and knowledge possessed by older people, and better overall management of this special component of our human resources.

Yet we are not alone in all of this. All of the advanced societies, from Western Europe to Japan, are experiencing the same type of age shifts in their populations and are encountering many of the same problems associated with these changes that the United States is. We have an opportunity to learn from them and they from us as we move into this age of the aged.

The Problem

For more than two decades, I have been concerned about the strong, persistent tendency for many companies, institutions, and government agencies to force older employees out of the workforce or to bribe them into taking early retirement. Who will pay for all of this idleness? In a single day, a productive, earning, contributing human being might become a fallow, consuming, disconnected retiree, a state in which many stay for the rest of their lives.

Social Security funds and pension benefits are not wealth except in the minds of the beneficiary. These funds are a call upon wealth. Real wealth is the goods that we produce and the services that we render. When a person leaves the workforce, he or she may become a total consumer rather than a producer. More dollars from pension funds released into the marketplace to chase fewer goods and services is the classic prescription for inflation and economic trouble. Older people who continue to contribute to the commonweal are a valuable national asset and should be treated as such by managers and policymakers at all levels.

While it is true that many people have joyfully sought the freedom of retirement as a way to escape the confinement, boredom, and sometimes onerous work of their jobs, others have wished to continue gainful employment and enjoy the satisfaction of comradeship, a satisfying routine, interaction with customers, or the pleasures of interesting and challenging work. Sadly, for such people, being pushed out has often been accompanied by the implication that they were somehow not as good as or as valuable as younger employees.

Early in 1990, the Commonwealth Fund, a New York-based philanthropic organization that has been studying older employees, reported that one-third of "career personnel" are retired by age fifty-five and that almost half the career jobs are over by age sixty. Once released, many of these early retirees never return to the workforce, and those who do return often have to settle for lower-paying jobs. Yet the fund reports that a national survey that it commissioned reveals that there are nearly two million American workers between ages fifty and sixty-four who are ready, willing, and able to return to work ("Millions of Older Workers . . .," 1990, p. 6). Such workers have been producing for most of their adult lives, seldom require any special training, and are often willing to do fill-in work (that is, flexible-schedule, part-time, or seasonal work). Though they have often been victims of age bias, these are proven people with much to contribute. Could this encouraged or enforced idleness be another example of some managements taking short-term gains while creating long-term losses for all of us? When a person wants to work but cannot, our loss is great. While some retirees continue to provide valuable services to our society, others do not.

I have found through considerable research a set of very complex interlocking problems related to how we manage or mismanage our human resources and the lives of many of our long-term employees, on the job and afterward. There is a great need for an examination of how those older employees who would like to continue working can be managed so that their productive potential continues to contribute to our gross national product (GNP) and our nation's social and economic well-being.

If the early-retirement trend continues, we will have more and more people being supported by a shrinking labor force and the continued idling of older people, as well as the waste of their talents and abilities even when working. Unless comprehensive corrective measures are taken, this situation could explode within a decade or two into a crisis involving severe generational conflicts, further productivity losses, greater intraorganizational strife as more people turn to lawsuits to resolve age disputes with management, a loss in national competitiveness, and the overall obsolescence of the fastest-growing segment of our workforce—older employees.

The older employee problem is not an abstraction to be solved by some government agency or personnel policy alone. It is an issue that each of us must face when dealing with an older employee, whether we be supervisor, co-worker, personnel specialist, or executive; whether we set policy or implement it; and whether we serve as counselor, friend, or a helping agent to older employees when they face the decision of whether to continue working. Each older person must also decide on how he or she personally will handle this challenge.

The plight of older employees faced with stereotyping, discrimination on the job, and in some cases declining capabilities who nevertheless could be productively employed is a very human problem. Much personal suffering can occur because of a lack of caring in the workplace, failure to see win-win options about job and work choices for older people, and insensitive, poorly conceived, and even discriminatory policies and their implementation. Ann McLaughlin, U.S. secretary of labor, summed it up well (Rones and Herz, 1989, p. i): "Older workers are a national resource. They are skilled and experienced. When they leave the workforce before they are ready, both they and society lose. . . . As we review the implications of an aging population, it becomes clear that we must pay particular attention to the problems of older workers. Public policy should strive to accommodate both those who are ready to retire and those who would like to continue to work. Institutional barriers must be lowered and innovative approaches developed. The efforts of private sector employers will be the major key to success."

The Challenge to Management

Until quite recently, much of this formerly minority resource—whether workers, professionals, or managers—has been, on the whole, poorly managed. For a long time, aging employees in our organizations have been largely cut off from job-related education, development, and promotional opportunities because "they're too close to retirement." With the continued aging of our workforce and the increasing clout of older employees, we can no longer afford to take a casual view of one of our few resources that is growing in quantity and quality as the years go by. Perhaps nowhere are new attitudes, new practices, and new visions more needed than in the management of older employees.

How productive our workforce remains (or becomes), the quality of working life experienced by all employees, and, in large measure, the future of our economy and society are highly dependent on how well older people, individually and collectively, are managed and supervised. It is clear that we will be increasingly dependent on older employees to produce for and manage our society. Above all, we need a more balanced look at our workforce if we are to gain maximum advantage from each of our age segments in the decades ahead.

To appropriately appraise this shift from a focus on youth to one on older workers, we need to deal with two preliminary questions: (1) What is different about managing an older employee? (2) Why is how we manage the older employee important to us?

What Is Different About Managing an Older Employee?

Older employees want most of the same things out of work that others want: income, dignity, a sense of belonging, security, a chance to contribute, recognition, interesting work, opportunities to show what they can do, companionship, respect, career growth, influence over what happens to them, and so on. These common desires of older personnel are shared with employed people of all ages, but (as with others) each person's list and priorities are special and individual. On the other hand, some things about an older employee are different. For instance:

- Older employees, by various definitions, are a legally protected class of workers, and how management relates to them definitely will affect the organization and those employed by it.
- They often have some options and protections that younger people may lack, such as vested pension plans and seniority rights.
- They are part of a growing political constituency that has and will continue to have a powerful effect on labor laws and public policy.
- They are and for some time to come will be one of the fastest-growing components of the workforce; consequently, organizations will be increasingly dependent on them.
- They represent a health and wellness influence on organizational operations that will grow as their average age and their numbers increase in the workplace.
- They are often subjected to many prejudices and stereotypes that hamper their ability to contribute to their employers' well-being.
- They represent a powerful potential for (often unexpected) productivity gains.

Why Is How We Manage the Older Employee Important?

Many of the characteristics of older people are particularly suited to the emerging information age: As their physical prowess, so appropriate to the machine age, declines, their institutional memory, ability to synthesize, and judgment tend to increase in value. As a society, we will increasingly have to invest in the productive potential of older people or see unnecessary declines in our gross national product while laying out increasing sums for the encouraged idleness of some of our best workers. Many employers must change many of their ways of doing business if they are to encourage older people who need or want to work to remain employed. Many questionable past and current management practices have greatly wasted the knowledge and ability of older people. Such practices need to be identified and remedied.

Managing a progressively aging workforce may be one of the greatest challenges faced by management in the next several decades. The productivity and wealth of any society depend on the effective management of its resources. We have reached the point in human development where our future hinges on how well we manage our most valuable form of capital—ourselves. In time, all of us who survive will be part of our older population. How well we live and relate to each other will depend in large measure on how well we manage.

How Old Is Old?

People in the United States not only are living longer; they are living younger. A person of fifty today is usually in better shape than the average forty-year-old was two decades ago. You have probably seen Grant Wood's painting *American Gothic,* in which a stern-faced farmer holds a pitchfork while his dowdy wife stands next to him. Colburn (1985, p. 12) points out that Jane Fonda, at the height of her success in selling her exercise videotapes, was at age forty-seven seventeen years older than that farmer's wife.

The notion that reaching a certain age renders one more useless than when one was younger is a relatively new one. Cooper and Torrington (1981, p. 2) have noted that "Until the end of the nineteenth century, people were not regarded as being old until they could no longer take care of themselves." For many reasons—some of them positive—this country has attempted to rigidly fix the point at which an individual presumably becomes less able and therefore retirable. It is increasingly questionable whether society can any longer afford to hold such a stance on working age.

When the Social Security Act was passed in 1935, a presidential pen stroke established age sixty-five as the accepted crossover point from working to nonworking (with a few exceptions, primarily related to disability, setting the age at sixty-two). Now federal law has abolished altogether any mandatory retirement age except for some special categories of employees. However, the Social Security system still uses the same general age categories. Ironically, just as Americans are tending to become physically and mentally more able at later ages, the early-retirement phenomenon in America indicates that the age at which a person is classed as old is coming down. So when is an employee considered old? The Age Discrimination in Employment Act includes everyone age forty and above. Nevertheless, though there is no firm agreement on any given number, there seems to be a consensus forming around the age of fifty as a way to distinguish between "middle-aged" and "older" employees.

Despite the law, few people in their forties see themselves as old, nor do most other people consider them to be old. Fifty seems useful, because many employees emotionally view the half-century mark as a watershed of their lives, and it is here that organizations begin to question the value of further investment in an older employee—especially organizations offering early-retirement options. But most importantly, it is at about fifty that certain types of age discrimination have traditionally become operable.

Many experts also view age fifty as a turning point in an individual's career. Traditionally, an employee is supposed to follow a steady climb up the ladder in experience, pay, or position, beginning in the early twenties and peaking in the late forties. At that point, one reaches a plateau, and if management policies take their usual course, a person thereafter is either static or moving downward; that is, receiving fewer promotions, fewer educational opportunities, and, perhaps, a decrease in responsibilities. This circumstance is based on the assumption that the individual is quickly approaching retirement or is in a state of declining abilities. Consequently, many employers set fifty-five as the age when employees may take early retirement, and this figure is built into some pension plans. Thus, for our purposes here, we will consider age fifty as the turning point (except when legal factors are involved), though the limitations of any such definition are quite apparent.

Need for New Visions

To successfully adapt to our rapidly changing world, we need a new vision, one that takes into account at least the following factors related to older workers.

The Knowledge Worker. The age of the highly trained and educated knowledge worker is surely here and will bear the brunt of our productivity challenge for decades to come. While service jobs may grow most rapidly, they only redistribute the wealth and make life easier. The generation of new wealth hinges on the knowledge and skills of the information age employee, whether it is the engineer designing a new product by computer or the researcher developing new superconductor materials. Will our rapidly aging workforce be prepared (educated and developed) to carry that burden?

The Learning Curve and Productivity. Every job has a learning curve. Generally, it is steep when a person is new to the job. That is, the employee's absorption of new information is very rapid at first. He or she learns many things and learns them quickly. Eventually, however, the curve tends to level off as one's work is mastered or to climb slowly as the job changes or evolves. For too long, the experience on which older employees have staked their claim to fame has often been an illusion. Thirty years of experience on a given job often meant one year of experience stretched out over thirty years, with only imperceptible real growth in learning occurring as the person aged. In the skilled trades and the professions, on-the-job learning did accrue over the years, but the great bulk of America's workers have been unskilled or semiskilled workers, with little change in their job over decades.

That picture, however, is changing. Old jobs are dying more

rapidly than ever. New ones are created rapidly. Rapid adaptation is becoming essential for all age groups. But what of older employees? Contrary to popular stereotypes, older workers can adapt successfully to new trades, master new skills, and learn as successfully as anyone—if proper training methods are used.

Lifetime Learning. A culture of continuing education must permeate the workplace and be operative for as long as the employee remains with an organization. Cutting older people out of available developmental and educational opportunities is indefensible.

Self-Investment. Older employees must also take greater responsibility for enhancing their own breadth and depth of knowledge and skills. Each employee and the employee's organization must cooperate in periodically rejuvenating the employee's learning through cross training, promotion, or even lateral transfers, to mention only a few of the devices that will accomplish that.

Changing Organizational Structures. The tall, hierarchical organizational structure is giving way to flatter, more versatile forms, where eternal career climbing may no longer pay off as the all-consuming passion of many younger people. Older employees tend to be more content with and in some ways more amenable to accepting the challenges of lateral transfers rather than climbing. Hence, they may flourish in an environment that is less structured.

Information Management. Peter Drucker (1988, p. 50) pointed out that older managers who have always found information scarce, expensive to develop, and slow in coming may now be swamped with it. Consequently, older managers may well need to be prepared to manage information more effectively if they are to stay on top of their jobs.

The Need for Wisdom. Information requires more than just management; it must be put to some useful purpose. Older employees may be uniquely qualified to make sense of our information glut. If they can stand back and put it in perspective, they can effectively direct its use. Meaningful experience, the ability to synthesize, and wisdom itself are somewhat related to age. But there is a whole emerging realm in adult education where these special abilities often found in older people can be heightened, focused, and directed toward constructive organizational ends.

Reversing Personal Curtailment. Rather than being viewed as a period of withdrawal, old age can be seen as a period of expanded productivity, joy, and accomplishment. Many older executives and business owners find this to be the most creative and exciting period of their working lives. Many retirees experience that same joy working in new and challenging fields. This notion of expanded mental capabilities and usefulness with age may well be the next great social movement in our society.

Self-Management and Expanded Personal Responsibility. Older people are increasingly finding that "if it's to be, it's up to me." This grasping of individual responsibility and declining reliance on institutions and organizations is a relatively new phenomenon in our general population. Self-assertion and taking personal responsibility seem to be a delayed reaction to the newfound independence inherent in a secure retirement income. Democratization of comfortable leisure, or at least the freedom to work at what you want, is creating a new social class who can and want to contribute to society.

Public Contribution by the New "Leisure Classes." Just as with earlier "leisure classes," many older people want to develop and use their talents productively, but not just to earn more income. For example, some enjoy the role of elder statesman, mentor, or ombudsman in the companies that employ them. A sense of mature responsibility is sure to grow in the decades ahead. We need effective general education to release the potential inherent in these emerging citizen-philosophers who do care what happens to us.

The Revolution Is Here

American society is in the throes of a major economic, social, and even political revolution—the equation of age versus youth has turned our world upside down in a relatively short period of time. In only a generation or two, we have gone from a youth-focused society to one where the aged wield primary power—and their power is growing. Does this mean generational strife, as some predict? The answer clearly rests on how we manage this shift in power.

Management implies directing effort to achieving some goal that has greater value than the energy, time, and resources expended to attain it. Whether we are managing to get to work on time, operating a university department, or directing the operations of a federal agency, it is expected that some kind of return will be greater than the investment we make, no matter how difficult it is to measure that gain. That return also involves a judgment regarding the relative value of the investment versus the end result. Therefore, when discussing the management of older employees, individually or collectively, we come quickly to the issue of how our effort is being directed and the value of that increment of return. Related, of course, is the question of whether, if we redirect that effort, we can increase our gain or the value of our return on the investment.

The answer to that question will affect each of us for decades to come. It will have a great influence on our gross national wealth, our level of international competitiveness, and the quality of work life for employees of all ages and possibly even the likelihood of intergenerational strife. This last point is critical. As the pool of younger workers shrinks and the economic burden of a ballooning retired population falls more heavily on fewer and fewer shoulders, the potential for civil conflict increases.

In a very real sense, our older employees are a key national asset, more vital to our future than oil or farmland or factories. Further, this is a workforce issue and a human productivity issue that includes everyone old enough to work and even many retirees who are still productive and contributing to our economy. And foremost, the effectiveness of our management of older people is a public issue of concern to everyone, because it affects everyone.

Whether we encourage older people to remain in the workforce or push them out as we have been doing will have a great impact on the expected labor shortages of the 1990s and beyond. While in periods of economic downturn it is difficult to promote a retired person's need to work, people have needs in addition to income, and organizations have needs in addition to structured forty-hour jobs. Flexibility in meeting the needs of all our people and organizations will require creative approaches. The good news is that there seems to be a substantial pent-up demand for work by America's older citizens.

The American Association of Retired Persons reports that 33 percent of its members fifty-five years of age or older regret having retired (Stephens, 1989). This report and that of the Commonwealth Fund mentioned earlier ("Millions of Older Workers . . .," 1990) make it clear that millions of older Americans want at least some work to do. Yet, as Ginsburg (1985, p. 42) reports, "Very few U.S. companies allow workers to continue part-time employment while drawing part of their pension. . . .—But it [has been] not uncommon for firms to have 'cordial compulsion' campaigns for early retirement. Forty percent of Fortune 500 companies have had them," before changes in the law discouraged such practices.

Pressures to abolish the mandatory retirement age are part of a movement away from the assumption that "everyone wants to retire" and its powerful corollary, "as soon as possible."

Advances in medical research, genetics, and pharmacology portend an exponential explosion in the numbers of people who will be healthy to a much later age in life. If we do not solve the problem of enabling people to work later if they desire, we may have a huge population of restless, disaffected older people demanding changes in the way we do business. This could become an enormous social and economic problem.

Finally, since it has been assumed that much of the cost of supporting a growing retired population would have to be offset by increases in worker productivity, we must increasingly draw on the special experience, knowledge, and abilities possessed in abundance by our older workforce. Research on older employees in recent years clearly indicates that our aging population can rise to the challenge if we manage our critical human resources more effectively. Few will escape the consequences of how well or poorly we manage older employees, not the newborn infant or the expiring octogenarian, for the issue involves our national health and wealth.

Chapter 2

Facing the Demographic Imperatives

The workforce effects of the recent increase in births will not be felt until the twenty-first century, by which time we will be living in a far different world. According to Goldstein (1988, pp. 41–42), "Through the year 2000 the labor force will increase at a slower rate than at any time since the Great Depression, at about 1.2 percent yearly growth compared with a 2.2 percent yearly growth in the 1975–87 period. Women will account for about two-thirds of the expected labor force growth in the 1990s. Hispanics will constitute about 29 percent of all employment growth until the end of this century while 11 percent will come from Asians."

Productivity is the name of the game when it comes to maintaining the health and balance of our society. And making a contribution does not always require that a person hold a job. Older retirees who do volunteer work contribute billions of dollars' worth of services to our gross national product (GNP) every year. Retirement need not be an endless round of golf, basket weaving, and travel.

A case in point was presented to me when I was chatting with a featured speaker at a management conference a few years ago. I said, "I understand you are going to talk about retirement." "No," he replied, "I'm going to talk about 'protirement.' Retirement is retreating from something—perhaps even a retreat from involvement in the most valuable part of our lives—our work. I want to talk about going toward something of merit and joy—not just toward death." If we are to adapt successfully to the changes inherent in workforce demographics, we need to alter our views and subsequently our organizational policies and actions regarding early retirement and a host of other aspects of work, productivity, and the management of older employees.

Our nation does not need another crisis, especially one that has been predicted and measured and one that can be resolved by a change of attitudes, policies, and behaviors. This particular impending crisis, of course, deals with demographic changes occurring in our workforce and throughout our society as a consequence of millions of individual decisions: some important public-policy decisions, and corporate and institutional decisions as well. This crisis is based on idle people who want to work and could work but for a variety of reasons are not able to work.

"In recent years, Federal legislation has been passed to allow or encourage workers to extend their work lives. Anticipating a dramatic decline in the ratio of workers to retirees when the baby-boom generation retires, Social Security regulations have been altered to encourage later labor force withdrawal and to increase penalties for early retirement. In addition, age discrimination laws have been extended to protect workers from mandatory retirement at any age. At the same time, however, an opposite and more dominant force has influenced workers' retirement age; many employers have made earlier and earlier retirement possible through options offered in their pension plans" (Rones and Herz, 1989, p. 1).

This productivity crisis has been rumbling from time to time for over a decade. It had a minor eruption a few years ago when the Social Security system was in trouble. Another occurred in the mid 1980s, when many organizations shrank their workforces, largely using "early-out" retirement options for senior and not so senior employees as a way of doing it. Other crises related to our aging population are probably not far off. Workforce statistics hint at the potential.

Workforce Changes

The background dimensions of this problem are clear and well charted. In the thirty-five years between 1950 and 1985, the segment of our population over age sixty-five more than doubled, from 12.3 million people to 28.5 million. By the year 2020, the numbers will have nearly doubled again, to 51.4 million, assuming no great advances in lengthening life. Yet the Social Security Administration reports that about 70 percent of the Social Security benefits are being paid to people under sixty-five, compared to only 2.2 percent in 1956.

From 1950 to 1985, the percentage of our total population over sixty-five rose from 7.7 percent to 12 percent. By the year 2020, those over sixty-five years of age are expected to be 17.3 percent of the population, or more than one in every six people, and the baby boomers will just be starting to have an impact on the over-sixty-five age group. But a more sobering thought is that, assuming no major changes in the laws, federal spending for pension and health care payments as a percentage of GNP, which was 9.3 percent in 1985, will rise to 11.8 percent, or about one dollar in eight, by 2020.

Table 1 offers a recent overview of the distribution of the U.S. workforce population over age forty-five. But the real stinger comes from U.S. Census Bureau projections, which indicate that the eighteen-to-twenty-four age group, from which employers usually draw new entry-level workers, will decline by 17 percent by the year 2000 as the baby-bust years take over. These projections indicate that for every six new entrants into the job market today, there will be only five in another decade. This drop may seem small, but it represents millions of workers and accentuates the shift in the average age of U.S. workers.

Early Retirement and Workplace Conflict

The changing workforce demographics have led to grim predictions of generational warfare as the burden of an ever growing number

Table 1. Labor-Force Status of the Civilian Noninstitutional Population Age Forty-Five and Over, by Sex and Age, 1987 Annual Averages (Numbers in Thousands).

Sex and Age	*Population*	*Labor force*				*Not in Labor Force*	
		Employed		*Unemployed*			
		Number	*Percentage*[a]	*Number*	*Percentage*[a]	*Number*	*Percentage*[a]
Total							
45-54 years	23,183	17,487	75.4	723	3.1	4,972	21.4
55 years and over	49,943	14,506	29.0	490	1.0	34,946	70.0
55-64 years	21,835	11,465	52.5	412	1.9	9,958	45.6
55-59 years	11,036	6,949	63.0	255	2.3	3,832	34.7
60-61 years	4,420	2,275	51.5	87	2.0	2,058	16.6
62-64 years	6,379	2,240	35.1	70	1.1	4,068	63.8
65 years and over	28,108	3,041	10.8	78	0.3	24,989	88.9
65-69 years	9,736	1,850	19.0	50	0.5	7,837	80.5
70 years and over	18,372	1,191	6.5	29	0.2	17,152	93.1
Men							
45-54 years	11,215	9,750	86.9	426	3.8	1,039	9.3
55 years and over	21,899	8,532	39.0	307	1.4	13,060	59.6
55-64 years	10,267	6,682	65.1	258	2.5	3,327	32.4
55-59 years	5,249	4,027	76.7	158	3.0	1,064	20.3
60-61 years	2,068	1,343	64.9	55	2.7	671	32.4
62-64 years	2,950	1,312	44.5	45	1.5	1,592	54.0
65 years and over	11,632	1,850	15.9	49	0.4	9,733	83.7
65-69 years	4,411	1,108	25.1	30	0.7	3,273	74.2
70 years and over	7,221	742	10.3	19	0.3	6,460	89.5
Women							
45-54 years	11,968	7,737	64.6	298	2.5	3,934	32.9
55 years and over	28,054	5,973	21.3	184	0.7	21,886	78.0
55-64 years	11,567	4,783	41.4	155	1.3	6,630	57.3
55-59 years	5,787	2,922	50.5	97	1.7	2,767	47.8
60-61 years	2,352	932	39.6	32	1.4	1,387	59.0
62-64 years	3,429	928	27.1	25	0.7	2,476	72.2
65 years and over	16,476	1,191	7.2	30	0.2	15,256	92.6
65-69 years	5,325	742	13.9	20	0.4	4,564	85.7
70 years and over	11,151	449	4.0	10	0.1	10,692	95.9

[a]Percentage of population. For the unemployed, this figure should not be confused with an unemployment rate, which is the unemployed as a proportion of the labor force.

Source: Rones and Herz, 1989.

of retired people is borne by younger wage earners. When the Social Security system was new, the ratio of active producers to retired workers was greater than 4:1. Today it is about 3:1. If current trends continue, the ratio will be 2:1 by the end of the 1990s. This shift is a primary reason for the increases in Social Security taxes paid by employed people in recent years.

To finance the mounting old-age medical and retirement benefit payments, both the taxable wage base and the rate of taxation have been boosted periodically. One expert estimates that these taxes must increase to between 15 and 20 percent of payroll by the end of this century to cover expected retirements. Yet companies and government agencies still try to persuade, induce, or even force people into early retirement. For example, in March 1988, with the U.S. Defense Department required to cut its worldwide workforce by 5 percent, many units were given permission to offer early retirement to thousands of civilian employees who did not normally qualify for it under federal rules. This has led to some employees who are in their forties being offered early-out retirement options. During this period of reduction (as with some previous ones), employees could retire on immediate (though sometimes reduced) benefits at any age after twenty-five years of service or at age fifty after twenty years of service.

In another example, during April 1988, the Senate Governmental Affairs Committee began hearings on a bill that would authorize early-out options to employees in all federal agencies. This bill would allow early retirement for people fifty-five years old with fifteen years of service or fifty-seven years old with five years of service. Previously, retirement was usually available only to those age fifty-five with thirty years of service. This bill alone would have offered early-retirement options to 400,000 government employees.

In 1989, the Small Business Administration received permission to offer early retirement to 500 of its 4,800 workers. It was reported (Causey, 1989) that it asked for the early-out option so as to avoid layoff procedures that would hit younger workers with the least seniority. For quite some time, the same thing has been occurring in private industry, institutions, and local governments whenever personnel cutbacks have been required. In 1990, there were several similar initiatives to enrich the incentives for federal employees to retire early. These options were related to Defense Department cutbacks anticipated as part of the so-called peace dividend growing out of events in Eastern Europe.

This brief history is offered to show the persistent appeal of early-retirement options no matter what their long-term economic consequences. Although the war in the Middle East closed out many of these movements, they could easily return with peace.

Employers have been responding to various economic slumps by the use of early-retirement incentive plans (ERIPs) as a way to reduce their payrolls or avoid layoffs (especially of younger employees). ERIPs provide incentives to employees to retire earlier than would normally be possible under their regular retirement plan. While some observers see ERIPs as beneficial to employees, others see them as a way to get rid of older employees.

The problem of personnel cutbacks is certainly a complex one, without easy answers, and there would probably be some criticism no matter what approach was taken. However, there are many assumptions made when the early-out option is used, such as that younger employees, with their careers ahead of them, will stay longer than older employees; younger people are inherently more "able" to do the job than older employees; older employees are close to retirement anyway; virtually all employees want to retire as early as possible; and older employees tend to be over the hill. Most of these assumptions are demonstrably false; even where they do apply to specific individuals, their generalized use leads to poor policies regarding early retirement, with implications such as the following.

First, the earlier a person retires, the longer he or she is likely to be tapping pension funds (many of which are not prefunded), drawing Social Security, and probably participating in federal medical plans. In general, we will all be paying something for the rest of the former employee's life. Although many who retire early will not be idle, people who take subsequent jobs tend to do so only for a relatively short time, may work only part-time, and seldom contribute to society at their former level of talent, experience, or productivity.

In a *Fortune* magazine article, Ramirez (1989, p. 187) reported on the work of Malcolm Morrison of George Washington University, who found that a retiring worker cost the company $40,000 a year for pension and health benefits if retiring at age fifty to fifty-four but only $30,000 a year if he or she left between the ages of fifty-five and fifty-nine and only $23,000 a year if he or she stayed on past age sixty. These data, drawn from employment figures at a large aerospace firm, showed that these cost declines occurred partly because pension and benefits were paid out over a shorter period of time: fifteen years on the average for a sixty-five-year-old, versus twenty-five years for a fifty-five-year-old. Other factors that reduce costs for older workers include less likelihood of children being covered by the medical plan and salaries plateauing after age fifty.

Second, using early-retirement options can severely hurt future operations of many organizations. These tend to eliminate the people with the greatest experience and organizational know-how. Also, while such personnel reductions were originally aimed at getting rid of higher-paid older employees and some low-performing individuals, it was almost always found that some of the best performers opted out, while less productive employees tried to hang on because of their limited ability to get other jobs.

Third, prior management policies, whether in government or the private sector, are often responsible for the crisis situations that make personnel cutbacks necessary. Bloated staffing and salaries in companies and a consequent inability to remain competitive, as well as unwise tax policies and increasing federal debt (the budget deficit) leading to meat-ax cutting of federal employees (Gramm-Rudman, for example), have produced manpower crises and consequent reductions in the employment of older workers. Thus, "early out" becomes "easy out" as the least objectionable way to reduce personnel.

General Changes in the Labor Market

How well we will be prepared to face the new century will depend on the type and quality of decisions that we make in the interim. Consider the following realities.

The life-span of both men and women will continue to increase, with or without any great medical breakthroughs related to the aging process. Life expectancy for the general population, which is hovering near seventy-five today, is expected to exceed seventy-seven by the turn of the century. This may not seem like much, but it can mean millions of people available for productive work of some type. But more startling indeed is the fact that men who today reach age sixty-five can expect to live to seventy-nine, while women who do so can expect to reach eighty-three on the average.

Minority aging warrants particular attention. McNeely and Colen (1983, p. 26) report that about 17 percent of the members of ethnic minorities in the U.S. population in the 1980 census were over sixty-five. But this proportion of our population is growing more rapidly than is the white population and has a younger population base, so that its effects will be greater as we move into the next millennium. Since a higher proportion of this population is disadvantaged, the economic implications for the future can be substantial.

The "old-old" already are our fastest-growing age group. John Keane (1985, p. 11), director of the U.S. Bureau of the Census, predicted that the number of those age 100 and over will be the fastest-growing age group in our nation, nearly quadrupling by the year 2000. Also, the number of people age seventy-five and over will grow from the 10.7 million people in 1982 to 30 million by the year 2030. If that seems like a long time, consider your own life expectancy and see whether you are likely to be around to pay the bills for such things as early retirement when they become due. If you are not, will your children or grandchildren be? Also, consider the fact that the United States has nearly 3 million people past eighty-five and that this number will be near 4.5 million by the end of this century. Surely efforts to keep those older people who wish to remain productive at much younger ages should be encouraged. People even past 100 years of age working and being productive if they so desire should not be an impossible dream.

The percentage of older men in the workforce has been steadily shrinking since the early 1900s. This was related to the influx of young immigrant labor until about 1925, and then to the increased number of women in the workforce (a trend that is still continuing), but now it is largely due to the availability of Social Security, employee pension plans, and, most recently, early-retirement options. The Bureau of Labor Statistics states that in 1900, 30 percent of men age fifty-five and over were not employed full-time (Copperman and Keast, 1983, pp. 19–23). Only 35 percent of people age fifty-five and older hold jobs today, compared to 45 percent in 1930. Also, the median retirement age for men keeps dropping, from sixty-five in 1963 to about sixty-two today, and though there are fewer data about women, they are expected to follow suit as more become eligible for pensions.

Women are predicted to maintain their current rate of participation in the labor force. The retirement situation is more complex for women. That is because many women in their fifties and sixties today have had very little paid work experience throughout their lives. As a result, they often do not choose a retirement age on the basis of their own work history or pension resources. Labor-force participation rates for women age sixty-five and over have followed the same trend as those for men—they have declined from a high of about 11 percent in the early 1960s to about 7 percent today. Participation rates for women aged fifty-five to sixty-four have changed little over the last two decades.

In 1900, only 20 percent of American women worked for pay outside the home, mostly in domestic service or semiskilled factory work, and most quit when they got married. By 1987, 56 percent of women were working (on the average, the woman was married, was a mother, and had a high school education).

The decrease in the number of younger workers in the years ahead is expected to affect the relative size of the job market itself. Walsh and Lloyd (1984, p. 35) point out that the Bureau of Labor Statistics projects that the labor force will grow from 110 million workers in 1987 to 131 million in 1995. But this constitutes a rise of only 1.5 percent per year. In the 1970s, on the other hand, the increase averaged 2.9 percent per year. This slowed growth rate virtually ensures that severe labor shortages will occur unless we encounter a substantial economic downturn. There are several signs, including lowered unemployment rates and regional shortages of entry-level employees, that this shortage of younger people is already occurring.

Age distortions will occur throughout the work force. According to Walsh and Lloyd (1984, pp. 35–36), the baby-boom generation will create a bulge of middle-aged workers of unprecedented proportions by the year 2000. And there will be far fewer young employees to fill entry-level positions. By 1995, individuals aged twenty-five to fifty-four will account for 73 percent of the workforce—up from 64 percent in 1982. The pool of sixteen- to twenty-four-year-olds will shrink by 14 percent during the next ten years as a result of the lowered birthrate during the 1960s and 1970s.

Overall, by the year 2000, only 39 percent of the work force will be younger than 35, as opposed to 49 percent at present, while the number of people between fifty and sixty-five will increase at more than twice the rate of the overall population. Consequently, the bulge of middle-aged workers will be arriving at the age when early retirement has its greatest impact, so that any age-related problems that we have now are likely to be accentuated. In addition, while the shortages of younger workers could be a boon to black inner-city youth, among whom unemployment has been highest, it may also mean that there will be greater pressure on employers to hire illegal immigrants in larger numbers despite the obstacles and penalties.

Research Findings on Workplace Participation

A close study of the research on older employees indicates a number of other influences operating to produce workforce changes and alterations in the labor market. According to Greene (1980, pp. 63–65), health does not play as important a role in an employee's decision to retire early as was once believed. Rather, it is the individual's actual and potential financial condition that primarily determines whether he or she will continue working. Generous pension and severance awards for early retirement, Social Security benefits, disability payments, and a comfortable level of personal assets all serve as incentives to leave the labor force.

For many, the option of working part-time at their current jobs, rather than retiring, is not available, according to Gustman and Steinmeier (1985, pp. 257–258). Blue-collar workers are the most likely to be so constrained; managers are least likely. Because lower-level employees are in the most financial need of work, once retired they are often forced, because of their age, to accept lower-paying jobs if they can find them or attempt to live off their pension and Social Security payments.

Workers of this era are in general a different breed from earlier generations. They are better educated and healthier. They will live longer, and many view retirement as an unfulfilling option.

Many older individuals would prefer to work, but given the emerging demographics, industry is not yet forced to seek them out and encourage them to do so. Forced unemployment for older workers is particularly stressful, since many are unable to find alternative adequate work, if any. Women, blacks, and Hispanics are particularly hard hit, because they often lack financial reserves, may lack pension plans, and generally find it harder to gain reemployment at an adequate wage.

The cost of underutilization of older workers in the United States is estimated to be $10 billion per year ("Benefits Important . . .," 1985, p. 15). Yet it is predicted that the cost of supporting older nonworkers will be $635 billion annually between 2010 and 2025 (in 1978 dollars), as compared with $112 billion in 1978. Conversely, Victoria Kaminski (1983a, p. 36) estimates that if older workers were to continue working, the GNP would increase by $200 billion a year by the year 2005.

According to Burkhauser and Turner (1982, p. 304), Social Security "comprises over 40 percent of all government social welfare expenditures and is the largest single government budget item," and this is increasing. Also, 9.9 percent of the total compensation dollar is currently paid for pension and welfare benefits that are age-related, and this percentage is likely to escalate rapidly in the next decade.

Paul Winston (1986, p. 68) reported on a survey of 236 certified employee benefit specialists that found that inflation in medical care costs was the greatest concern for employers. Other areas of concern included "potential cutbacks in Medicare reimbursement and the potential for Medicare to assume a secondary payer status for all retirees." It is not surprising, therefore, that the majority of the respondents did not favor any laws mandating cost-of-living provisions for private pension plans or that they favored legislation that would modify the current funding limits for retiree medical benefits to allow for health care inflation. Also, there has been a significant increase in the use of early retirement to reduce current costs. "In 1985, 38 percent of companies with 500–999 employees and 44 percent with 1000 or more employees had, or were considering early retirement programs. In 1989 the figures were 61 and 55 percent" (Stephens, 1989, p. 5).

Implications of Current Research

What are the implications of these projections? This question has at least two facets: how industry will adapt to these changes and the financial burden to society. The situation as currently projected is to a great extent the result of the large influx of young workers that occurred in the 1970s because their availability provided a large pool of fresh labor to support the steadily growing pattern of early retirement. Other factors favoring this trend were high levels of unemployment and pressures by labor unions favoring younger employees. However, the organization of the 1990s will be increasingly dependent on older employees and must compete with other companies for a continually shrinking pool of younger workers. In the face of the growing number of older employees who will opt to continue working, it must begin to devise new methods of recognizing merit—or risk losing many of these younger employees. It must also adjust the workplace to meet the changing physical and emotional needs of older workers. And it must adjust to the reality that the older worker of the future will not fit the compliant stereotype of the past.

The baby-boom generation is better educated than older generations have been, and its members grew up in an era of protest, self-actualization, and women's and minorities' rights. Therefore, these are not individuals who will accept unequal treatment on the basis of age without resorting to legal or extralegal means. In addition, industry must deal with the costs of updating the skills and knowledge of older workers as these increasingly become obsolete. And companies may also have to pay rising health and pension costs.

Whatever changes organizations make in the structure of the workplace and work schedule, we need to take the issue of older employee productivity seriously. We need to make it worthwhile (at least in terms of psychic income) for the older employee to continue to produce and to enable that employee to perceive the satisfactions to be derived from such activities. It has to be a truly natural win-win outcome for both older employees and their organizations, or it is not likely to work.

Chapter 3

Shedding Common Myths About Older Employees

While the behavior of every age group is stereotyped by others to some degree, no group is as negatively affected by such generalizations as the elderly; at least other age groups are expected to outgrow their idiosyncrasies.

Older people are often perceived as poor, isolated, senile, unhappy, and unhealthy. As employees, they are often viewed as unmotivated and as less creative and less productive than younger workers. Certainly, these are not characteristics that lead to promotions or to selection for new learning opportunities.

Several studies have shown that managers sometimes engage in age discrimination without being aware of it. For example, Rosen (1978) reports on a 1977 survey that he conducted of 1,570 subscribers to the *Harvard Business Review*, in which he sought to assess the degree to which age discrimination affects managerial decisions. The respondents were divided into two groups and each group was asked to evaluate a series of problems involving poor worker performance and decisions regarding training and promotions. The problems presented to the two groups were virtually identical except for the age of the employee involved in the incident—one-half dealt with a younger worker and the other half with an older one.

In each of the situations, the older employee fared worse in the respondents' evaluations, regardless of his or her qualifications. When both an older and a younger worker were failing to adequately perform the job, the older employee was seen as resistant to change, and the respondents recommended reassignment. Those surveyed believed, however, that the younger worker could benefit from an "encouraging talk." Similarly, the older, equally qualified employee was perceived as less motivated to keep up with changing technology, less creative, and less able to deal with job-related stress.

What this and other research reflects is the Catch-22 nature of discriminatory thinking. There is a tendency among some managers (as well as perhaps among most people in general) to believe that workers gradually lose their abilities as they age. Because advancement is based on the organization's view of the employee's potential, older workers are not considered to be candidates for such opportunities; rather, they are seen as obstacles to the company's growth. For example, a study of 142 managers by Rosen and Jerdee (1979) found that managers were more willing to suggest retirement to employees the closer they were to age sixty-five, regardless of the individual's performance or sex.

In many cases, the ideal candidate for a particular job is believed to be an individual in his twenties with a few years of work experience. Daniel Knowles (1984) suggests that many personnel specialists and managers have set their minds on this image and will not even consider an older worker who is better qualified and willing to accept the proffered salary. Moreover, having been raised in a society where "ageism" is rampant, older employees themselves begin to act the part expected of them.

Cultural Notions About Age and Work

The mistaken notions about older people are so numerous and widespread that not all of them can be covered in a single chapter. Therefore, specific assumptions related to productivity, health, and learning will be developed in subsequent chapters. Here we explore

eight of the more general concepts that many people perceive as characterizing aged employees and the negative impact of such generalizations on older employees in the workplace:

1. Older people should retire to make way for younger employees.
2. Most older people are pretty much alike.
3. The basic job needs of older people in general are different from those of younger people.
4. As people age, they tend to focus on the past.
5. Most older employees cannot or will not change to meet the changing needs of the organization. They prefer to coast and shy away from promotions or challenge.
6. Age is a disease—a slow but continuous process that cannot be reversed.
7. Old age is (or should be) a period of relative calm and stability—and that's what old people want.
8. As people age, they become more critical, complaining, and suspicious.

These eight commonly held beliefs, gleaned from various publications of the National Council on Aging, lay an "apparently" rational foundation for grouping all older employees into a single bag that can be nicely labeled and put on a shelf without feelings of guilt.

Before examining the truth of such generalizations, consider their implications. Discrimination affects the older worker's self-image and employment status. Consequently, many older employees internalize society's biases toward them and behave in such a manner as to reinforce these myths. Older individuals, it has been found, suffer from depression to a much greater degree than younger people. And many of them believe that their level of competence will begin to slip as they grow older. For example, Tavernier (1978, p. 46) notes that a survey of 1,285 managers from Denmark's 150 largest companies revealed that nearly half the managers under the age of forty expected to experience a decline in their competence as they aged. The respondents were also asked how they would react if their company offered them a lower-status job with a 10 percent pay cut "in order to make room for a younger and 'better' employee. Half of those over 55 years of age said they would accept the situation. Only 15 percent said they would work harder to get promoted."

More concrete results of ageism concern older employees' reemployment rate, their potential income, and their chances for promotion. "Unemployed workers over 45 can expect to wait at least four times as long for new jobs as workers under 20 years of age" (LaBerge, 1977, p. 54). When they do finally find work, the job most often will be lower paying and carry less status than their original position.

Coser (1984, pp. 131–132) noted that "educational level is not related in the same way to retirement intentions of men and women. Male prospective retirees tend to have less education than those not planning to retire which is consistent with [their] occupational differences. However, female prospective retirees are likely to have more education than women who have no intention of retiring." She explains this contradiction by examining occupational differences. "Men's educational level is usually matched by their occupation," and it is men in routine occupations that are more likely to retire—if they can afford to do so. "In contrast, women's educational level is usually not matched by the socio-economic level of their occupation. Women generally are [more] likely to have routine occupations and those who are better educated tend to be dissatisfied with the relatively low level of employment available to them" and therefore tend to retire earlier if they can afford to do so.

And, finally, the situation regarding promotions can be dismal. For example, one manager in her fifties described her superior's consistently excellent evaluations of her performance. She was told she was one of the top three performers in her department and their strongest manager. In spite of this, "She was denied a promotion on the basis of the superior's *feelings* about her age rather than on the basis of her performance" (Macleod, 1983, p. 58). It is no wonder then that the senior employee's output and attitude may deteriorate, leaving the organization to deal with a worker who has become a liability.

For its part, society, in an attempt to cope with the growing number of retirees, has developed community and educational programs that encourage the elderly to be passive and dependent. The programs often segregate older individuals from other age groups and focus on activities rather than the development of marketable skills. At least one author (Peterson, 1983, p. 296) has suggested a different orientation: participation and self-actualization. He believes that the skills and abilities of older people are valuable and that they should "continue to participate in the mainstream of society because [they] . . . may help overcome some of the societal problems facing the nation." This can be done through their mentoring of the young, volunteer work, and teaching special subjects.

None of this denies that aging sometimes creates problems for some individuals. Certainly, one does change as one grows older. The goal here is to separate myth from reality and "what counts" from that which "makes no difference." Accordingly, we want to ask, what are some of the real problems that confront the elderly?

Aside from the physical changes that the older person experiences, the process of aging may also be characterized, to differing degrees, by loss and social disengagement. For those who opt to retire, there is frequently a financial loss and, perhaps, a loss of status and authority. There is usually a change in living arrangements and community, caused either by the individual moving or by his or her children leaving the home or area where they all once resided. And, finally, there may be the loss through death of one's spouse, contemporaries, siblings, or parents (Knox, 1977, p. 529).

Myths that pervade this culture—the elderly are poor, lonely, unhealthy, institutionalized—become realities only as a function of a given person's life history. Most older people live independent, socially active lives that are well above the poverty level (money worries are often a greater issue for younger people). Only a very small percentage of the elderly live in nursing homes or other institutions. Against this background, we can examine the specific stereotypes that are often used as justifications, either consciously or unconsciously, for discriminating against older workers.

1. *Older employees should retire early and make way for younger employees.* Aside from being a self-serving battle cry for some younger people, this belief clearly has wide currency among some top-level managers, human resource development professionals, and others concerned with the long-range health of the orga-

nization. Why else the push for early retirement even when such programs will cost the organization so much, long into the future?

Often buried in this cry are the assumptions that older people cannot contribute much to the future of the organization, that the future depends on the young, and that the needs of the young are more important than the needs of the elderly (they've had their chance, now give us ours!). The general rationale of those who believe that the old should give way to the young is that the young have many more years to give to the organization, that they will eventually take over anyway, that they are inherently superior performers (because they are young and full of energy and good ideas), and that they will grow discouraged and leave if their way upward is blocked.

As turnover statistics indicate, although the young may have more years to give, they tend not to give them to their first or second employer, and turnover rates tend to be lower among older workers than among younger ones. There is also considerable question about the young being inherently superior performers except in jobs requiring great strength and agility—a lessening requirement today. (How much does a byte weigh, anyway?) Also, good (sound) ideas usually spring from the rearrangement of knowledge and experience in novel ways to solve current problems, and older employees tend to have a lot of each. In reality, some people do become less competent as they age, but much depends on what they are doing and whether the particular abilities that are declining are directly related to their job. The great number of executives, political leaders, and scientists who capably lead their organizations until they are well into their eighties or nineties shows the fallacy of assessing contribution on the basis of age. An executive who opts for early retirement at fifty-five may be contributing less than executives who strike their stride at fifty-five and continue their high performance rate into their eighties.

In some cases, an increasingly marginal employee might well be able to come up to employment standards with a change of job or assignment. Most people who enjoy reasonably good health can be useful and productive to the very end of their lives. They may even become more capable as they age. The notion that most people become incapable as they grow older is ageism at its worst. We need to consider each case individually; in the era of the Age Discrimination in Employment Act (ADEA), the penalty for not doing so has become substantial.

Two final points are pertinent here. First, much of this "make-way" viewpoint is based on the assumption that there are a limited number of jobs and if one person (presumably old) holds the job, another person (presumably younger) is denied the position. Also, we are all familiar with the depiction of the organization as a pyramid and the implied conclusion that there are fewer and fewer jobs available as one moves toward the top. In some instances, this is the case. But there is seldom, if ever, a fixed correlation between the number of jobs available and the ages of those who hold them. The job market contracts and expands as a function of general business conditions, entrepreneurial effort, government policy, and so on and is always in a state of flux. Simple one-to-one job thinking is erroneous except possibly within a given organization. Even there, laying off an older worker would hardly guarantee that a younger person would get the job. Job requirements are far more complex than that.

Second, it has often been found that the jobs at the top of the organization are the hardest to fill. These positions require a breadth of experience, wisdom, and maturity seldom yet developed by younger people. American companies have been involved in encouraging early retirement for years, and there is scant evidence that these actions have improved these organizations' performance. And while some younger individuals may have gained, society is paying a heavy price for this loss in productivity, gross national product, and taxable revenues. Setting older people aside in favor of younger ones can be very costly.

2. *Most older people are pretty much alike.* The notion that older people are alike, which allows people to stereotype them, flies in the face of logic and common sense. In reality, we are most like one another when we are babies, because so little has happened to make us distinctive. As people grow, they acquire skills, knowledge, and experiences that set them apart from other individuals. Time also allows our genetic differences to manifest themselves; consequently, as we age, we become less, not more, like each other.

A study conducted of the elderly in northern California

further establishes this point. The researchers, according to Maas and Kuypers (1974, pp. 5, 215), examined ten different life-styles of 142 people born in the early 1900s. They discovered a great deal of diversity in the living and working arrangements of these individuals. Those who were financially secure were able to choose whether to retire or to continue working. The ability to choose, however, was considered an essential right by these individuals. Similarly, the selection of housing and leisure-time activities covered a broad spectrum. It is interesting to note that none of those surveyed said that he or she would opt to live in a "high-rise multiple-dwelling unit restricted to aged residents." The authors conclude that, as with any other age group, the needs of the elderly cannot be planned for in a "monolithic way." Because the psychological and physical well-being of older people varies immensely, it can no longer be assumed that the "package" approach—one type of health care, work, leisure-time activities, and housing arrangement—will satisfy those needs. On the job, these differences cry out for individual treatment—a look at each person and his or her needs and abilities as unique. This notion of individual differentiation with age is upsetting to some managers because it makes sweeping generalizations and blanket policies difficult to apply. It requires that we devote more personal attention to the differing needs of each employee. But if those needs are attended to, it also allows each employee's potential to be used by the organization to a greater extent.

Considerable research suggests that the production of innovative ideas is more a matter of personality than of age and that the source of the best ideas may not necessarily be restricted to the bright young person. Unfortunately, the habit of offering suggestions may have been trained out of some older employees, and the challenge to many supervisors might be to tap into that unique reserve of know-how so that it can be successfully applied in a current context.

3. *The basic job needs of older people in general are different from those of younger people.* Despite the potential for ironic contradiction between this point and the last one, many people believe that the basic needs of old people are different from those of young people. Yet people of all ages share the same needs for the basics of life—food, clothing, shelter, and good health. Equally important

are the psychological requirements for security, love, companionship, belonging, self-respect, and the respect of others, as well as the need for recognition and achievement. These fundamental human needs are not lost with age. While there are some obvious differences in specific needs, such as those related to the type and amount of insurance coverage required, family needs and other obligations may be more important than age differences.

Where the needs of the various age groups have been shown to be different, it has not always been to the elderly's disadvantage. For example, a study of 3,053 workers was conducted to determine whether there was any relationship between age and work values. According to Cherrington, Condie, and England (1979, pp. 618–622), younger workers place more importance on money, on the value of friends, and on the acceptability of welfare than on work. Older workers, on the other hand, gave work's moral importance and craftsmanship ("work values traditionally taught and considered important in an industrial society") the highest value. They concluded that work values were a result of one's historical experiences, the different types of socialization one receives, and maturity. If, as has been shown here, older employees value the quality of their work over the amount of their pay, then some of the traditional arguments for hiring a younger worker over an older one become specious.

Of course, some of the needs of the elderly are different because of changes in their physical condition or situation. For instance, they generally require a different type of insurance coverage. Most older people do not need obstetrical coverage but would be interested in a greater amount of hospital insurance. Somatic changes also may create a need for some physical alterations in the workplace; a particular older person may prefer a slower-paced and less stressful job. None of these differences, however, is sufficient to justify society's transformation of the elderly into a subspecies possessing lowered life-style expectations.

4. *As people age, they tend to focus on the past.* The statement that the elderly "live in the past" ties in with the other stereotypes of them as out of touch and, perhaps more significantly, out of reach. Focusing on the past has come to be synonymous with senility in the viewpoint of some people. One survey of traits that

are believed to characterize the elderly discounts this explanation and offers instead the theory that the process of life review or reminiscence serves a useful function of helping the individual to gain perspective on the meaning of his or her life. It has nothing to do with brain disease. And, as we will learn in later chapters, this process of synthesizing past experiences allows the individual to approach new situations with a clearer understanding of how to handle them. Young people reminisce about high school or college days (or earlier), so reminiscing may well be a lifelong pattern for some, but the young also have a lot less to reminisce about.

5. *Most older people cannot cope with changes in the organization.* People's ability to handle change is related to how well they handle stress, their tolerance for ambiguity, and the value that they receive from the changes themselves. If a person has experienced job change as mostly negative, it should not be surprising that he or she views change as bad news and may resist it. This calls for greater and more reasoned explanation by management of the purpose behind the change and the nature of the change itself.

While a tolerance for ambiguity is important for everyone, people need to be able to make sense of what is going on about them. A sound systematic plan for change, broadly understood and implemented in an orderly fashion, reduces ambiguity and the seeming chaos that often accompanies organizational change. Younger people who are action oriented rather than contemplative might like the excitement of chaos. But someone who has had to make change work and who has suffered from poorly planned and implemented change may not be as enthusiastic. Also, when change is related to age differences, it often favors the young, so older employees' reluctance may only reflect common sense.

Finally, prolonged or excessive stress over a number of years does lessen a person's physical capacity to be resilient. And older employees are less likely to be given stress-management training than younger people are because of the types of discrimination previously mentioned. Stress-management techniques, methods for visualizing end results, and meditative (relaxation) exercises can go a long way toward helping an older person manage change effectively.

6. *Age is a disease—a slow but continuous process that can-*

not be reversed. Eisdorfer and Cohen (1980, p. 50) suggest that any discussion of an older person's physical or psychological well-being requires a consideration of that person's past to understand his or her current situation. While it is possible to isolate a time period in one's life for self-examination, "it is impossible . . . to do so without risking some distortion." There are also some somatic changes that accompany the aging process. Vision and hearing acuity may diminish; the skin becomes less elastic; there may be degenerative changes in the joints and vascular changes that can affect the supply of blood to the heart and brain (U.S. Department of Health, Education, and Welfare, 1978). Despite such changes, age is *not* a disease. Aging is a process. The physical or mental problems that one confronts as one grows older are a function of many factors; for example, one's genetic makeup, socioeconomic class, diet, amount of exercise, and life-style.

While at least one often quoted study (see Fallcreek and Mettler, 1984, pp. 1–10) has found that most older people (80 percent) suffer from some chronic disease, the research studied more nonworkers and institutionalized individuals than employed people (which is common for general studies of the elderly). However, the study included the less noted observation that about two-thirds (67 percent) of those reporting chronic conditions indicated that those conditions did not interfere with their ability to remain active. In addition, some people who quote the 80 percent statistic ignore the reality that many of those people with chronic health problems developed and experienced some of these conditions long before they could be classed as elderly. For instance, we should realize that diabetes is a chronic ailment, yet hundreds of thousands of afflicted employees of various ages carry out their daily work satisfactorily for decades, without their chronic ailment interfering with their output. Age, therefore, should not be considered synonymous with disease or pathology.

7. *Old age should be a period of calm and stability.* Many believe that older people can no longer handle the changing demands of the workplace. The belief that older people desire a quiet, reflective life-style may certainly be true in some cases, but this does not mean that *all* wish to retire, as some claim when pushing for the early retirement of others. However, many older employees have

a need for stimulation, an opportunity to use their imagination, and even challenge. How else can they feel that life is interesting and rewarding? In fact, this is exactly why many people look forward to retirement. It is often seen as the first chance in their working lives to escape monotony and boredom—to do something different. The belief that older people want to sit in a rocking chair and do nothing is largely an outdated model of reality carried over from a time when people had to suppress their thought and feeling in order to survive under autocratic and most often unimaginative management.

Today, "quality managers" can make a person's job challenging and rewarding by the delegation of decision-making authority, the use of problem-solving task forces, and the equitable distribution of varied and interesting assignments. There is not much current reality in the belief that older people want repose above all.

8. *As people age, they become more critical, complaining, and suspicious.* In most cases, these descriptors do not apply solely to the older individual. Research has found that, barring some debilitating disease, personality traits tend to remain stable across the adult life span. One study revealed that the elderly described themselves in nearly the same way as they had when they were younger.

What this emphasizes, again, is that aging is a process. Most physical and mental changes cannot simply be deemed reserved for old age. Rather, context is almost everything when one is attempting to understand and describe an individual's life status. However, if older employees are shunted aside in the workplace and their ideas and experience discounted, as often happens, it should not be surprising that they become more critical, complaining, and suspicious of management and even of other employees who treat them similarly.

Older workers of today also differ a great deal from their counterparts of earlier decades. Rosow and Zager (1980, p. 5) of the Work in America Institute believe that "they are healthier. . . . They began working later than their predecessors, so the extension of work life may not mean an actual lengthening of career. And although the average level of formal education of older workers several decades ago was far below that of younger employees, the gap has been closing and will close even further in the 1980s."

What does all this mean with respect to the adaptability of the older employee? A study by Rayburn (1983) found that there was little relationship between the age of top executives and a company's financial success. Specifically, she discovered that there was no statistically significant difference between the "sales, assets, net income, stockholders' equity, and number of employees, for companies whose top executive is over 65 years of age and those firms with younger top executives" (p. 14). This, she believes, supports the concept that "older top executives do not suffer a decline in intelligence or capability" (p. 15). Her study also included an examination of whether there is a relationship between the "promotional expenditures" of a company and the age of its management. Her findings did not support the hypothesis that if managers grow more conservative as they age, they will hesitate to spend large sums of money on advertising campaigns.

It would seem, then, that the older employee can adapt to changes in the workplace very well and in a manner that allows him or her to compete successfully. While many older people prefer to slow their work pace, this is a function of their specific needs. It does not, as we continue to emphasize, reflect the situation as a whole for *all* older individuals. What is essential for the elderly, as for any age group, is the possibility of pursuing whatever life-style and work style best suits their needs and abilities.

Facts and Fallacies About Older Employees' Job Attitudes and Performance

Below are listed a series of additional questionable but common beliefs about older employees in the workplace. They add a special dimension to the negative additional sources of antiage biases. Here they are given with their countervailing reality.

Fallacy: Older people want to retire as soon as possible.

Fact: Some do. But a 1986 survey by the Administrative Services Society indicates that half of the retirees over age fifty-five would prefer to work full-time and continue to use their job skills. This is consistent with other surveys that say that many would like to continue to work part-time and some to work at less strenuous or more interesting jobs (Blocklyn, 1987, p. 17).

Fallacy: Older workers are interested only in a progression from work to retirement.

Fact: Many older workers have been living what Kenneth Dychtwald (Dychtwald and Flower, 1990, pp. 92-99) calls a "linear life plan," by which people learn for fifteen to twenty years, work for thirty to forty years, rest for a while (retirement), and then die. However, an increasing number, up to 30 percent by some estimates, start new careers after formally retiring on a pension and/or Social Security, go back to school, or seek out part-time work for as long as they are able.

Fallacy: Older people seek leisure and want to avoid responsibility.

Fact: Some older people may long for a life free of responsibility (perhaps we all do at times), but a survey conducted at two large companies found that more than 20 percent of their employees are now caring for an elderly relative ("More Firms Aid Workers . . . ," 1987). Also, large numbers of older people are dedicating a great deal of their time and other resources to caring for children, grandchildren, and even great-grandchildren.

Fallacy: Older workers enjoy relatively high incomes and therefore are too expensive to keep on the payroll when younger employees could do the work for less.

Fact: In the fall of 1984, the U.S. Senate Special Committee on Aging (1984) released a study showing that, overall, older employees do not earn more than younger workers and that (depending on the employer) often at about age fifty, real earnings begin to decline with age; the cost ratios most often favor older workers where a generous medical or retirement plan is involved (the medical plan is most important for lower-paid employees, and the pension plan is the greatest factor for higher-paid employees).

Fallacy: If layoffs were determined solely on the basis of performance, older employees would be hurt.

Fact: Grumman Corporation, for instance, found that when it laid off workers on the basis of detailed performance evaluation, the average age of the workforce went *up* from thirty-seven years to forty-five years. There is considerable documentation that older workers are extremely productive.

Fallacy: Younger employees discriminate most against older employees.

Fact: Most age discrimination in the workplace—in educational opportunities, in promotions, in changing job requirements—is based on decisions of managers who are themselves over forty. Younger managers often lack the power to set policy or to approve its implementation.

An Age for Achievement

Dispelling myths and stereotypes about age is not enough. We need a positive focus on age and the abilities that develop with age. We need to generate a positive self-fulfilling prophecy about aging—a prophecy of old age being potentially the most productive period of our lives, when all of our talents and development reach fruition. Old age can be a period of expansion, fulfillment, and achievement for those who believe it and desire it.

I remember my mother saying with a wistful smile when I was very young, "Life begins at forty." I'm not sure that many people believed that at that time, but nonetheless, for many it proved true. Now that I am more than two decades past that crossover point, I can say that for me, a fuller life began at fifty and has been picking up speed ever since.

A new age-related phenomenon has developed in recent decades—a host of people looking forward to the joys of retirement. But all too often, behind that joyous anticipation lurks the relief of going *away from* something—work, an onerous job, the controls and limitation of the workplace—rather than *toward* something positive. Old age should not be a burden; for many it is becoming a period when old dreams are rediscovered, dusted off, modified to reflect a greater sense of the world, and pursued with passion.

We have been told about the countless examples of high achievement and public service on the part of noteworthy individuals. For example:

- Conrad Adenauer was chancellor of West Germany until he was 87.
- Irving Berlin was still working when he died at 101.
- Hulda Crooks, 93, has climbed ninety-seven mountains, including Mount Fuji in Japan, since she was 65.
- Charles de Gaulle was president of France until age 79.
- Nobel scientist Barbara McClintock is 90 and still working.
- Claude Pepper was still leading the fight in Congress to protect the rights of the elderly through legislation at 89.
- Robert Sprague, founder of Sprague Electric (now part of Penn Central Corporation), at 90, still serves as a director of the company and writes books on skiing. He also works nearly full-time in the company's patent department.
- Jane Stoval, 104, started as a milliner but became an author, senior golf champion, and student pilot at 89.

Is this burst of learning, skill development, personal growth, and contribution only for the exceptional? Not at all. There are also chief executive officers of major corporations, creative writers, artists, actors, and politicians whose careers have run into their nineties. Also, for each of these distinguished names, there are thousands of older people doing exceptional and valuable work late in life. And the numbers are growing as more and more older people are "finding themselves" at last. Increasingly as we age, we need to create a healthy, positive image of ourselves, so that our abilities, despite problems, are continuously growing. This bounty can be harvested on the job for millions of people.

A quotation from Stephens (1989, p. 1) in the bulletin of the American Association of Retired Persons (AARP) is revealing: "Corporate America continues to give high marks to its senior employees. Yet employers are doing little to strengthen the role of older Americans in the workplace." Is something strange going on?

Chapter 4

Addressing the Issues of Health and Wellness

Every organization has a responsibility and challenge to do what it can to enhance employee health. This responsibility does not diminish as the workforce ages, nor does it necessarily become any more difficult. Unfortunately, the realm of health and wellness is an area where myths and misconceptions about older workers and their value in the workforce often find fertile ground.

Not surprisingly, supervisors with their responsibility to ensure that the work gets done each day, are much concerned about employee illness and absenteeism. Excessive sick leave, tardiness, time off for doctors' appointments, and low levels of output because the worker is "not feeling well," even though present, all reduce productivity. Ill health in the supervisory and managerial ranks is also of great concern, for low levels of energy, absence, or on-the-job illness can adversely affect decision making, continuity of operations, or output. Since frequent and severe illnesses are often associated in people's minds with advanced age, the treatment of older employees has long been influenced by the belief that older employees represent a far greater health risk than other personnel.

Yet considerable and growing evidence indicates that many of these attitudes and beliefs are not well founded. The health of the elderly is changing rapidly for the better. Most of us have known a spritely octogenarian who still does his or her own housework, attends the family business daily, or works part-time in a store or office. Perhaps we have heard of someone "way past sixty-five" who performs heavy work, walks long distances each day, or "hasn't missed a day of work in the last fifty years." Such people are often regarded as exceptional or remarkable. There is evidence, however, that in the decades ahead such people will become commonplace. And, as we will demonstrate later, the elderly compare quite favorably with young workers when it comes to sick leave, tardiness, and low performance because of "not feeling well."

An individual supervisor, the managerial team that runs an organization, and the policies and procedures under which all its employees operate can all have an effect on an employee's health, attendance, and productivity. In the sections that follow, we consider the special and genuine problems related to the health of older employees.

Work as a Contribution to Employee Health

We have generally sensed that work is a healthy activity and that prolonged idleness can debilitate the body, mind, and spirit. While this viewpoint can certainly be carried to extremes, we know, deep down, that if humankind had no work to do, it would invent it out of boredom. This idea might be challenged by those who view their work as only onerous, demeaning, and unrewarding, but think of how many people serve in voluntary organizations, take on difficult, demanding hobbies, and invest considerable time and effort to generate wealth far beyond what they will ever use. All this is work: the expenditure of time and energy for some useful purpose.

When we get past the notion that work is something that we *have to do* in order to survive, we acknowledge that work, usually through employment, offers a person a wide range of rewards that meet a variety of physiological and psychological needs. This ability to master our situation and to meet our own needs provides a healthy balance in our life, an opportunity to grow and develop, and often the physical and mental challenges that keep us alive and alert.

At an elementary level, employment offers the regularity or rhythm of activity that may be missing in a retiree's life. This regularity is important to many who have based their life on routine, but it is also of importance to many others as a way of keeping their physical (and psychological) systems in tune. Further, for many, work provides physical and mental exercise that keeps their body and mind from atrophying. And for older people who lack adequate resources or income to play or work as desired, a job may mean the difference between want and adequate shelter, a healthy diet, and even survival.

For most, income-producing work means freedom from fear—it means meeting the inherent need for security that is so strong in humankind. Regular work, however, is associated not only with income and financial security but also with the sense of calm that comes from knowing that there is something waiting for us to do, something that has value to others. The awareness that a paycheck is given for value received is very explicit and concrete. This sense of worth and utility is clear for every day of employment, and this builds self-confidence, good inner feelings, and a secure belief that anything so necessary is not likely to be swept away.

Another important aspect of work that contributes to health is the inherent and genuine stroking that comes with possessing a job. The companionship, sense of acceptance, and feeling of belonging that friends at work bring to each other provide the mind-body link that can counteract forms of marasmus, or wasting away, that come to some who live isolated lives. The hunger for meeting these fundamental needs can help keep us healthy.

Thus, having a job maintains self-esteem and pride—that sense of distinction and accomplishment that virtually everyone needs. Though a job may be little valued by its holder until it is lost, even retirement is seen as something earned through work. Some types of work provide far more healthy recognition and challenge than others. Boring, dead-end, highly regimented work affords little in the way of health-generating good feelings, while highly exacting, intense, and unrewarding tasks can create debilitating stress and tension. Therefore, the kind of work and the way it is organized, paced, and supervised can have much to do with whether it contributes very much to the physical and mental well-being of the employee.

Capacity Devaluation

Older people disabled by accident or illness tend to be treated differently from younger people with the same type of disability. Our society's orientation toward chronic conditions, impairments, and capacity losses leads to barring many displaced or disabled workers from jobs. We mistakenly consider impairment as a disability, and this distortion leads us to regard impairment as the only real criterion of disability. The focus on medical impairment directs attention away from job performance requirements, an individual's adaptability, and the flexibility of job requirements to the more definable but less adaptable condition of impairment. Thus, if a person were to suffer a severe (say 50 percent) loss of hearing, the impairment would be seen as a disability, regardless of whether the impairment actually reduced the person's ability to do his or her job, whether the job could be modified to permit adequate performance, or whether the person was able to compensate for the impairment.

Further, research by Lawrence Haber (1970) of the U.S. Social Security Administration found that older workers who believe that their capacities are devalued by others and that therefore it will be difficult for them to keep or find work tend to accept illness and incapacity as a socially acceptable way out. Such a person tends to turn him- or herself into the kind of individual the situation requires—a disabled one. Haber says, "The acceptance of disability and the requirement of proofs by regulatory agents are also consistent with increased commitment to behavior and attitudes appropriate to incapacity" (p. 180). "The association of aging with capacity loss leads to the identification of chronological age as, in itself, a measure of capacity" (p. 168).

"Sadly," Haber finds, "the evidence on older worker attitudes suggests that self-regarding attitudes are fixed early in the course of incapacity" (p. 177). However, he also notes that "we can successfully intervene in this self-devaluation of older people and minimize its effect, especially at the outset of incapacity . . . rather than as a restorative treatment after they accept their disability" (p. 181). Thus, he makes a clear distinction between capacity loss and disability. He states that "a substantial proportion of older men [and women] become severely disabled who might otherwise make a more productive adjustment to disability. Employment and rehabilitation practices, however, systematically limit [their] adjustment opportunities, . . . and negative self-evaluations lead to inflexible and maladaptive responses" (p. 180). Health and work attitudes play a critical role in the success or failure of older people to continue to work regardless of the capacity loss involved or the extent of physical recovery. In addition, Haber cites studies in Britain that found that attitudes (emotional problems) of older working men were more important factors in hard-core absences from work for sickness than the original physical condition.

The amount of time off work for illness or injury also affects productive reemployment. "It appears that if a man has three months off work at any time in later middle-age, there is a [substantial] risk he will never return to work again" (Haber, 1970, p. 180). This fact has led many researchers to suggest that, as hospital patients generally recover faster if they get up and around soon after surgery, disabled or ill older employees should be allowed to return to work (or at least given something productive to do) as soon as is medically feasible. The longer a person remains idle, the more likely idleness is to become a lifelong pattern that often leads to further decline and possibly to an earlier death.

Since these facts about health and wellness have been known since at least the late 1960s, why are people so slow to adopt policies that would improve the productive lives of many older employees? Part of the answer may be ignorance among policymakers, but much of it also seems related to our general tendencies to accept the ill health of older employees as natural or inevitable and to expect them to retire or get along as best they can.

When President Carter signed ADEA legislation in the 1970s,

many of the bill's strongest backers linked premature retirement with ill health and early death. Physicians share this concern.

While physiological changes are most pronounced and most associated with age, they vary markedly among individuals of the same age. This suggests that we should focus on the health and wellness of each individual rather than on the age group to which an individual employee belongs.

The Disability Issue

According to the U.S. Social Security Administration, approximately half of the older workers who retired in the early 1970s did so because of disability. But as the U.S. economy shifts from physically demanding jobs to those in the information and service industries, more people will be able to work longer. The percentage of workers sixty-five and older in finance, insurance, real estate, and wholesale and retail trade already is nearly quadruple the proportion of such workers in all other industries combined.

Current governmental and private programs to improve health conditions in the workplace (such as asbestos removal) and prohibitions against the use of toxic and carcinogenic substances in manufacturing and processing industries should have a substantial long-run beneficial effect on the health of older employees. Similarly, while 85 percent of workers over sixty-five suffer from chronic diseases such as declines in sensory processes (especially vision), declines in the immune system that can lead to kidney or cardiovascular diseases, and degenerative diseases such as rheumatoid arthritis, such conditions can often be controlled medically so as to not impede a person's ability to work. A successful cataract operation on an eighty-year-old may restore that person's effective vision to its level at age forty.

Some older employees become trapped in a downward health spiral when hit by unemployment or the threat of it. The anxiety and stress of an anticipated layoff can demonstrably increase the likelihood of employee illness. If such a layoff actually occurs, it compounds the likelihood of psychologically induced sickness (which is a physical illness nevertheless). Since most employees' health insurance benefits are a function of their employment, loss of employment tends to lead to reduced health care. Consequently, such illness and reduced care make reemployment even more difficult. This downward health spiral seems to be a major factor in forced labor-force withdrawal by many older employees.

Age provides a poor indicator of an individual's health. Some people's health declines rapidly with age, while others experience little or no decline for decades. In the general population, there is a tremendous variability in wellness among older people. Among the working elderly, there is even less correspondence between age and ill health. When considering employee age and ill health, we should recognize that, first, unhealthy workers of any age tend to leave the workforce, so that those that remain are in better than average health; second, absenteeism and turnover, which are often associated with ill health, are less common among older than among younger employees; and, third, when poor health leads to poor performance, taking corrective measures that protect the interests of both parties is a major management responsibility.

Some authorities claim that health is the overwhelming factor in the retirement decision. While surveys generally show that health is *stated* as the overwhelming factor, Rones (1978, p. 4), discussing a Social Security retirement history study, suggests that the health factor may be exaggerated because "social pressures from a work oriented society may induce some older people to cite it, rather than a desire for increased leisure." The study found that of retirees who stated that they had no current health problems limiting the amount or kind of work they could do and that their health was *better* than that of their peers, about 10 percent of the men and 13 percent of the women nevertheless stated that health was their primary motive for retirement. Of those with no current health limitations who reported their health as the *same* as that of their peers, 13 percent of the men and 22 percent of the women reported health as their primary reason for retirement. Rones cites the study's conclusion that "Unless the health of all these people [23 percent of the men and 35 percent of the women] has improved since retirement, health status should not be accepted as the complete explanation for their early retirement decision" (p. 4).

Retiring "on" disability and retiring "because of" disability may be two quite different things. However, a kinder assumption is that even to those workers who retire on disability, health might be a way of resolving the psychological dilemma caused by the conflict induced by early life messages about "keeping one's nose to the grindstone," rather than a desire to escape from an onerous work situation or to enjoy more leisure.

Intellectual Decline

There has long been a popular notion, based on some rather faulty early research, that people hit their mental peak during their twenties and then begin a gradual steady slide downhill until death or senility occurs. Such a belief can in itself needlessly damage people's health. For instance, when an older person becomes disoriented, begins to forget, repeats things frequently, or experiences a substantial personality change, many supervisors, co-workers, and even family and friends tend to regard such behavior as an inevitable part of old age. The older person may easily accept their assumption and consequently not seek medical attention for symptoms that in a much younger person would be considered serious signs of some sort of breakdown.

In reality, where intelligence tests have been administered to people as they grow older, researchers have found that most people maintain their intellectual ability through their sixties and often beyond. Some current evidence suggests that there may be some general decline between ages seventy and eighty as a result of normal aging but that it is usually not severe enough to impair a person's job performance. And even such decline may be lessened as more older people maintain their general health longer.

Prominent researchers have concluded that any decline in intellectual ability, when disease is absent, is probably a result of apathy, boredom, and disuse of the mind. The only aspect of intellectual ability that appears to genuinely decline with age is speed of response. When rushed by others, older people tend to respond poorly. However, if there is evidence of rapid (noticeable) mental decline, it is important to consider illness, not age, as a likely cause.

This leads us to consider senility. Many people believe that senility is inevitable in people beyond a certain age. In reality, less than 5 percent of our population will become senile, and some of this is reversible. Senility results from a brain illness or disease and is not a direct consequence of normal aging. "Organic brain syndrome" (OBS) is a brain disease that causes memory loss, impaired thinking capacity, and disorientation. OBS comes in two forms. *Chronic* OBS is currently considered irreversible and appears to be caused by interference with the blood supply to the brain or by a disease that kills the brain cells. It may also be related to a person's genetic makeup. *Acute* OBS is generally reversible and may be caused by infection, malnutrition (often a result of poor eating habits), or a reaction to incorrect medication. If an employee develops significant signs of senility, it is important that he or she be encouraged to seek prompt medical diagnosis and attention. It is all too common for people in the workplace to express surprise at how quickly an older individual went downhill mentally (especially after an illness) without it occurring to anyone that the person may have a treatable medical problem and everyone tragically assuming that this deterioration is the inevitable consequence of age.

Heredity and Health

When we turn to physical health and vigor, we encounter a reality and a very common myth whose mistaken application can cause unfortunate consequences for organizations. The reality is that long, healthy life tends to run in families. The myth is that beyond a certain age (often specified as fifty-five, sixty, or sixty-five, depending on whom you are talking to), the physical health of many people goes steadily downhill, chronic diseases increase dramatically, and becoming bedridden for long periods of time is virtually certain.

Sadly, people often use the reality that one's heredity affects one's longevity and health to reach strange conclusions. For example, some people who know that early heart attacks run in their families often despair and wait fearfully for the inevitable to happen. Conversely, some people who are genetically well endowed (with four healthy long-lived grandparents) perceive themselves as immortal and neglect the health measures that common sense should dictate.

But our genes are not the only things that affect our lives. Diet, exercise, family life, how we manage stress, and our social support system greatly influence how long and robustly we live.

The facts that, *as of today,* men tend not to live as long as women, that blacks and some minorities tend to die earlier than whites, and similar statistical data are sometimes used by personnel specialists and supervisors for questionable purposes.

What some people perceive as memory loss in some cases may be only a slowing of response or inattention when information is first offered to us. With advanced age, usually age seventy or above, the normal loss of brain neurons, the circuits that control memory, may be great enough that memory loss of 10 percent or more may occur, especially in our short-term memory.

Some people's brains are better at some things than others. Some are good at formulating concepts or organizing information, while others may excel at storing detail. Unless our memory loss interferes with our work or daily life, we should accept it as one of life's minor irritations and possibly look for other causes than age, such as stress, grief, fatigue, alcohol, or some other problem that can lessen our abilities in general.

Today, since genetics cannot yet be used for accurate predictions of individual health or longevity, it might be most practical to strive for a healthy life-style and expect the best.

GULHEMP: The Antidote

Instead of making assumptions about a person's ability to perform on a job, why not measure that person's ability to do a given job? Youry (1975) describes a "unique system for testing an employee's physical condition and providing a parallel analysis of a particular job" (p. 5). It "aims to match workers to specific jobs, to underscore an individual worker's physical capacities for job performance, and to make it clear to all concerned that capacity and ability—not chronological age—are the determining factors in job performance" (p. 5).

This technique, developed by Leon Koyl, has been successfully applied in industry for more than twenty-five years in the United States and Canada. It is known as GULHEMP, for *G*eneral physique, *U*pper extremities, *L*ower extremities, *H*earing, *E*yesight, *M*ental, and *P*ersonality. The *M* and *P* factors have not been utilized in the system for some years because of possible conflict with federal equal employment opportunity requirements. They have largely been replaced by performance testing—if the "person-job match" is good in other respects, testing is done of the person's ability to perform the job or tasks directly correlated to job tasks to see whether mastery can be achieved.

The magic of GULHEMP lies in its positive approach: It emphasizes what an individual, regardless of age or disability, *can do* on a specific job. To appreciate the uniqueness of GULHEMP, contrast it with most employee health evaluations. Typical health reports focus on the negative aspects of a worker's physical state. They note such things as "heart condition" or "emphysema" and abound with limiting statements such as "avoid high-stress work" or "cannot lift heavy loads." Therefore, supervisors and managers glancing over the typical medical report learn only what the worker cannot or should not do. In the absence of any positive information, is it any surprise that supervisors tend to take a negative view of older employee capability?

GULHEMP does not imply indifference to a person's medical ailments. Nor does it deal in false optimism or paint a rosy medical diagnosis that is dangerous. By contrast, the process starts with a first-class head-to-toe medical examination. It "checks hearing and visual capacity, heart and pulmonary functions, ability to lift and push and the range of the individual's mobility" (Youry, 1975, p. 5). It includes blood, urine, and other lab diagnostic tests that are part of a conventional physical exam. When health problems are detected, the employee (or prospective employee) is notified, and a nurse refers the person to other medical practitioners for treatment.

The next step in the GULHEMP process is to analyze a particular job to obtain an accurate profile of its fitness requirements and to determine whether the person in question can do that job. A detailed study of the work to be performed is generally conducted by experienced job analysts or industrial engineers. A specialist starts with the U.S. Department of Labor's *Dictionary of Occupational Titles* (1991), which supplies basic information on the job requirements of more than 30,000 jobs. But the analyst also studies how and under what conditions a specific job is performed in the environment where the person is expected to work. A work sheet is created that lists the physical demands of the job, environmental factors, and perhaps hazards that an older person may be particularly exposed to. These analyses have been helpful to the employer or prospective employer by identifying hazards and recommending ways to meet the Occupational Safety and Health Act's requirements for a safe work environment.

In a classic program, GULHEMP was used to help older people stay employed (by redesigning work so that a person with diminished abilities could still do the job), take a new job with the same employer, or find a job that the person could demonstrably do. Success was substantial. In 1970, "the GULHEMP system became the focal point of operations for the Industrial Health Counseling Service (IHCS) in Portland, Maine" (Youry, 1975, p. 5). The Maine Employment Security Commission received a grant from the Manpower Administration of the U.S. Department of Labor and contracted with the National Council on Aging to set up an experimental project to determine the effect of the GULHEMP process on employment of elderly workers. In two years, "almost 100 Portland firms had subscribed to the service, and more than a thousand middle aged and older workers who up until then had been unable to find jobs because of their age found work" (p. 5).

Local firms that used IHCS services paid a reasonable fee for both the physical exam and the job analysis. In one month, 137 middle-aged and older unemployed people applied for work at the Portland Unemployment Security Office. Even the 30 percent of them who were between ages forty and forty-five were considered too old for certain types of jobs by many prospective employers. However, many such employers tended to change their minds when confronted with the GULHEMP concept and the results of the employees' physical exams. As Youry pointed out, "Age is never a barrier to working, only physical limitations are. And these can be measured and fully compensated for by using a yardstick called GULHEMP" (p. 9).

Supervisors and managers in many firms need to be confronted with the reality of GULHEMP if they avoid working with or employing older employees because of presumed physical incapabilities. GULHEMP has demonstrated that it is an effective way for firms and governmental agencies to invest in the future of older employees. It helps create independent people able to work and produce and to pay taxes to help support our society.

Health Versus Work

Many older people are showing that the common belief that old age is a physical toboggan slide is outdated. Today, many people are actually improving their health as they get older because of their increased attention to good nutrition, exercise programs, and the use of stress-management techniques. Many researchers firmly believe that while illness and decline can occur at any age, half or more of the decline experienced by older Americans is due to inactivity, boredom, and the belief that infirmity is inevitable. Active, involved, intellectually challenged employees with an effective social support system in the workplace need not necessarily experience a decline in their ability to get the job done.

Sheppard (1971, p. 26) reports that of 2,123,000 males over sixty-five in the labor force, about 67 percent reported that they had no chronic health condition or any that limited their activities. Of 55,000 that were unemployed and seeking work, 58 percent indicated no chronic or limiting conditions. But most striking was the finding that of 5,431,000 men not in the labor force through retirement or for other reasons, 38 percent had no health condition that would keep them from working.

The critical point is that, while most employees who are out of the labor force report health problems, a substantial proportion report no chronic health problems or conditions that limit their ability to work. With this enormous healthy but aged resource idle, we may need to ask ourselves what can be done to encourage at least some of these people to become producers again. It is clear that many people work, produce well, and enjoy their jobs despite chronic physical problems. Perhaps management's concerns about the health and wellness issues in today's workplace are overdrawn. As our workforce ages, we may need to be more realistic and focus not on employee illnesses as such but on how they affect work output in individual cases.

Toward a Healthier Future

Numerous drugs improve memory in both humans and animals, but some have severe side effects or create only small, brief changes. However, other drugs, such as nimodipine, do not have strong side effects. While this drug has not yet been thoroughly studied for its effects on human beings, there is considerable promise that research will ensure that, in time, even in those rare cases where memory loss affects work output, such disabilities can be overcome.

Forecasts of the effects of medical research on our aging workforce in the next two decades are startling and heartening. But even without such a medical revolution, there is much that employers can do now to encourage good work from older workers.

Part Two

Older Employees and Organizational Success

We should grab the opportunities offered by older people who want to work. No matter what our job, we can encourage and support policies that gain the special productivity dividends offered by older workers. Some of us will be in a position to design and implement such policies. A pervasive organizational culture of invitation, inclusion, participation, personal development, and opportunity for older people should parallel that offered to all other employees.

The next five chapters deal with special factors influencing the structure of such a culture: the realities of and potential for older employee productivity; the key ingredients in older employee health and wellness and what the organization can do to help; the training and educational methods most suited to effective learning by such personnel; a variety of special ways in which supervisors and others can lift older worker motivation and morale; and important program elements for achieving age-neutral human resource management. The information offered here is research based and theoretically sound and has been practically applied in a wide variety of successful organizations.

Chapter 5

Realizing the Potential of Older Workers

What kind of output can we expect from an older employee? While many assume that ability to produce declines with age, in many fields the opposite is true. If productivity is defined as the value of the work received for the money or resources expended, age may have little bearing on it. An experienced auto mechanic of sixty-eight may return several times the value in marketable labor that an eighteen-year-old just learning the trade might, even taking into account wage differentials. Similarly, an older salesperson might well be able to outsell a younger competitor for a variety of reasons related to experience, know-how, and empathy, whereas in a job requiring considerable physical strength, a younger employee might have an edge. In any of these cases, it is necessary to evaluate each situation on its own merits to achieve justice to the individual and to the organization.

Factors Favoring Older Employees

What is the general productivity record of older employees? Where do their strengths and favorable work attributes lie? Where can management focus its attention for greatest payoffs from older employees?

Because of their greater experience, older employees usually have a more farsighted view of their work. Perhaps because they know that they cannot find a new job as easily as younger people can (and they are not as inclined to look), their attitude toward their work tends to be more accepting and responsible. In addition, if they have invested a number of years with the organization, they tend to be more loyal to the company and to require fewer inducements to remain with it.

According to Yolles, Krinsky, Kieffer, and Carone (1984, p. 18), by the time they reach their middle years, most employees have developed work habits that enable them to produce at a steadier rate and achieve consistent quality. Given the right environment, the output of such workers can remain of a high quality. Older workers also have some advantages with regard to accidents. Norman Root (1981, pp. 30–31) reports that a study based on data collected by the U.S. Bureau of Labor Statistics "involving the analysis of more than one million workers' compensation records, from agencies in thirty states, concluded that younger workers are hurt more often but less seriously than older employees." While older employees' injuries tended to be more severe and long-lasting, especially in industrial accidents, these employees often developed techniques for avoiding accidents that younger employees had not yet mastered. This was particularly true when the older employees had long experience at the same or a similar type of work. The same findings hold true for illness.

Management may therefore see a statistical trade-off between younger, more accident-prone employees and older, safer workers who, if injured, would experience a longer recovery period. The matter of accidents becomes a nonissue, however, when the organization assumes responsibility for providing a safe work environment. In addition, office work, work in familiar surroundings and less stressed atmospheres, and self-paced (versus machine-paced) work tend to decrease the likelihood of accidents, as do good physical condition, agility, and alertness on the part of the individual. Also, older employees themselves will often sense when and whether they are losing their capacity to master their work situation and will be open to or even suggest work reassignment or changes in work methods or equipment that will increase the safety quotient of their job—if management is amenable and open to such changes.

The older worker usually shines brightest when it comes to absenteeism and tardiness. Wall and Shatshat (1981, p. 28) report that Bankers Life and Casualty Company, which has a policy of hiring older employees, conducted a six-month study and found that 27.1 percent of the elderly had perfect attendance, a record matched by only 10 percent of those under sixty-five years of age. Gerald L. Maguire, director of Bankers Life Corporate Services, said that his company has found that when older workers seem to be skipping, "It's not often age-related." Moreover, the rate of separations (discharges, quits, and disciplinary layoffs) is highest among those age twenty-five and under and very low among those over forty-five except for early retirement situations in recent years.

Tomorrow's Older Leaders

At the executive end of the employee scale, according to Deutsch, Shea and Evans, Inc., a prestigious, worldwide, executive search firm, there are often better reasons for hiring older rather than younger managers (Verespej, 1975). The company concluded that among other advantages, "they are the last generation to retain the traditional work ethic." They also have better attendance records and are sick less often. They are more experienced in the means of getting things done "within the system—and they are less prone to view the job as a stepping stone to a better job with another company" (p. 34). Sally Jacobs (1984, p. 24) makes the following point:

> Although people are retiring at ever-younger ages, there are nevertheless lodged in the upper echelons of companies . . . a handful of senior executives who not only do not lose their potency with age; but . . . thrive on the passing of years. We are not talking merely old; we are talking *Really Old.*
>
> As they move into their eighth and even ninth decades, these men, these Methuselahs among executives, are considered no longer merely old, but genuine

> phenomena. Their ability to work and their level of activity defy rational explanation. They thrive on a level of activity that would exhaust folks half a century their junior.
>
> For their companies, they provide the invaluable perspective of several score of years in the business. And the confidence they have developed in the course of that experience often enables them to be more innovative and receptive to change than their younger colleagues.

Age, therefore, should not be considered a sufficient explanation for change or decline in an individual without other supporting data. As J. Sonnenfeld (1978, p. 91) citing many studies, has said, "The high variation of . . . performance within age groups compared with the variation between age groups suggests that individual differences are much more important than age group differences. The need to evaluate potential on an individual basis, and not by age group, has been convincingly established in these studies."

The Expectation of Decline: Fact and Fiction

For many people, the expectation of physical and mental decline becomes a self-fulfilling prophecy—the expectation of an event tends to cause it to happen. We are all fed a great deal of negative and often false information about what happens to us as we grow older. As we have noted, the elderly are portrayed as more rigid, less able to learn, and more forgetful than younger people. A study by Dubin, Shelton, and McConnell (1978, p. 43) found that the younger the survey respondent, the earlier these effects were believed to occur. Twenty-five-year-olds, for example, believed that the effects of aging could be seen at thirty-five and that by forty-five the person is "on his way over the hill."

For many people in our population, these stereotypes are accepted as reality, so that each tiny ache or pain or lapse of memory that they experience is taken as a sure sign that they are getting old and consequently cannot perform as well as they had previously. As a result, their spirits flag, their self-image suffers, and they may produce the very effects that they fear. They also often get reinforcing negative feedback from their contemporaries and may return the favor.

While many older people are experiencing active, healthy, fully involved lives, with no hint of decline, such cases are often dismissed as exceptions, because "everyone knows" that one's abilities decline with age. All of this is despite the fact that there is no conclusive evidence that age causes changes in abilities and behavior (rather than being a contributory factor in specific cases).

A 1987 survey of human resource managers nationwide by *Personnel* magazine, as reported by Blocklyn (1987, p. 16), revealed that 14 percent of the respondents found older workers more productive than younger workers. Not surprisingly, they attributed this high productivity to experience, reliability, maturity, and a strong work ethic. However, the 6 percent of the respondents at the other end of the scale, those who found older workers less productive, did not necessarily feel that this was the result of diminished abilities on the part of the workers. A resistance to change (an attitude that in itself can be changed) and other negative attitudes, rather than lack of ability, created the problem. Most importantly, however, 80 percent saw little difference between the productivity of younger and older employees.

As we have noted, the *decremental theory of aging* assumes that abilities decline as workers age. But many researchers have noted that the greater an individual's experience, skill, and competence, the smaller is his or her decrease in productivity with advancing age. For example, Giniger, Dispenzieri, and Eisenberg (1983) reported on a study of 667 garment workers that examined the variables of worker productivity, absenteeism, accidents, and turnover. Of these workers, 212 held "speed" jobs and 455 held "skill" jobs. A cross-sectional design was used, with the workers divided into six age categories. It was hypothesized that declines in physical abilities with age would be greater on speed jobs than on skill jobs. However, this was not the case. Older workers surpassed the younger workers on both speed *and* skill work. When partial correlations were made between experience and performance that removed the influence of age, it was shown that experience rather than age determined performance.

While several studies in different industries have noted a modest reduction in speed of performance among elderly workers, the research cited above offers the employees' accumulated experience, better work methods, and consistency of output as inducements for the retention of highly experienced older employees. Yet, lest we conclude that such reality applies only to production workers, consider the following. In an article entitled "Does Life Exist for Copywriters over 45?" Fields (1978) indicated that there has been no problem placing writers forty-five and older if they have stayed up to date and demonstrated through their proof books and other evidence that they can still come up with fresh, creative conceptual campaign ideas. The author cites several examples of older writers who competed successfully with much younger candidates and produced much more reliably for their employers.

Furthermore, at the managerial level, research has found that older employees are able to discern the value of information more accurately than younger decision makers. The quality of their work is high, and they seek relatively large quantities of information when formulating their decisions. On the downside, senior managers appear to be less confident of their decisions and more willing to alter them.

The critical factors are the job that the person is doing and the person him- or herself. Many conditions can affect the older worker's performance level. For example, education, health, level of activity, and socioeconomic class are known to have a significant impact on one's intellectual performance. In this respect, the elderly are as different from each other as are members of any other group. Those who come from an advantaged socioeconomic class and who therefore have the luxury of greater flexibility in their lives tend to maintain their level of intellectual competence. However, even for the majority of people, it has been shown in studies cited in the special report on aging by the National Institute on Aging (U.S. Department of Health and Human Services, 1982, p. 1) that intellectual ability not only is maintained as one grows older but, in some cases, is actually improved.

Rix (1979, p. 787) quotes the late Ross McFarland, one of the most noted researchers in the field of ergonomics, who said, "Compensation takes place for every [physical] decline." Rix also states that "experience and judgment may be much more relevant to a particular job than the ability to lift 100 pound weights." Supervisors and managers who expect good performance usually get it; those who do not expect it do not get it.

What the Older Employee Can Contribute

According to Robert P. Hagen (1983, p. 5), older people are generally credited with "excelling at such work as teaching, counseling, craftwork, working with younger people, historical research, and filling judicial and administrative roles." It is in the role of mentor, however, that some older workers can be of greatest service to the organization. Many older people develop, on or off the job, skills related to coaching, counseling, and communication that could be useful to the organization. For example, Kevin, a young man in his late teens, had dropped out of school and had a record for job-hopping when he was hired as a plumber's helper by a medium-sized contractor. He was assigned to work with John, an older and experienced plumber. He quickly noted that John did not "put him down" as the other journeymen did to their assistants. John taught him many things about the work, including the "why's," and exhibited persistent, reliable attention to details. Kevin quickly noted that "John was the only lead man who did not 'rip off' the company by sitting in the truck drinking coffee half the morning." Kevin developed a deep respect for John and his ways and in time came to emulate him and the type of work that he did.

The value of encouraging older high performers to develop their coaching and training skills is another argument for a supervisor's being aware of *all* the abilities of his or her employees, rather than simply those necessary to do the job. Choosing an older person for special tasks, however, should be done carefully because of other people's possible perception of the assignment. Three other characteristics of the older employee also require special consideration.

Maturity. A solid body of research indicates that older employees tend to make up their minds more slowly than younger ones but consider more factors when doing so. Their judgment tends to be sounder, though they are less inclined toward risk, particularly impulsive risk. This does not mean that older people are inherently more conservative than younger people. Taking advantage of one's lifelong experiences should not be confused with fear. Timidity, uncertainty, or a tendency to avoid hard decisions is most often a lifelong behavior pattern that affects some people and not others. Moreover, training in problem-solving techniques may improve the older employee's ability to make decisions more quickly and systematically. Mature behavior and judgment in its workforce can be a primary asset to the organization.

Synthesis. Older employees have collected a lifetime of observations, facts, and data. At some point, often at about fifty-five to sixty-five years of age, they may begin to synthesize this learning in comprehensive ways. Older people begin to build elaborate and often elegant systems of thought that allow them to extrapolate and draw new conclusions about their experience and learning. These insights form the basis of a mature personal philosophy that can be of value to the organization. This is particularly a period when older managers can make their greatest contribution toward influencing the direction that the organization or the organizational unit will take.

This ability of older people to synthesize is a natural result of processing their experience. It is, however, rarely recognized or realized, and few have been taught a systematic way to do this. Assigning problems to older employees (without excessive pressure and deadlines), sharing current information with them, and seeking their counsel can go a long way toward encouraging such distillation of experience and the fabrication of new approaches to solving organizational problems.

Creativity. It takes ideas to come up with ideas. A large part of creative thought emerges through the process of association; that is, seeing the similarity or dissimilarity between new ideas and the things that we already know. This is not merely a process of analysis but often involves making the intuitive leap between what is and what could be. The more experiences we have stored in our mind, the more we are likely to see a connection between a need and a unique solution. Experience not only leads to more reasoned decisions but also imbues the worker with a greater sense of self-confidence. If such employees are allowed flexibility in assignments and deadlines, they can pursue more creative solutions to company problems than might the younger worker who is hampered by inexperience and anxiety about pleasing superiors.

Keeping the Older Employee Productive

Organizations keep older employees productive in essentially the same ways as other employees are kept productive—by providing them high but achievable goals, giving them recognition for accomplishment, making them fully functioning members of the work group, removing their fears about security, providing them meaningful work, keeping them informed, and offering them opportunity.

Unfortunately, both employees and managers have sometimes stopped looking at the future of the older person. Assumptions about retirement, investment in the employee, and even the employee's ability to produce will long precede a decline in the employee's ability or willingness to contribute. If management and employees could agree to a moratorium on assumptions about an employee's age as it relates to his or her abilities, both might be better off. If the organization would do more work-oriented preretirement counseling as part of its ongoing career counseling, years before retirement age, it might learn more about what each individual needs and wants, both before and after retirement. This could also increase employees' awareness of available options, the need for planning, and the reality that the need to be productive does not stop at a specific age. An increasing number of older people are beginning to insist that they not be sidelined.

In an analysis of several studies on the attitudes and performance of older workers, DeMicco and Reid (1988, p. 60) stressed the point that "job satisfaction reflects the employee's response to the job or to some aspect of the job, so that day-to-day events might affect an employee's level of job satisfaction." Organizational commitment, on the other hand, is more global in nature, reflecting the worker's effective response to the organization as a whole, and is less subject to change on the basis of transitory events. "Since commitment is connected to lower turnover, lower absenteeism, and better job performance, an employee's willingness to make a commitment to the organization is a valuable attribute. The mean level of overall organizational commitment in older workers . . . was found to be higher than reported in previous research." Therefore, committed older employees may well be more productive and enduring in their output than younger, less committed employees.

More companies faced with legal obstacles to enforced retirement are beginning to plan for the long-term "full use" of employees up to the day when they leave the workplace. This should reduce the tendency to expect coasting in a person's last few years. Management needs to continue to invest in its valuable older human resources, and employees need to continue to invest in themselves as long as they are employed. To do less will cheat both.

Chapter 6

Successful Health and Wellness Programs

Since, by federal law, most employees can work as long as they wish so long as their performance meets explicit work standards, the continued health of older employees is critical to both employer and employee. Here we move from the macro view of health and wellness issues of older workers to specific things that organizations can do to maintain or improve older employee health.

A 1989 AARP-sponsored poll of 400 companies (Stephens, 1989) lists the rising cost of health care coverage as one of the primary obstacles that impede the full use of older workers in American business. Helping employees maintain their health and vigor through preventive measures and wellness programs will certainly contribute to at least slowing, if not checking, the continued rise in health care costs, for these programs are highly cost-effective. Many excellent companies are working as partners with their employees to accent health and wellness, while others are simply continuing to pay the fare for ill employees.

Many firms, government agencies, and institutions have developed highly successful, beneficial, and rewarding programs that help their employees reduce their illnesses. These programs have ranged from no-cost activities, such as lunch-hour aerobics classes taught by volunteer instructors, to complex stay-well programs whereby employees receive free physical examinations, considerable training in health-producing activities, and the use of elaborate exercise and weight-control facilities and equipment. In many such cases, the employer benefits by measurable improvements in attendance, higher personal output, lower medical costs and improved organizational morale. However, the greatest long-term companywide gain is probably the mutual caring that grows out of this type of support for employees' health.

When it comes to older employees, some special efforts might well pay off. Since such personnel may have less experience in engaging in employer-sponsored activities, they may feel unduly self-conscious and be pessimistic about their health and their ability to improve it themselves. However, these are merely problems to be overcome. And often they are very much problems of certain individuals rather than characteristics of older employees as a group. Much depends on how individual older people perceive themselves and what they feel able to do about their physical condition. Here, for example, the use of the term *wellness* is useful, for it reflects a focus on positive proactive measures rather than the reactive, curative (after-we-are-ill) approach with which many older people are most familiar.

Employee Health: Perception and Reality

Rubenstein (1982, p. 33) reports on a study that found that people aged fifty to seventy perceive themselves as healthier and feel relatively younger than those under twenty-five. In many respects, the image of the enfeebled older person has been replaced by one of a tanned, golf-playing Florida retiree. But this last image no more characterizes all of the elderly than does the wheelchair-bound stereotype. The reality is that many older people, especially women, live at or near the poverty level, and a good percentage suffer from chronic illnesses such as arthritis, high blood pressure, or diabetes.

Colburn (1985, p. 14) says, "Older Americans are seven times as likely as young adults (aged 17 to 44) to have a heart condition or high blood pressure, and 10 times as likely to have diabetes or arthritis." Yet these statistics are often irrelevant when we are considering a specific older individual.

Eisendorfer and Cohen (1980) state that some elderly people with serious health problems may be deluding themselves about their condition. In a Duke University longitudinal study, 44 percent of the aged who were actually in poor health rated themselves as in good or excellent condition. Consequently, as far as behavior is concerned, perceptions may be more important than reality. "It also may be that many of the elderly, along with the rest of society, accept disease as a normal part of aging rather than as something treatable, which in most cases it is" (p. 56).

Most important is the fact that many of the diseases experienced by the elderly tend to be "life-style" illnesses; that is, they can be prevented or improved by medical technology and by the individual, the community, and the organization taking a more responsible role in altering unhealthy modes of living. The key to improved health may well be not the illnesses that a person experiences but how that person regards his or her illness and how he or she decides to live and act.

Rubenstein (1982, pp. 32–33) reported on an extensive *Psychology Today* survey of 25,000 respondents that reported that, "For both men and women, feelings of health and vitality increased with age—even though the incidence of chronic illness also rises. People under 25 said they feel several years older than their real age; people in their thirties felt about five years younger; and people in their 40s about 10 years younger. In their 50s people feel 13 years younger than they are, and those over 70 feel about 17 years younger." Also, older people expect to live longer than younger people. *Psychology Today* found that those under twenty-five expected to die at about age seventy-three, while those who are over seventy expect to last, on the average, to eighty-six. Since it is well established that the longer a person lives, the longer that person can expect to hold on, positive expectations may enhance a person's actual durability. The authors offer a powerful thought as to why older people seem more healthy: "A more disturbing and probably more accurate explanation . . . is simply that health pessimists die sooner, leaving only the optimistic vital people to tell the tale of old age."

The foregoing suggests that employers in general and supervisors in particular can have a positive impact on the health of older people by encouraging them to take a more positive, upbeat approach and being supportive of their efforts to improve or maintain their health. In contrast, saying, for instance, "Jim, you'll never be able to quit smoking after all these years" is a destructive and often nasty way to treat a person who would like to do whatever it takes to live longer. "There may be a special place in hell reserved for downers—they never get to meet anyone—complete loneliness is what they have earned for the way they have treated other people's aspirations," said one health-oriented supervisor (personal communication).

Taking Charge

How do people go about trying to control their health? The respondents to the *Psychology Today* survey (Rubenstein, 1982, pp. 30–31) said that "diet, exercise and positive thinking are very important." And why should feelings of good health and health itself improve with age? Again, "Older people seem to care for themselves better than young people. They take more preventive measures, like getting regular checkups, eating breakfast, getting enough sleep and using their seat belts." Also, "people over 60 exercise more than those in their 40s or 50s, eat to excess less often, and seem to be less self-conscious and neurotic than younger people." For example, while people under twenty on the average reported twelve medical symptoms, only four were reported by those over seventy.

In 1981, the National Health Interview Survey, conducted by the National Center for Health Statistics, stated that eight out of ten elderly people asked to compare their health with the health of others of their age described their own as good or excellent. Only eight percent rated their own health as poor in comparison to that of others of their age. These and other data reported in the survey led the staff of the U.S. Senate Special Committee on Aging (1984, p. 52) to conclude that "an individual's evaluation of his or her own health is often the most important assessment of personal health status." Even though they may have a physical limitation, most Americans evaluate their health favorably, and this belief tends to help them perform more effectively.

Two results of such studies that may have profound implications for the future are that of people sixty-five and older, those with higher levels of education tend to rate their health more favorably than those with less education; and those who are currently employed rate their health status better than do other older people. Overall, the majority of Americans of all ages agree that elderly Americans are healthier today than they were a decade or so ago. However, we should not overlook another reality about health and wellness. Wilbur Cohen, former U.S. secretary of health, education, and welfare, has said that "while it is true we're a healthier, more able, population, that doesn't mean everyone" (Colburn, 1985, p. 14). Organizations and supervisors at all levels may well encounter older employees whose health and wellness problems are critical. Here the task is to detect the problem early, counsel the employee in a healthy, productive way, provide whatever support is appropriate to resolve the problem most expeditiously (that is, medical attention, sick leave, and so on), and, where possible, take whatever measures are necessary to maintain health and productivity.

Stress and Wellness

Of particular importance to older employees is the fact that many types of illnesses have a cumulative aspect. Excessive negative stress, whether it comes from the work itself, an arbitrary supervisor, bad personal habits, a troubled home life, the invasion of disease germs, or excessive eating, appears to be basic to triggering illness. If the stressors (the external sources of the stress, such as tobacco smoke) are not controlled, if a person becomes ill and does not receive prompt and adequate medical attention, or if the person does not learn to invoke what Dr. Herbert Benson (Benson and Klipper, 1975, pp. 25–27) calls the "relaxation response," that "natural and protective mechanism against overstress which allows us to turn off harmful bodily effects of stress," so as to manage his or her internal reaction to stress, that person's body may, over time, lose its ability to respond effectively to stress, and consequently the person may become ill more frequently.

Fighting off a particular illness may result in the development of antibodies to that disease, thereby providing a form of immunity to that specific ailment, but that victory does not enhance one's general health. In addition, calling on the immune system to tackle one disease after another or (as may be the case for a person with an unhealthy life-style) several stressors at the same time can lessen the body's resilience—its ability to respond effectively to new assaults. This is especially true where one organ, such as the lung or heart, is constantly subject to abuse—that organ may lose its ability to bounce back in the future. While organs that are no longer under assault, such as the lungs when freed from smoking, have restorative power, the earlier in life one stops smoking, for example, the greater is the body's ability to heal.

In a special report on aging, the National Institute on Aging (U.S. Department of Health and Human Services, 1982, p. 21) indicated that people commonly assume that when older people are stressed, they tend to use escapist fantasy, hostile reactions, denial, and withdrawal. However, scientists found that older and middle-aged adults are somewhat less likely to use these coping mechanisms than are young adults. The report describes the findings of two researchers, Robert R. McCrae and Paul Costa, who studied three categories of life stress: *threats,* such as those posing a present or future danger; *losses,* requiring adaptation to a harm that has already occurred; and *challenges,* which open up favorable but taxing opportunities. They found that older participants tended to use less positive thinking and less self-blame and humor than did younger subjects. They were also more likely to take things one step at a time.

The findings indicated that age itself was not the cause of most of the results. Instead, the researchers discovered that individuals of different age groups faced different kinds of stress. Older people experienced fewer challenges and more threats than the younger groups did. Losses were about equally frequent among all age groups. The type of stress influenced the type of coping mechanism selected. Faith tends to be a more common choice when threat is the stressor, whereas rational action and humor are more common when the stress is a loss or a challenge. "When these factors are taken into account, most of the age variations in coping disappear."

Undue physical or mental stress on an older employee can often be reduced by job redesign or by voluntary downgrading. The employer that ignores workplace stress on older employees may be risking lower productivity, increased workers' compensation costs, and premature loss of some of its best employees.

Special Problems

Dr. Herbert S. Parnes (1980, p. 27) argues that investing in the health of the labor force would significantly reduce the labor-market disadvantage of older employees and reduce public dependency when unemployment results from health decline. "Long term policies to improve the health of the workforce should be encouraged, not only on humanitarian grounds, but because bad health deprives the economy of otherwise willing human resources. The principal causes of illness and death among older people are related in large part to the character of the individual's life style. Increased research on effective methods of influencing the health related behaviors of individuals early in life would appear to have potentially high payoffs." Employer efforts to offer training, support, and guidance in these directions can help greatly. The current trend toward employee assistance programs is another positive sign of employers' interest in the relationship between health and productivity. Though often based on efforts to solve performance problems, as with drug and alcohol counseling, these and other types of assistance can contribute mightily to general workplace health.

Among the problems that companies will face increasingly in the future are two for which answers are at present scarce: how to deal with terminally ill patients on the payroll and how to deal with the increasing number of older people classed as handicapped. The AIDS epidemic has brought the issue of terminally ill employees to the forefront of human resource managers' thinking in recent years, but the problem of terminally ill employees would have received increased attention in any event as our population aged and laws to protect employment of the elderly increased in power.

Changes in the laws governing the employment of the handicapped will gain increased pertinence as people work longer. Several major corporations, especially 3M and Control Data, have found it efficient to implement an internal rehabilitation program in the hopes of retaining disabled employees and keeping them productive. Characteristic of such efforts is a search for positions throughout the organization where the valuable skills and abilities of older employees can continue to be used.

Another growing area of concern is the issue of elder care. For the seven million households caring for a disabled elderly parent or relative, family obligations often turn into highly stressful, full-time jobs. If child care was the employee benefit of the 1980s, many experts predict that elder care will be the benefit issue of the 1990s and beyond. Though many companies are resisting elder care benefits because of the already high cost of health care, the costs of increased absenteeism, tardiness, phone calls during working hours, employee stress, and shortened hours are exacting their toll. And some employees are in dual-dependency families, where they are responsible for children as well as for older relatives. Any form of wellness program that helps such employees cope may well be worth the investment.

Stay-Well Programs

In recent years, a growing number of firms have developed employee health programs that concentrate on improving and/or maintaining employee health by encouraging healthy habits and preventive medicine. Such programs are often free to all employees, and in a few companies, such as Control Data Corporation, the program is open to spouses as well. Employers gain much from promoting employee health and wellness, such as decreased absenteeism, reduced insurance costs, more consistent productivity, higher morale, and lower peripheral costs (such as hiring temporary personnel to fill in for ill employees). But employees can gain even more: greater ongoing health, feeling physically better more of the time, a prolonged life with fewer bouts of illness, and the good feelings that flow from self-mastery and personal achievement. Most of these programs are based on the following premises:

1. *Wellness* is our natural state and can be preserved through alertness, healthy habits, and early attention to developing illness or health problems.
2. *Life-style*—that is, the habits we engage in every day (smoking or not smoking, what we eat or drink, and so on)—has a major impact on the likelihood of illness and the length of our lives.
3. *Change* for the better, personal (and even family) habits, can be achieved through positive encouragement and strong support from employer, co-workers, and supervisors.
4. *The workplace* is one of the most effective environments to encourage wellness, because so much of a person's time is spent there, because work requires a high energy level, and because the potential for transmission of disease from person to person is very high.
5. *Stress* as a primary precipitant of illness can be great or small at work, but it is there that the management of stress can be dealt with most effectively.
6. *Training* in how to manage one's stress, how to give up smoking, or how to properly engage in an exercise program can most effectively be offered by an employer.
7. *Support systems* such as medical examinations, employee assistance programs (drug or alcohol counseling), and the dietary offerings in the employees' cafeteria are only a few of the ways that companies and government agencies are encouraging health and wellness among their employees.

At the core of stay-well programs is the paramount belief that each individual is ultimately responsible for his or her own health and wellness, and to an incredible degree each of us need not be passive or dependent on medical professionals for maintaining our health. Doctors may be needed to cure our illnesses or disease once they have a hold on us, but proactive health habits can often be used to avoid that eventuality.

Wellness promotion in industry has taken hold because of the observable gains derived by both employees and employers. Dr.

John P. McCann (1981, pp. 39–40), president and chairman of the board at Control Data's Life Extension Institute, has stated that "the reason for this increased interest . . . comes from four factors: 1) the escalating costs of a sickness oriented health care system; 2) the limited availability of health care professionals which, in turn, has resulted in an increased need to rely on self-help; 3) the emergence of a more sophisticated [health care] consumer; and 4) a changing value system that places more emphasis on fitness, good appearance and moderation in many aspects of human behavior." McCann also says that "Society in general and industry in particular are embracing the concepts that: 'to stay well' is less costly than 'to get well;' to *prevent* is more rational than to *cure;* and that a healthy lifestyle enhances the chances for improved health, longevity and the quality of life." McCann's view is backed up by the reality that "the cost of a sickness oriented health care system" is approaching a half trillion dollars a year and that less than 3 percent of that is spent on the *prevention* of illness.

While major corporations such as Control Data, Johnson & Johnson, Prudential Insurance, General Foods, Kimberly-Clark, Sentry Insurance, and Xerox have exemplary comprehensive long-term programs in health promotion, many other organizations are doing their part. Thousands of companies, institutions, and government agencies offer stress-management training, promote employee sports teams, sponsor after-hours aerobics courses and encourage employees to attend organizationally sponsored programs to fight alcohol and tobacco use, dietary problems, and drug abuse.

Nothing in a sound wellness program discourages seeking medical attention when needed; such programs simply discourage passively waiting until illness takes hold before doing anything about it. The development of health-producing habits and a focus on illness prevention are becoming the first and second lines of defense in the struggle for wellness. For older employees, this shift in orientation from a concern about illness to active efforts to generate health is critical.

According to Shea (1982, p. 23), "older employees, especially less sophisticated individuals, tend to have lifelong conditioning to the illness centered medical model of treatment. Further, any poor health habits they may possess, have generally been reinforced by decades of practice and social confirmation. And finally, early life conditioning has led many to deny symptoms, avoid going to doctors (males especially), and to disregard the advice they do receive." While these generalizations do not apply to the many individuals who are taking their health opportunities seriously, they do apply to a vast segment of today's older workforce. Therefore, the design of a wellness program can be critically important to older employees in particular, since this is a population where health issues are considered to be most serious.

Designing a Wellness Program

Whether an organization offers a comprehensive stay-well program such as Control Data's or can afford only limited assistance, several elements of a good design can have particularly beneficial effects on an older employee without a great investment in resources or facilities. Several of these elements are discussed below.

Developing Health Risk Profiles. Drs. Lewis Robbins and Jack Hall have developed a process for identifying risk factors for all the major causes of death; the process, which is now computerized, can provide a comprehensive profile for each person at a modest cost (McCann, 1981, p. 41). In many programs, participants have their blood pressure taken and a blood sample drawn and analyzed, as well as being weighed and measured. By filling out a questionnaire on his or her life-style, mental outlook, and medical and family history, each person provides information that leads to a profile that not only identifies personal health risks but compares chronological age with "risk-age." Perhaps most importantly, the profile shows how a person's "risk-age" can be reduced if he or she changes certain behaviors. Most organizations follow up this type of profiling with programs and supportive systems that help people change their behaviors for the better. It should be no surprise that the earlier an older person is profiled, the more profound the effects of the changes on that person's health will tend to be.

Managing Personal Stress. When a person learns to use the "relaxation response" (various meditative methods that produce a state of deep relaxation), avoid excessive behaviors (such as eating too fast), give up self-destructive habits, cope effectively with external stressors that cannot be eliminated, avoid being drawn into negative interpersonal transactions with others, and take on healthy, satisfying behaviors (such as exercise or a productive hobby), that person's health usually improves dramatically.

Modern advertising would have us believe that headaches and upset stomachs are inevitable and that miracle pills will end the problem almost instantly. However, a headache or an upset stomach is a symptom, not a disease, and pill popping never gets to the source of the difficulty. "Pills (unless prescribed by your physician for a specific basic ailment such as arthritis) should be kept as a *last* resort and only used as temporary relief while the source problem is being dealt with," a renowned internist said recently (personal communication).

Every day, thousands of people are learning to effectively manage that great cause of illness—stress. When allied with solid medical treatment for existing specific ailments, stress-management techniques can lead to a healthier, happier life. Unfortunately, many older employees have been bypassed by such education and believe that discomfort and illness are inevitable "for one my age." Organizations offering stress-management programs can help these individuals particularly.

Democratization of Wellness Programs. A few decades ago, company health clubs were almost exclusively for executives. More recently, mid- and lower-level management as well as some professionals have been invited in. Yet, increasingly, organizations are coming to truly depend on *all* of their employees, not just those they consider to be their elite. Nissan USA, for example, offers all its facilities and health programs to all its employees. But health and wellness programs do not necessarily require paying for expensive recreational facilities. Some of the wellness training and exercise programs can be delivered by outside agencies at their own facilities, such as the local school system, local recreation clubs, social agencies, or community colleges, at reasonable costs.

Developing a Comprehensive Long-term Program. A comprehensive long-term program is not necessarily an expensive one or an involved one. It basically requires surveying employee needs or interests, identifying all of the components of a sound wellness program, designing the optimal sequence for providing them, and working out a delivery system that balances costs against anticipated results and organizational resources. An organization that has a company (or designated) doctor or nurse, for instance, can offer the services required for a health-risk profile inexpensively, and the results themselves may lead many employees to take remedial action on their own. Similarly, a smoking-cessation program offered through the auspices of the American Cancer Society a couple of times a year may be sufficient to meet one form of employee need. The organization's tuition-refund program may also be expanded to cover health-related learning outside the work environment.

Changing the Subculture and Developing Peer Support. Programs aiming at altering a person's habitual behavior seem to work best when there are considerable peer support, an absence of negative messages from authority figures, organizational support, support at home, plenty of opportunity to practice the new behavior, and a network of similarly inclined people. Unfortunately, older employees may lack some of these supports, as, for instance, if they are widowed. But the most important consideration may be that planners of such life-style-change training ensure that the program has ongoing aspects that help participants stay with the new behavior. A person not only needs to learn what to do and how to do it but often needs help from people with similar problems to practice techniques and strategies for success. The new healthy behavior also needs to become "normative" for the subculture in which the person works. Here the supervisor can do much to encourage older employees to continue the new behavior and perhaps also run interference for those prone to accept negative peer pressure.

We Will Pay Either Way

According to Miller (1986, p. 396), "In the United States the cost of health care for people sixty-five and over accounts for . . . one third of all spending for personal health care. Per capita the cost for the elderly is more than three times the cost for Americans *under* sixty-five." Since germs are broadcast by everyone who is ill, how can we pass up opportunities to create a total healthy workforce and workplace throughout the organization? Preserving the health of older employees makes sense.

Overall, there is a great deal that virtually any employer can do to assist older employees to improve their health and wellness quotient. With constructive programs, policies, and support, they can help improve the lives of their members in profound and long-term ways. But the most effective programs will be those where the mode is one of partnership. Employees have at least as great a responsibility for their own health as anyone else has; working together, both employer and employee will benefit.

Chapter 7

Training and Education

"You can't teach an old dog new tricks." Well, perhaps not, but since we are dealing with developable human beings and not "old dogs," the use of this cliché is not only insulting but irrelevant. Most people go on learning virtually to the end of their days and adapt to life continuously. They may resist learning some things, as most of us do, and be uninterested in learning others. But most older employees are quite interested in learning "new tricks" if they see a gain and if the required effort toward new mastery does not exceed what they are willing to invest. Coperman and Keast (1983, p. 23) state, "Although not conclusive, available research indicates intelligence and learning ability do not necessarily decline with age and that learning techniques that complement and use prior learning, may reduce the cost of such development efforts."

Each older person, just as each person of any age, learns some things faster and better than others, has preferred learning methods, and finds different subject matter difficult or easy. And though there are certain factors that make older people different from younger people, when it comes to job training and education, these differences need not lead to a lack of success in employee learning.

The Problem for Management and Supervision

Investing in the continued training and development of older employees is likely to be one of the most difficult and stubborn problems faced by management of organizations, despite their increased dependence on an older workforce. Rosow and Zager (1980, pp. 24–25) point out that discrimination against older employees in offering opportunities to acquire new skills and knowledge is well documented. Worse, denying such opportunities to people in their late forties and beyond was until a few years ago openly and unassailably practiced on the rationale that investing in an employee who was approaching retirement was silly and certainly not "good management." Reserving training slots or educational opportunities for younger, less seasoned employees was rationalized by other, often unconscious, biases. Younger people were considered inherently sharper, better able to grasp the material, and less resistant to applying new methods or techniques.

Along with these assumptions went the beliefs that older people are set in their ways, experience declining intellectual and reasoning abilities, have poor memories, and do not do well in classroom settings. In fact, as Keyfitz (1984, p. 229) says, "Previous societies have had every interest in inculcating unadaptability. What good would it have done in medieval times for a cabinet maker to change over to tailoring in mid life? As long as the cycle of each generation was shorter than the cycle of technical change, a shift of occupations would have been sheer waste. We are the inheritors of a deeply imprinted premise that no one over 50 can learn anything. . . . How adaptable and trainable are workers in their forties [and beyond], millions of whom can expect their occupations to be undercut by technical change during the remainder of the century?" Consequently, managers and staff personnel have assumed that they were putting their money where the payoffs were and that that was good management. However, when it became evident that learning opportunities were one of the criteria for assessing age discrimination, some rethinking became necessary.

When personnel specialists and managers began to look deeper into the learning abilities issue, many were quite surprised to find that in many cases, their assumptions were false, their conclusions erroneous, and their behavior unfair. Additionally, since many of these inaccurate notions are common throughout our society, they were also held by the very employees who were being discriminated against and who therefore did not presume to challenge such "self-obvious truths."

Workers and managers alike generally assumed that older employees were short-timers, while younger employees had their whole working lives before them. Of course, few considered that turnover is greatest by far among younger employees and that the gracious manager who reserved learning opportunities for younger people was often preparing personnel to work for their competitors, where an employee of fifty might have ten, fifteen, or even more than twenty years of service ahead of him or her over which to recoup the organization's investment. The challenge before us is to ensure that older employee learning is effective and returns paybacks to the organization.

Obstacles to Developing Older Employee Knowledge and Skills

According to Rhodes, Schuster, and Doering (1981, p. 21), training and development for older employees may range from the learning of totally new skills to development of safer job behaviors to counter declining physical capabilities, from updating an engineer on a new technical process to providing remedial education to a service worker through a local community college. Whatever the problem, it takes imagination, awareness, and real knowledge of older workers to design programs that produce payoffs.

Today, there is considerable evidence that older people, many still in the workforce, are interested in lifelong learning at quite advanced ages and make excellent students. A recent AARP-Andrus Foundation study, reported in *Modern Maturity* magazine ("Older Students . . .," 1990, p. 97), found that mature adults (age sixty and over) made a positive contribution in college classes that they were auditing without taking examinations. More than 75 percent of the faculty members conducting these courses at Wichita University in Kansas said that these older students were at least as quick to learn as younger ones, and 64 percent said that they seemed more motivated. Sixty percent of the faculty members said that older students made a positive difference in their classes.

More than half the older students interviewed said that they attended campus events, read the student newspaper, and regularly used school facilities such as the student center and library. They also reported that while the learning provided the greatest benefit, they enjoyed the people on campus the most. The researchers also discovered that older students were in the majority in many of the physical education classes. So much for the idea that older people, whether employed or not, are uninvolved in life and resistant to learning new things.

Goodrow (1975, p. 421) says, however, that older adults often regard any type of testing procedures as threatening, and such evaluation often causes them to reject educational efforts. He has found older men to be especially reluctant to engage in any activities that threaten their self-image or are embarrassing. Many senior people are unfamiliar with current educational methods, and their apprehension about their past rote learning and evaluation must be overcome before they feel comfortable in a new learning situation. In addition, quality measures of attainment can be achieved in other ways than testing.

But what of the older person who is already on the job and needs to stay up to date? In an article titled "Accelerating Obsolescence of Older Engineers" based on a classic study of 2,500 design and development engineers in six organizations, Dalton and Thompson (1971, pp. 63-65) point out the need for companies to be involved in adult education in larger and more creative ways. They cite the common complaint that some companies expect engineers to take a course or two every year until retirement, despite evidence that such effort will not improve their performance rating or lead to advancement. And while the company may pay for books and tuition, these are only a small part of the cost to the individual who must sacrifice personal and family time to attend classes and do homework.

As a consequence, the authors recommend what many companies are currently doing: using cable TV, videotaping lectures and demonstrations, using in-house people as instructors, and setting up TV classrooms in their plants to receive closed-circuit programs from local universities. With these methods, travel time is virtually nil, costs are often low, and personal sacrifice is minimized, so that employee bias against continuing education is reduced.

Dealing Realistically with Older Learners

In a series of classic studies of verbal learning in older people (Ross, 1968, p. 265), the authors evaluated the effects of "challenging" versus "supportive" instruction on participants. They reported that when aging individuals "are placed in an evaluative situation and told that their performance will be compared with others," great insecurity and stress become evident. Related research showed that anxiety depressed performance most when the material was difficult or complex. Older people did best when they received initial instruction in a considerate, supportive way and worst when the instructions were "challenging." However, when the material had been learned and had only to be relearned (refreshed), challenging instructions did not have the same negative effect. The researchers suggest that perhaps on relearning, the material no longer seemed as difficult or novel as it did the first time. The authors conclude that new and better ways of developing older people may well reduce the performance gap between the generations. Other researchers, such as Taub and Long (1972), suggest that differences in anxieties, work methods, and strategies particularly affect the testing of memory.

But where does all of this lead us? Typical laboratory experiments concerning aged learners have often been based on very artificial tasks designed to eliminate as much as possible the effect of prior knowledge on the experiment; the measurements have largely reflected current ability to perform the task rather than the potential for long-term mastery; and most of these studies on human learning ability made no provision for adapting the methods of instruction to be most suitable for older subjects.

Sheppard (1971, p. 18) discusses the work of Meredith Belbin, who has commented on two other aspects of such studies that would tend to bias their results against older learners. First, older adults do not like tasks that appear to them to be meaningless and strange, and therefore some of the performance decline is known to be related to a negative reaction to the nature of the material (the tasks often involve learning a series of nonsense phrases or the memorization of sets of random numbers). And, second, many older adults are out of practice when it comes to learning and first need time to get back into the swing of things before being tested. On this last point, most such experiments that showed older people at a disadvantage were of very short duration and thus did not allow the test subjects to get back into a learning mode. Sheppard also points out that when factors such as education are held constant, age differences related to performance become less important. Overall, teaching methods that match the learning styles of older people appear to be the most productive.

Learning Styles and Productivity

A series of generalizations about the way older employees tend to learn can provide guidelines for the design of developmental experiences or training programs for older employees. These guidelines can provide the basis for effective programs that allow for individual differences and strengths.

1. *Older employees tend to learn best at their own individual pace.* Work by Canestrari (1963, p. 167) indicates that a self-paced learning schedule allows older people to make the correct responses that are in their repertoire and consequently perform better than they do with externally paced tasks. Self-paced learning methods tend to serve older learners well because they are noncompetitive and minimally stressful: The consequences of error are not critical or threatening, since learners are able to practice the learning task until they get it right.

As Haberlandt (1973) notes, self-paced learning does not necessarily mean slow learning, and it often means good learning. A common complaint about older learners is that they often resist new learning. Often, however, the problem is not resistance but the need to reconcile new information or behavior patterns with old, and what may be needed is a chance to ponder and to adjust. Being allowed to do so at a comfortable level can lead to high performance. Programmed Instruction and similar techniques, where appropriate, have been found to be very suitable for training older personnel.

2. *When there is a need to unlearn or relearn, systematic adjustment is required.* All of us, at almost any age, have developed not only habits but investments (emotional and otherwise) in certain ideas or ways of doing things. To change means loss, as well as possible gain. Change also produces stress. Often a person needs to work through that sense of loss as well as to adjust to the discomfort of unfamiliar behavior patterns.

Supervisors and trainers can facilitate these adjustments by clearly indicating early in the program the nature of the change and why it is necessary; involving the person in planning the change; focusing more on what happens—the results—than on how the learner chooses to effect that outcome, unless time, safety, or monetary constraints rule out the employee's preferences; encouraging movement toward the change; and reducing or removing obstacles to effecting the change (environmental, personal, and interpersonal). One should allow the older person sufficient time to adjust to and get comfortable with the change and provide feedback that supports the new learning. It is also helpful to create a vision of what it will be like when the change has been made and to help the employees imagine themselves performing the new tasks successfully.

3. *Material should be relevant and realistically related to job needs.* Sheppard (1971, p. 19) found that older employees tend to have a low tolerance for abstract and "nice to know" material. When Belbin's Discovery Method (discussed later) was used in teaching job skills, such as machine operation, it "produced superior results in every type of comparison (including completion rates, accuracy of measurements, and the time required for test assignments on the machines) against the use of traditional methods of instruction when comparable groups of older workers were in training." In contrast, paper-and-pencil testing is often seen as abstract and unrelated to job performance, unless calculations or such written material are part of the daily work assignments.

4. *Learning assignments requiring memorization often require more practice for older employees.* Though there are disagreements in the literature on whether older employees have their greatest problems with long-term or short-term memory, Taub and Long (1972, pp. 497–498) argue that much is known about ways to compensate for memory problems that can help older people perform better than anticipated. First, older employees can substantially improve their memory and therefore their performance through practice. Second, extensive practice of a memory-related task often allows an older employee to match the performance of younger workers. And, third, research indicates that even a few practice sessions may be enough to produce a long-lasting, productive effect on the memory performance of older personnel.

It helps to provide opportunities to practice new knowledge or skills so that they appear naturally in the learning sequence, are not threatening to a person's ego or social status, and are clearly and directly related to the desired outcome. Also, where memory is involved, a trainer should include cues at critical points for reinforcement, provide an overview of the whole job so that the parts fit in where appropriate, and consolidate learning before moving on.

5. *Learning ability most often declines through lack of practice.* Knox and Sjogren (1965, p. 136) claim that research clearly establishes that "adults who continue to participate in educative activities learn more effectively than similar adults who do not." Just as our muscles tend to atrophy from disuse, there seems to be a similar weakening of our mental capacity if it is not used. People should jog their minds as they do their bodies.

According to Rosow and Zager (1980), for management this highlights the issue of denying learning opportunity to employees who are advanced in age. This behavior obviously produces a self-fulfilling prophecy, where it gets harder for an older person to be ready for schooling—and to do less well if the chance does come along—which in turn leads the supervisor to conclude that more such efforts would be wasted. Instead, we need to seek out opportunities to keep an older person's learning ability alive. This includes challenging work assignments as well as an opportunity to attend various types of developmental programs.

6. *Testing and evaluation tend to be very stressful to older*

employees, and learning falls off rapidly as a consequence. Though most people find testing stressful, older people seem to be particularly susceptible. This seems to be tied to self-image, a strong need to save face, and a fear of looking bad before peers. One of the compensations of aging is the respect and deference sometimes shown to a person because of his or her age. To jeopardize that social standing can be very threatening.

Closely related to this phenomenon is older employees' tendency to avoid such risks as trying to guess the right answer. When the risk of mistakes is high or the pace fast, they might not respond at all to test questions out of fear of being wrong. This has been one reason for some low test scores among older employees compared to those of younger people. Older employees tend to cease functioning or miss opportunities to respond when their stress level is high. It is as though they are saying, "Doing nothing is not as bad as being wrong."

In general, older employees do not like to be compared to others and seem to learn best when measured against their own previous performance. This does not mean, however, that they have any aversion to meeting high job-related standards; it is simply that they would rather do it in their own way. As a matter of fact, a chance to show what they can do, if the task is clearly job-related and they have had time to develop mastery, is well received by them.

7. *Participative teaching techniques that accent the learner's previous experience and accomplishments lead to high performance.* Learning methods that lead the learner through a series of positive learning experiences as a participating partner have high appeal to older workers—once they get used to the techniques. Many older employees have been raised in schools where the instruction was presented in a teacher-child mode, with the instructor imparting information top down rather than sharing it as an equal.

Knowles (1981, p. 168) says that the more the older learner can be brought in as an active partner in the learning process, the better the results. Small-group discussions, simulations, group exercises, and sharing between participants work well. However, people whose experience has largely been with passive learning may need time and opportunity to get used to this more responsible mode of learning. Obstacles for some older workers also include the attitude that schooling was something completed long ago, the expectation of long lectures, and the unwillingness to spend personal time in learning. Active, participative methods may also help overcome a tendency to doze during long training sessions, problems with verbal learning (retention), and low reading levels or unfamiliar vocabulary.

Like most of the rest of us, older learners respond best to praise, rewards, recognition, and a psychologically supportive environment. Such an environment is easiest to attain with active and participatory teaching methods because more of the learner's behavior is apparent with such methods.

Other Design Considerations

In an older population, where diversity between individuals tends to be greater than among other age groups, providing more options in media and methods, greater flexibility in teaching approaches, and more attention to individual differences and needs can produce substantial payoffs. Some considerations to keep in mind are outlined below.

Generational Differences. Generational differences count in training and education. During the first quarter of this century, six to eight years of schooling was considered adequate. The ability to read, write and do sums was thought to be sufficient for most jobs. The Great Depression and World War II elevated the population's notions of what constituted educational adequacy to a high school diploma. The educational provisions of the GI Bill after World War II, the growth of community colleges, and related developments in employee training raised national expectations to include a college education for virtually everyone determined enough to get one. Today, advanced degrees are the popular vision. Increasing technological complexity and work specialization caused similar developments in training.

Cognitive Styles. Cognition—the mental process or facility through which knowledge is acquired, as through perception, reasoning, or intuition—is often related to the type and extent of education that a person has received. Once acquired (usually by maturity), a cognitive style tends to persist unless substantial efforts are made to change it. Therefore, cognitive style may also be somewhat related to generational differences, with the more formal styles of analysis and synthesis more common in the younger (and more formally educated) portion of our older population. Sorting learners by cognitive style is sometimes feasible and worthwhile (if the numbers to be trained or educated are substantial), and teaching methods can be varied to emphasize the strengths and abilities of each type. Offering supplementary assistance where needed is also important.

Brinley, Jovick, and McLaughlin (1974, p. 183) point out that "the failure to reason well may be due to a failure to remember, which is in turn a clue to failure to reason well, and so on." Here, poor reasoning ability is not an inherent problem but rather a reflection of lack of knowledge of ways to handle data efficiently or to reason logically. Therefore, the use of mnemonic (memory-assisting) devices and techniques for coding data for mental storage can greatly affect performance. Information about various methods of studying can be helpful to some older employees as well.

Contributions to Learning. When we look at the age spectrum of older employees, we notice immediately some additional generational differences as well as substantial individual variations in background and experience that can bear on course design. These can include broader life experience for some of the younger ones, greater exposure to continuing education, and technological experience in particular disciplines. We can see these variations as problems (the potential for boredom by some as we bring others up to speed) or as opportunities. However, in general, a person's prior learning is a valuable resource and a motivator that should be built upon.

Gender, Culture, and Ethnic Differences. Some of the research (Murray, Powers, and Havighurst, 1971; Covey, 1980) indicates differences in the learning patterns of males and females within our own culture that result from the socialization process that we were exposed to as children and later in life. For instance, among older employees, the macho male self-image may produce less tolerance for potentially embarrassing situations and less sensitivity to the feelings of others when the course focuses on learning that may involve such hazards or needs. Though many of these gender-related social differences are changing in our younger population, it may take decades before the impact is significant in our older workforce.

Similarly, within some ethnic groups, participants may expect and even demand greater focus on lectures, rote learning, and even negative criticism. Individual attention to people from other cultures and at least a chance to talk out their feelings about seemingly strange training methods may prove very helpful to such individuals.

The Key Role of the Supervisor or Manager. While we have focused on formal training and education programs, much of the really significant on-the-job learning results from people's watching and listening to their supervisors. What tasks are assigned, how much real authority to choose methods is passed down, how much information is shared about plans, objectives, and requirements, and how much encouragement, support, and recognition are offered often determine how much and what kind of significant learning occurs on the job. Over the years, this supervisor-subordinate relationship is the key to most of the real learning that keeps an older person up to date.

Successful Teaching Principles

The purpose of training and education is not testing—it is to produce successful job performance. Unfortunately, many people overlook this obvious consideration and do things that turn off older learners, ignore their need for clear-cut, demonstrable success, and overlook some rather simple things that can add to older employee learning. The following are guidelines to some of the more effective training methods:

- Look for possible physical causes of impaired learning; use them for problem solving, not as an excuse to avoid developing a person.

- Provide an overview of the job to be done, fitting it into its place in the scheme of things.
- Relieve learner anxiety before the program starts.
- Allow for learning by easy stages of increasing complexity.
- Introduce new subjects clearly, and relate them to prior learning.
- Offer variety in teaching methods, but be cautious of abrupt shifts in logic or ideas.
- Point out and discuss tasks involving "association" or "discrimination" before the task is tried.
- Use large print on written materials and exercises and leave plenty of white space.
- Use overhead slides with large print or computer graphics unless the group is very small.
- Stay flexible and focus on the individual as much as possible.
- Consider your efforts as a challenge to be met.

There are exceptions to all generalizations and because of their varied life-styles, differing processes of socialization, and diversity of life events, there may seem to be more exceptions than similarities between older individuals. Use this diversity as opportunity. Whether you are planning and conducting developmental activities for one individual or for a thousand, good teaching techniques can have very substantial and long-term payoffs with older employees.

Discovery Learning

In the years since the concept of learner-centered education and training was developed, it has led to a number of very productive approaches for use with older employees. One of the most impressive is the "discovery learning" method attributed to Meredith Belbin.

Older employees have a rich experiential background to call on, but they have seldom adequately organized or evaluated it. Hence, their prior learning may be vague or disorganized, so much so that they may find it very difficult to communicate it to others. Many older people, especially if they lack rigorous academic preparation, possess insights that deal with specific incidents rather than relate to a broad range of general situations. They have a hard time drawing principles and general conclusions from their experience. In fact, the rambling stories some people tell represent an effort to extract such general principles, sometimes without success. Consequently, a trainer may need to help employees to reexamine, articulate, and generalize what they have learned from their previous experience before new knowledge is added to it.

The Discovery Method has been used to help older workers (and entry-level young employees as well) to discover for themselves answers to a series of problems in a developmental order. Each problem is relatively small and generally sequential and involves a meaningful whole, rather than being a subpart of something that lacks meaning by itself (as is common in many types of training and education). Belbin's method concentrates on creating a series of concrete, specific, meaningful tasks that require increasing sophistication. The instructor tends to keep a low profile but is supportive and encouraging. The instructor's role is primarily planning and creating the experiences, shielding the participants from interference, and providing cues or hints on approaches to solving the problem as needed. The instructor also provides quick feedback on mistakes so that incorrect learning is minimized. Participants in such programs are provided with a clear goal for each task or job, allowed adequate time to practice, and given an opportunity to consolidate their learning before they undertake a new task. Time and effort are also expended in overcoming any anxiety or reluctance to participate that the learner exhibits.

The Discovery Method has been found to work well with virtually all adults but particularly with older people because of its practical "applied now" approach. This method has been demonstrated to work effectively in many types of employee development programs in the United States (for example, Corning Glass, Exxon, and LTV Electronics), Austria, Sweden, and the United Kingdom, among others. In a series of field experiments coordinated by Europe's Organization for Economic Cooperation and Development, the Discovery Method has been shown to work well with employees past forty. More recently, application of this method in the United

States has been extended from its original base of primarily blue-collar production, service, and maintenance personnel to a wide variety of employees, ranging from newly hired college graduates to executives preparing to assume new managerial roles in different departments, such as moving from research and development to manufacturing.

Discovery learning, with its strong emphasis on older people discovering for themselves rather than having the instructor explain how the new task is to be performed, is producing some cost-effective and valuable side effects. The method reduces short-term forgetting, involves the participant more actively in the learning process, and produces greater older employee performance. It is particularly effective with people who are being prepared to handle new technology, perform redesigned work, or take on greater responsibility. In such cases, the best method for doing the new work is seldom clear. Older employees with a rich experience base but no training on the exact way to do the new job often develop highly creative methods of accomplishing the task that decrease the cost and effort required and increase their sense of ownership of and commitment to their new work.

The notion of some management personnel that older workers do not adjust successfully to changing technology is disproved by the results of a training program described by Anderson (1983). In the early 1980s, a prominent southwestern bank designed a training program to facilitate its efforts to introduce on-line banking, which required computer training for its employees. As Anderson points out, most members of the "precomputer generation" (approximately 36 percent of the U.S. population, including eighty-one million over age forty—thirty-five million over sixty) have little or no computer experience. The bank designed and conducted an effective training program, and the great majority of participants completed the training with ease. "A few, however, appeared fearful and were unable to use the new system effectively" (p. 21). Most of those were between the ages of forty-five and fifty-five and had been in their jobs for some time. Some of these older individuals believed that they could not learn. According to Anderson (p. 22), the problems encountered with these employees included the following:

- Reluctance to participate fully in the training
- Avoidance of using the system
- Hesitancy to solve problems encountered during training
- Reluctance to change old habits, behaviors, or procedures
- Increased errors and mistakes

Unwilling to accept defeat, the project team revised the training in such ways that in time all the employees were using the system effectively. One of the key factors in their success was allowing their older personnel to adequately practice the new skills and behaviors. The message seems clear: Very few older employees need be put out to pasture because of obsolescence or lack of learning ability if their organizations invest properly in their continued development.

Chapter 8

Motivating and Building Morale

Whether an older employee chooses to remain with an organization or leave it, stay productive or coast to retirement, accept or seek early retirement or reject it, or maintain professional competence or lose it most often depends on the interplay between the employee and his or her manager as well as between the employee and the culture and policies of the employing organization. That employees' motivation and general morale are influenced by how they are treated, the incentives (or lack of them) offered, and their perceptions of what their future holds in the organization is clear.

Motivation is defined here as the physiological and psychological needs that incite a person to actions aimed at satisfying those needs; and morale is the state of the spirit of an individual or group, often exhibited in enthusiasm or lack of it for performing assigned tasks. Issues of motivation and morale center around how we feel about things, which is often more important than the things themselves. Money is sometimes listed as a motivator, but how a person feels about a given amount of money leads to action or the lack of it. We recognize that the key issues in these feelings are their intensity and how strongly we feel about competing options. Management tends to offer certain types of incentives or inducements aimed at evoking certain types of behaviors that they consider desirable, but there is no certainty that these will work. A chance to earn overtime pay may greatly appeal to one person and have virtually no impact on another. So we have a theory of margin about motivation—at what level we have to set the incentives to achieve the behavior that we need and what kinds of incentives we have to offer.

All of this sounds very mechanistic and impersonal, but every day millions of older employees are faced with choices in the workplace, and the choices that they make from their individual perspective affect the quality of life for them and cumulatively the quality of others' lives as well.

Keys to Motivation and Morale

We need to recognize three very important things about motivation and morale, particularly as they relate to older employees. First, in a very real sense, all motivation is self-motivation and very personal. Truly, you cannot motivate anyone except yourself. Management, for example, may provide incentives or disincentives (often rewards or punishments) to a person, but it is that person who chooses whether or not to be motivated. We commonly speak of "motivating another person," but in a pure sense, people choose their own behavioral responses, though they may do so subconsciously and therefore "feel compelled" to react in a certain way. The difference between self-motivation and external motivation often may not have much practical consequence, but understanding it can help us to recognize that people can reject our efforts to motivate them.

Second, an obvious factor, but one that is often overlooked, is that motivation can as often be negative as positive. The supervisor who says "I want motivated people" assumes positive motivation from his or her own perspective. Many managers have highly motivated people who are busy withholding commitment, diverting their efforts into personal pursuits, and spending their job time in social interaction with co-workers. Apathy implies a lack of motivation, but it is often based on discouragement and despair, so that neither the employee nor the organization benefits.

Third, there is a small but significant difference between motivation and morale. Motivation tends to be goal-oriented, an incitement to action, whereas morale is a more generalized phenomenon related to the condition of a person's involvement with or commitment to goals. Thus, when a person is demotivated, his or her goal may be to do nothing except draw a paycheck and fill a job slot. When a person's morale is low, it is difficult to generate the energy or focus required to accomplish tasks.

The Motivation Paradox

Curiously, we tend to pay lip service to the value of morale and motivation and then ignore them when making personnel decisions. Obviously, some organizations do not consider morale and motivation as income-generating resources; if they did, they would behave quite differently. This paradox is exemplified by a survey of company executives conducted by the Conference Board (Bernstein, Anderson, and Zellner, 1987). Among the 363 companies responding to the survey (mostly firms with more than 1,000 employees), the majority of the executives expressed positive perceptions of older employees. Yet the researchers found that in 1985, the time of the survey, these firms were "not yet actively encouraging older workers to remain in the workforce" (p. 50). Most of them continued to have mandatory retirement policies and pension plans designed to promote early retirement. For example, only 4 percent of the firms had offered any workers incentives that would discourage retirement before age sixty-five. And when such incentives were offered, it was usually only to individuals or small groups of employees with rare skills or very high performance records.

Of the 97 percent of these firms that had pension plans, 62 percent included early-retirement inducements; in only about 30 percent of the firms was the opportunity available for older workers to transfer to less demanding jobs. It is clear that the gap between attitude and policies about older employees is a wide one. It is also doubtful that the legislative changes eliminating age as a factor in mandatory retirement have altered the difference between what some management say about older employees and how they would treat them if they could. Such mismatches are bound to affect the morale of older employees and how they are motivated to respond to their management. What is needed is greater congruence between words and actions. Fortunately, there are several hundred excellent firms, including Grumman, Polaroid, Johnson & Johnson, and Travelers Insurance, that have long maintained congruence between their appreciation of their older employees and their policies.

Age and Motivation

One of the most difficult determinations when one is comparing the motivations of older and younger employees or delineating the distinctive characteristics of older employees is whether these differences are generational (and therefore eventually a passing phenomenon), related to life experiences (such as motivational differences between men and women), a social phenomenon (a function of how people were raised), or a consequence of managerial behavior.

A spokesperson for SAGA Corporation, a California-based food-service company, says that older workers are in some ways easier to manage. "They fit into the system better," are less mobile, and are "not as concerned about the self all the time" (Cook, 1980, p. 45). Similarly, a study of absenteeism in a large food-processing plant reported by Giniger, Dispenzieri, and Eisenberg (1983, pp. 469–475) found that older workers had better attendance and health records than younger employees and attributed the difference to the older people's "stability, more serious attitude toward work and mature judgment."

In *The Aging Worker,* Doering, Rhodes, and Schuster (1983, p. 34) offer the concept that "a *need* is an internal state that makes certain outcomes or job characteristics attractive." Most motivational theories are premised on the notion that people do things to meet their needs. More than sixty empirical studies on "need importance" and "preferred job characteristics" show some important differences between young and older employees but fail to explain why these differences occur. For instance, older workers report higher levels of work motivation and job involvement. Age and commitment are closely related, which is often seen as a function of "company loyalty." Older employees have a far greater tendency to stay with a given employer, but this may be for their own purposes.

In a similar finding it was revealed in several studies that older workers had a particular need for security and company affiliation and a lower need for self-actualization than younger workers. However, this was found to be more closely related to the stage of their career and influences of their life cycle than the fact that they were older. It is also possible that these differences flow from workplace conditioning and social values.

These same studies found that there were no consistent differences between younger and older workers' satisfaction with pay, promotion, supervision, and co-workers. However, older employees consistently expressed greater overall job satisfaction and satisfaction with the work itself, with satisfying work the major ingredient in overall job satisfaction. One interesting note: A survey of white-collar workers showed that age, job tenure, and job satisfaction were related in a positive "straight-line" correlation, but male satisfaction was more closely related to age than tenure, while for women the opposite was true.

Organizational Demotivation

Understanding of older employee behavior and the motivations that underlie it is especially critical when it comes to high-tech and professional personnel, since our future will depend on having them in the workforce over the long term. Dalton, Thompson, and Price (1977) note that they have often seen a "negative spiral" when an employee receives a low evaluation rating, is left on a dull assignment for too long, or is passed over for promotion. Though such employees may initially put out greater effort, if they do not see prompt positive results, they may develop a "what-the-heck" attitude. This generates a lower rating, less self-confidence, and consequently a still lower rating.

Dalton, Thompson, and Price observed older engineers and found that they tended to be pessimistic about their future and expected little positive reward for greater effort. They found that older employees were much more likely to believe that they would not receive rewards or recognition for an outstanding job on a piece of work than were younger employees. They remarked that engineers and other knowledge workers tend to work as part of a large effort where there are no clear performance standards, output is hard to measure, and therefore judgments of a person's contribution tend to be subjective. Further, they maintain that in recent decades, young engineers or engineering supervisors could easily move to another company and often to a higher salary and level of responsibility if they became dissatisfied. Many managers therefore used substantial salary increases, new and exciting projects, and promotions to hold on to these younger personnel. They also often used higher performance ratings for younger engineers to justify their actions. Older workers, on the other hand, often feel locked in by pension benefits and a general lack of job mobility and have been taken for granted and passed over when the goodies are passed out.

Heneman (1973) conducted an exploratory study of male and female department managers in a large retailing organization using "expectancy theory" as his basis. He found that older managers perceived less relationship between their performance and desirable outcomes on the job than did younger managers. He noted that "managers' performance may 'count' very little regarding changes in the nature of the job as well as transfers and promotions" (p. 33) and observed a "feeling that as one grows older, behaviors often do not result in the outcomes toward which they are directed; that one is not master of one's own destiny" (p. 34). He suggests that management look carefully at policies and practices that result in older employees perceiving their work situation so negatively and revamp their approach to produce greater older employee motivation.

Achievement Motivation

In a report on maintaining professional and technical competence in older engineers, Dubin, Shelton, and McConnell (1974) point out that achievement involves competition to meet a standard of excellence and postulate that people who are highly motivated tend to be attracted to activities that require skill and excellence in their performance. In addition, a major long-term motivator is advancement on the job. As well as the potential for advancement being highly valued, the good feelings generated by being advanced or promoted tend to last for a long time. DeMicco and Reid (1988, pp. 57, 60), who conducted a survey of workers in the hospitality industry, report that "over a quarter of the older employees were dissatisfied with the prospects of advancement on the job." They cite with approval the "Colonel's Tradition" at the Kentucky Fried Chicken Corporation (where founder Harlan Sanders *started* franchising his special chicken recipe at age sixty-six)—a program for employing older people that features positions with flexible hours, a variety of duties, and opportunities for advancement.

In early 1990, when I was doing research for an article on the desire of older people to continue working, I interviewed a manager who was seventy-five. He said, "My former employer forced me to take early retirement twenty years ago. At that time, Days Inn was the only outfit that seemed to look favorably on my experience. I started as a night auditor and have had five promotions since then. In this organization, moving up is based on performance. The statistics and my health indicate I could have another twenty years to go. Who knows—perhaps by then I'll be running the whole company." For those who are motivated to move up and think that it is possible, the achievement motivation may never die.

People who have a high level of achievement motivation see themselves as potent in relationship to their environment, are quite active, are future-oriented, want to take personal responsibility, are willing to engage in moderate (or calculated) risk taking, and seek very specific, concrete feedback on the results of their work. The capacity for taking pride in accomplishment is critical.

Achievement motivation in many workers has been found to decline very sharply after age forty as a result of a decreasing sense that job success is possible or meaningful. The level of aroused achievement motivation is a function of the expectancy of success and the subjective incentive value that a person attaches to that success. Since older employees' social and occupational roles are seen by themselves and others as less demanding, their motivation goes down. However, achievement motivation training, designed to elicit and reinforce patterns of thinking and behavior that characterize high achievers, encourages self-confidence and stimulates and reinforces achievement thinking. With this type of training, a person learns a new vocabulary for dealing with his or her inner thoughts and feelings. It helps participants to develop self-understanding through games and simulations, encourages personal goal setting and planning, and provides group support. The original research on this type of training (McClelland and Winter, 1969) indicated that it is effective in increasing the motivation of older employees but that the organizational climate strongly affects their motivation as well.

In a study using expectancy theory to determine the influence of training methods (interactive tutorial methods versus video modeling) and trainee age on the acquisition of computer skills, Gist, Rosen, and Schwoerer (1988) "found that older employees may not expend effort to learn new skills and abilities unless they have a positive expectation that skills mastery is attainable. This supports earlier research that found that older workers were not likely to volunteer for training programs because they had little confidence in their learning ability. . . . It seems likely that training approaches that integrate mechanisms for building self-confidence with training content may be superior to training approaches that only focus on training content" (pp. 257–258).

Avoiding Obsolescence

Dubin, Shelton, and McConnell (1974, pp. 7–10) point out that technical obsolescence often reflects inadequacies in the work environment that contribute to underuse or misuse of human potential. Studies of professionals considered to be "over the hill" identify the following factors.

Lack of Use of a Specific Skill. People commonly experience loss of proficiency at skills that they are seldom called upon to apply. However, it is not uncommon for a supervisor (especially one with an age bias) to assume that a deficiency in one skill characterizes the whole person, without specifying the full range of skills truly required for the job, and to evaluate the person's capacity as similarly deficient in all of these areas. Job specifications commonly state many skills that the employee will never use on the job.

Functional or Organizational Obsolescence. When older employees see no chance for advancement or challenging work, they may respond by working only hard enough to keep their jobs. Though many people argue that older employees do not want to advance or deal with challenges, there is little evidence to support this contention. However, if people believe that their aspirations will not be fulfilled, they may withdraw from active involvement, become dispirited, and lose energy. Withdrawal from the fray can be face saving, and eventually such people may come to believe what they have been telling themselves and others.

Managerial Bias for Youth. The manager of professionals who usually gives challenging jobs to younger employees deprives the senior person of a chance to learn, change, and grow and thereby produces the obsolescence manager's deplore.

Lack of Adaptability. One's degree of flexibility may be partly a personality trait, but adaptability can generally be learned, and people can become more flexible if they believe that they can. (In later chapters, I discuss some of the ways in which older employees can increase their adaptability.)

While older employees may not be motivated to do what management desires, they *are* motivated. In a repressive organizational atmosphere, people may be motivated by survival and security needs—not taking risks and doing only enough to hold on until retirement. If their jobs are not challenging or if the rewards seem destined for others, employees may well strive to maximize satisfaction of their social needs. Virtually everyone is motivated; if people can get their achievement and recognition needs met only off the job, that is where their motivation will be directed. Managers must determine whether they are encouraging or discouraging the positive motivations of older employees.

Quite logically, an older professional will not invest time in learning new skills or technology if not given an opportunity to use them on the job. Dalton, Thompson, and Price (1977) suggest that challenging assignments should be divided evenly between young and old if the entire workforce is to remain viable. The howls of indignation that this suggestion brings from some people often illustrate the depth of bias for youth and against age. Dalton, Thompson, and Price also point out the advantages that can be gained from pushing engineers and scientists into new areas of work at about ages thirty-five to forty-five to avoid boredom and to regenerate enthusiasm. Some managers should examine the way their managing contributes to the very problems that they are lamenting, suggest these authors.

People should be approaching their greatest period of creative work as they reach advanced age, if these abilities have not atrophied. They have more experience to draw on and can often synthesize to a superior degree. But because they may have received less education than younger people, they continue to perform less complex tasks of an earlier era, and they have been socialized out of creative thinking (especially on the job), some older employees may appear unable or unwilling to generate creative answers to problems.

Alpaugh, Renner, and Birren (1976) note the tendency among some older workers to prefer to deal with less complex visual stimulation, to exhibit a cautious desire to avoid ambiguous situations, to employ a strategy of cognitive and affective load shedding, and to be unwilling to put up with the dissonance often required to reach a creative conclusion. These authors acknowledge that education can be used to stimulate greater creativity in older adults, but they stress that it must address stimulation of their motivation as well as their abilities. The question, therefore, is not whether a person is motivated but how he or she is motivated and toward what.

Stimulating Motivation and Morale

Below are listed a number of ways that employers can help older employees with their problems of motivation and morale. Some are best done by staff personnel and others by an employee's supervisor.

Asset Counseling. Helping older employees to develop an inventory of personal job-related assets and letting them talk freely about it with others can help a great deal. At first, people may see little that they have to offer, but as they explore various facets of their life, work history, education, and hobbies, the list will grow and often along with it their self-image.

Achievement Motivation Training. Litwin (1970) describes achievement motivation training as "a specialized educational approach organized to elicit and reinforce patterns of behaving and thinking that characterize high achievers" (p. 65). He offers considerable evidence that this training produces noticeable behavioral change within the following year in approximately 60 to 70 percent of course participants. Older workers experience increased confidence in dealing with changing and difficult circumstances and the ability to establish realistic and personally meaningful goals—critical to a sense of dignity and pride in their ability to use their talents and resources.

Preventing Obsolescence Before It Begins. A philosophy of lifelong learning inaugurated early, before a drop in performance ratings, can help keep employees (especially professional people) and managers from becoming obsolescent.

On-the-Job Training. On-the-job training for older employees tends to be the most effective way of preventing obsolescence. One of its benefits is that it provides opportunities for peer reinforcement. In addition, inclusion in such training in itself can help cure many motivational problems.

Sabbaticals. If the half-life of technical knowledge is ten years or less, part-time, occasional training may not be enough. Sabbatical leaves for full-time study every five to ten years may not be too high a price to pay to keep a high-tech workforce at top performance. Full-time study of lesser duration may be an option, especially for new skills that are hard to learn on a part-time basis. Older employees often do best on self-paced full-time study. Sabbaticals or full-time study can be seen as both a reward and an incentive. Sabbaticals may be expensive, but they may also be the most economical way to extend a person's high performance. For example, the performance ratings of engineers with master's degrees tend to hold up ten years longer than those of engineers with only bachelor's degrees. This is true for engineers who receive their master's degrees in their thirties or later as well as for those who receive them in their twenties.

Performance Evaluation Systems. Performance evaluation systems should focus on the future rather than the past and should emphasize the positive. The process of ranking employees against each other ensures that some will get the message that they are inadequate and thus causes demotivation. Performance appraisal systems should not destroy the anticipation of older employees (or any others) for success and rewards. Positive reinforcement is important in any plan for motivation.

Supervisor Counseling. Consultation with older employees may reveal that they desire to learn new areas, practice newly learned skills, and perhaps even enter a new field. Supervisors can be helpful by practicing nondirective counseling techniques that stress active listening (without expressing opinions about the suitability or feasibility of the employee's aspirations) and providing reflective feedback on feelings and objective information about appropriate organizational resources available to the employee.

Motivation Is Personal

According to Robert W. Goddard (1987), numerous studies show that younger workers respond very unfavorably to jobs that they see as insignificant or meaningless, while older workers do not. Among senior citizens, the most frequently mentioned reasons for continuing to work are "to remain active and engaged, to enhance meaningful life experiences, to socialize, and to alleviate depression." Goddard states that "The motivation of . . . older employees varies but is largely dependent on recognition of their accomplishments, publicity among their peers, financial rewards, and consultation by management" (p. 34). He suggests the following positive ways in which supervisors can improve older worker motivation:

- Seize opportunities to provide positive reinforcement of older employees' self-image through special recognition for things the employees do well.
- Refer to older employees questions that fall into their special area of competence.
- Bring older employees to meetings where they can act as advisers on a particular issue or subject area.
- Consult with older people as a way to check out your own plans and programs.
- Involve older employees in work-oriented study groups.
- Keep older employees well informed about events and problems in the group, department, or overall organization.
- Discover talents and skills that may be transferred to the workplace by exploring older employees' activities and satisfactions away from the job.

These and similar ideas can enhance older employee morale and motivation considerably. In addition, an in-company task force or a group of supervisors can generate a list of techniques that have specific application in its own environment. This obviously involves supervisory training in motivating older employees and incentives for supervisors to deal fairly with older people. The fact that a youth preference is not only dangerous but organizationally defeating in our emerging labor market needs to be communicated forcefully.

Chapter 9

Appraising Older Employee Performance

How can an organization be managed so as to ensure age fairness to all its employees? How can the rights of older employees be protected without infringing on the rights of other age groups? Even an organization that is doing everything possible to avoid age discrimination in employment can take many additional steps to ensure a productive and viable workplace with a culture and climate that promote age cooperation and harmony. A defensive legal posture may be necessary at times, but it is still a primary managerial responsibility to ensure that standards for employee performance and productivity meet the interests of both the employee and the organization. This means both practicing age-neutral employment actions and seeking out the challenges and opportunities inherent in an age-diverse organization.

Managing Performance

Since not every older employee produces adequately, decisions must be made when an employee does not meet the organization's standards. The task then is to deal with the older employee as an individual rather than as a statistic and to resolve each productivity issue as fairly as possible. A useful procedure for dealing with unsatisfactory performance is to (1) define the gap between the job requirements and the person's output in terms as measurable as possible, (2) determine the cause (insofar as is possible), (3) decide whether it appears to be a temporary problem (as with an illness), (4) inform the person of the discrepancy between his or her performance and the standards, and (5) mutually plan for and work toward a satisfactory resolution. Ideally, this means helping the employee to close the gap between job requirements and his or her output—to be successful on the job. Generating an imaginative win-win outcome reflects managerial competence.

If the cooperative approach fails to close the productivity gap, disciplinary action and possibly termination procedures may be necessary. With older workers in particular, the emphasis should be on resolving the problem of unsatisfactory performance to avoid violating legal constraints of the ADEA regarding discipline and termination. General guidelines for taking fair and legal actions require that

1. Performance standards are clearly established.
2. Each employee's output is monitored and measured, in some verifiable fashion, against the job standards.
3. All employees doing similar work are evaluated according to the same standards.
4. The gap between job requirements and the employee's performance is clearly documented and communicated to the employee.
5. There are no factors such as faulty equipment or unsafe working conditions that may adversely affect the employee's performance.
6. Reasonable efforts have been made by the organization and its management to help the employee correct the peformance problem.
7. All aspects of the employee's performance, including absences, have been documented, and the documentation shows fairness and an age-neutral approach.

8. Such documentation does not begin when the employee files a grievance but is undertaken as soon as performance becomes unsatisfactory.

This performance-based approach generally makes certain that age itself is not a factor in the adverse action—that output or service is the only issue. When undertaken correctly and convincingly, the adverse action becomes merely an expression of the organization's legitimate right to get the job done well. The above guidelines can be applied humanely and fairly to all employees.

This approach does not mean favored treatment for the elderly; rather, it means establishing realistic job criteria that must be met and then evaluating each person's ability to perform that job as fairly as possible. If older people have physical infirmities that would prevent them from performing the work at hand without special equipment, for example, they should be treated as any other handicapped people would be, with the provision of reasonable accommodations, and not punished for being older.

As employment decisions in such areas as promotion, training, and discharge are increasingly challenged in the courts, the basis for such employer actions is being called into account. The key question is whether the individual was being judged on the basis of performance or of some other, more suspect criteria. Organizations that have solid performance measures that are communicated and fairly applied to all employees tend to be in a far more viable position than those that do not. Unfortunately, many performance appraisal systems are deficient in provable standards and are all too often inconsistently applied. Where age could be a factor in a dispute over a personnel action, weakness in performance appraisal leaves the organization and its managers vulnerable.

Creating an effective and clearly verifiable performance appraisal system and using it as a primary basis for all personnel decisions is certainly a tough task. To get supervisors, personnel specialists, and managers at all levels to use any appraisal system consistently is also a great challenge. The following sections discuss some of the primary aspects considered by experts to be the basis of a solid performance appraisal system.

Performance Appraisal and Evaluation Systems

Schuster and Miller (1981, pp. 580–581) claim that the employee's performance appraisal is by far the most crucial element in a defense against a charge of age discrimination. To be an effective tool in such litigation, the procedure used in evaluating employees should involve clear criteria that are consistently applied to all employees. If possible, it is best to follow some standardized model of evaluation, such as that published by the American Management Association (Humple and Lyons, 1983).

Under the ADEA, the employee has the initial burden of proof to establish a prima facie case of age discrimination. In general, the employee must demonstrate the following elements to establish such a case: (1) membership in the protected group; (2) discipline, discharge, or failure to receive a promotion; and (3) previous or present ability to do the job. Once evidence is presented to this effect, the burden is on the employer to offer rebuttal evidence. This is best done through a showing of an objective, fairly applied, and regularly administered system of performance evaluation.

While the courts have not required that employers maintain a highly formalized appraisal procedure, evidence of such a system does carry substantial weight with the courts. In *Stringfellow* v. *Monsanto Co.*, 320 F. Supp. 1175 (W.D. Ark. 1970), and in many subsequent cases, the courts were impressed by the company's use of a standardized evaluation technique (Schuster and Miller, 1981, p. 564). Generally, the courts seek three characteristics in appraisals: reasonableness, reliability, and relevancy. According to Walker and Lupton (1978, pp. 78–79), the first characteristic applies to the method's acceptability to its users. The system should have a clearly stated purpose and should have fairness and objectivity as its goal. Secondly, the evaluation technique is deemed reliable if appraisals of the same individual are "consistent among different raters and over a period of time. They should contain a minimum of subjectivity that leads to distortion." And finally, the system should be evaluating only those aspects of the work that are necessary to the successful performance of the job. "Personality traits, race, sex and age are rarely relevant to job performance."

To achieve an appraisal procedure that is reasonable, reliable, and relevant, management should, at a minimum, review its job descriptions to ensure that they are nondiscriminatory as well as specific. They should include descriptions of basic activities or roles required in the position and other, similar positions; special activities required that are unique to a given location, process, project, technical requirement, and so on; identifiable or measurable outputs, or products or services, resulting from performance; and skills, abilities, and knowledge actually necessary for successful performance (specifying skills, knowledge, years of schooling, or academic degrees that are not clearly related to satisfactory job performance may not be adequate proof).

Dubé (1988, p. 203) believes that if performance becomes an issue, "rarely should a standardized [performance appraisal] form be simply checked or circled. . . . Supervisors should be required to provide a written narrative comment, including specific reference to performance deficiencies during the period under evaluation. . . . Supervisors should be trained to write appraisals as objective reports of *performance* not as rewards or concessions. If an evaluated position lends itself to quantitative measurement, the measurement should be made and included in the evaluation."

The organization should, in addition, offer extensive training to supervisors and others in all aspects of the appraisal system—including its objectives and means of implementation. Some companies conduct mock evaluation sessions to develop appraisal counseling skills that are taped and then discussed with the supervisors. It is crucial that supervisors understand the importance of administering the program regularly and in a manner consistent with those of their colleagues. As is common practice in larger organizations, employees should be evaluated at least once a year, and the evaluation report should be retained for three or more years. Again, such appraisals should be written.

In each of the major personnel actions—promotions, layoffs, and discharges—the employer is required to make a contrary showing when confronted with a charge of age discrimination. The consistently well-documented performance evaluation sheet offers the best means of making this showing. For example, when an older employee is passed over for a promotion, the employer must show that the complaining employee was not as qualified as the candidate selected. Here, it is not the employee's performance in his or her present job that is the principal criterion but rather the employee's potential performance relative to that of other employees. With respect to layoffs, according to Schuster and Miller (1981, pp. 568–581), the employer is required to demonstrate that the laid-off employee was not as qualified as those selected to remain. Finally, defending an outright discharge will involve more than simply a showing that the employee was performing at a minimally acceptable level. This type of personnel action will probably require a further demonstration by the employer that the decision was nondiscriminatory.

How important is performance appraisal if push comes to shove on an issue of the performance of any older employee? According to French (1982, p. 20), *Gill* v. *Union Carbide, Inc.*, 368 F. Supp. 364 (E.D. Tenn 1973), is a good case example of the kind of impact an effective appraisal system can have. *Gill* involved an allegation of age discrimination by four discharged employees. In finding for the company, the court cited three characteristics of the appraisal system that it believed upheld the company's argument that it was nondiscriminatory: (1) the evaluation procedures related logically to the work being done, (2) the system was regularly implemented without favor to any particular group, and (3) the workers had been informed of the appraisal method.

In contrast, Perham (1982, p. 62) notes a termination suit involving General Motors that shows how local management's failure to fairly evaluate an employee's performance can backfire. One year before he was fired, the employee was given the highest possible rating. "But six days after his termination his former boss assigned him the second lowest of six possible ratings." Needless to say, the company lost the suit.

In sum, in most ADEA cases where the employer has prevailed, it has been the combination of a regularly administered, written appraisal system and the credible testimony of the supervisor that has tipped the scales in the employer's favor. Alternatively, cases where the employee has won have been characterized by a poorly documented system and noncredible supervisory testimony. Schuster and Miller (1981, pp. 575–576) offer as an example such testimony in *Buckholz* v. *Symons Manufacturing Co.*, 455 F. Supp.

706 (E.D. Wis. 1978), where the only evidence of poor performance by the employee was written by a younger manager who, it was shown, stood to gain by the employee's discharge.

Overall, a good performance appraisal system—one that actually measures an employee's contribution to meeting specific and fair organizational needs—will, by its nature, contribute substantially to age-neutral human resource management.

Supervisor Readiness

Almost any aspect of an older person's work life can be enhanced if his or her supervisor is ready, willing, and able to act. Most are willing, but some it seems, are lacking in the areas of being ready and able.

Because of ineffective management practices, some supervisors allow themselves to be overwhelmed and consequently become burned out, tired, and unmotivated to make any special effort. This is despite the fact that many older, highly experienced people are available to help share the load. The common belief of supervisors that they should do everything themselves wears them out and defeats them. They then become angry when called on to do more, which gets in the way of their objectivity, saps more energy, and turns their outlook even more negative. If they were to relax, see the older person as an opportunity rather than a problem, and begin to think about and search for positive elements, they might regain the optimism required to solve any personnel problems that they encounter.

Two other problems may afflict the supervisor: concentration on an older employee's negative attributes and a general reluctance to believe that older people can succeed. Long-standing prejudice and age bias can often be overcome if everyone focuses on the positive advantages of age. Weatherbee (1969, p. 35) discusses the thoughts in this area of psychologist Carl Jung, who noticed that "after life's mid-point, people may develop their previously neglected, less rational [creative] side for a new meaning. It is precisely this late development of instinct and the subconscious that, superimposed on earlier experience, sharpens judgment and understanding." For a supervisor to fail to stress this positive potential is self-defeating.

Finally, much is being written today not about a fear of failure but about a fear of success—success that matches capability. To many, this may sound strange, since we are often preoccupied by a fear of failing. But the other side of the coin, a fear of winning really big, is more subtle and harder to pin down, though just as invidious. Why do people back off from opportunity, retreat when winning, and have vague premonitions of disaster when things are going well? Success at a high level may not match people's self-image and may therefore lead to discomfort when they start to "get too big for their britches." Unless these issues of success are dealt with, many supervisors—and consequently their older employees—may never get to enjoy the greater fruits of their labors and abilities.

Guidelines for Avoiding Charges of Age Discrimination

The following guidelines offer an overview of the suggestions made in the literature for avoiding a suggestion or charge of age discrimination.

1. The concept of age neutrality should be built into all phases of personnel and management policies. For example, Humple and Lyons (1983, pp. 64–70) say that decisions regarding promotions and training for the older employee should be made in the same manner as they are for any other worker, regardless of how close the employer believes the worker is to retirement. This will ensure that older workers will have access to career opportunities consistent with their aspirations, abilities, and potential.

2. As a general rule, managers should be made aware of the provisions of the ADEA and should stay up to date regarding developments in the act. Snyder and Brandon (1983, p. 45) suggest that supervisors review such sources as the "ADEA Update" of the General Counsel for the National Commission on Aging, which appears frequently in the journal *Aging and Work*. In addition, managers should be familiar with their own state's age-discrimination laws.

3. Supervisory personnel should be sensitized to the fact that any deprecatory age-related remarks, made in either a formal or an

informal setting, may set up the organization for a lawsuit or weaken its position in such a suit. While most managers are aware that age references cannot be made in, for example, job advertisements or performance appraisals, many do not pay as much attention to casual references in internal memos or offhand remarks (Snyder and Brandon, 1983, p. 45).

4. Also important is that personnel departments establish and document a track record of disseminating frequent and widespread information about their antidiscrimination policies. If an age-discrimination lawsuit is filed, courts tend to look favorably on evidence of a long-standing organizational policy of nondiscrimination and may assess any damages accordingly.

5. An employer may want to consider placing qualified older workers in personnel positions to serve as watchdogs, trainers, or facilitators of ADEA goals.

6. If an employer believes that a certain job cannot be successfully performed by workers over a certain age, concrete documentation to support this decision should be available. In most cases, it is better to "performance test" each employee's abilities rather than establishing a hiring cutoff based on age.

7. Using written tests as a hiring criterion is often risky. Such test material may not correlate with job requirements; more importantly, results of such tests are usually inadequate as predictors of job performance.

8. Snyder and Brandon (1983, p. 45) suggest that employers should periodically review the age of their employees on a unit-by-unit basis to determine whether older workers are adequately represented. This information can provide good statistical evidence if the employer can show that such representation has been achieved.

9. Since, as discussed earlier, most ADEA lawsuits involve allegations of unfair terminations, the work performance of a replacement employee should be measurably superior to that of the former incumbent. And, as always, the performance differences between the two employees should be carefully recorded.

10. If an employee is transferred or offered a demotion in lieu of being laid off or fired, the reasons for this, too, should be documented so that no argument can be made that an employment alternative was not offered.

11. Bakaly and Grossman (1984, p. 46) suggest that if a discharge is unavoidable, the employer should first consider the possibility of a voluntary retirement or resignation. In such an event, the employee should be requested, without pressure, to sign a waiver stating that the retirement or resignation is in fact voluntary and that he or she has no further claims against the organization. The wording of such a waiver should be reviewed with an attorney. Inducements might also be offered to the employee.

12. Bakaly and Grossman further say that when any disciplinary action is taken, the supervisor should be able to point to some progressive disciplinary system whose guidelines are known to employees and are fairly applied. Such a system typically involves such provisions as "an oral warning for the first offense, a written warning for the second, suspension for the third, and termination for the fourth" (p. 45). At each step, the action should be documented and discussed with the employee, and the employee should be given an opportunity to correct his or her behavior.

13. Finally, they suggest that to further reduce the need for legal action, the employer may wish to consider resolving employee-employer problems through an internal grievance and arbitration mechanism. Besides the obvious savings of litigation costs, another important advantage for the employer is that an arbitrator, rather than a jury, will hear the case and that the arbitration process usually involves several steps aimed at resolving the issue.

14. Employers should be aware that employment actions directed at management-level employees should be just as age-neutral as those aimed at other workers. "According to the House Select Committee on Aging, managers and supervisors are the most likely victims of age discrimination" (Humple and Lyons, 1983, p. 68).

15. Humple and Lyons also note that "a notice regarding the ADEA must be posted in an obvious spot in every organization, employment agency or union hall covered by the Act" (p. 69). Lawsuits have been lost because of the employer's failure to post this notice.

The very act of consciously applying some or all of these guidelines as organizational policy creates heightened awareness of

ADEA issues in the organization and indicates that the organization is taking a proactive approach to age neutrality and fairness.

Creating an Age-Fair Employment Climate

In summary, the primary methods for creating an age-fair employment climate in the work place are the following:

1. Revising policies and procedures to make them age neutral
2. Training supervisors and managers in the rights and protections of the ADEA and how to handle age problems on the basis of good management practices—free of personal biases and assumptions
3. Developing uniform standards of performance and behavior
4. Striving for objective performance measures
5. Focusing organizational attention on the productive contributions that can be made by older employees
6. Striving to reconcile differences between older and younger employees that are related to age
7. Balancing the age-attribute scale by taking advantage of the special characteristics of older employees—their experience, insight, stability, and loyalty—and giving fair attention to these special attributes

Training supervisory and management personnel in ADEA requirements and appropriate responses is critical. They should not be left to guess at appropriate forms of behavior. Today, the ultimate logic of managing well is the antidote to possible ADEA problems. But more important perhaps is the sense of organizational justice that these actions can produce.

Part Three

SUPERVISION AND LEADERSHIP

Leadership, teamwork, and the search for productivity generally converge at the front line of managing older employees. It is at the individual contact points between the organization and its workforce—where the work gets done—that the application of policies and procedures and the employee's reaction to them become critical. And it is here that we encounter several critical questions regarding the one-to-one management of older employees: How do we resolve the "managerial leadership" paradox of treating older employees equally with other producers yet acting in such a way that their special needs can be met at the same time? How do we develop successful work teams that incorporate the special contribution that older employees can make, resolve age-related work-group conflicts if they arise, and train our older workers (and others) for group-centered leadership as this practice is developing in the workplace? How do we deal effectively with the "retired-on-the-job" problem and other low-productivity issues? How can we help older employees to consistently achieve the highest possible level of performance of which they are capable? How can organizations prepare for and encourage older employees to continue working? How can investing in our older workers build a more positive future for ourselves, our organizations, our nation, and our society? What payoffs can we expect if the investment is made? What will happen if the investment is not made?

Productive answers to these questions can determine just how feasible it is to encourage some older employees to keep working.

Chapter 10

Ensuring Success on the Job

The supervisor's job has been described as getting the work done through other people, effectively applying the organization's policies and procedures, and, more recently, providing the aid and support needed by employees to meet organizational objectives. These views assume that the supervisor will operate within the law and the other constraints placed on the organization by society, so that the organization can fulfill its mission without distraction. In our context, this means having a firm grasp of the organization's responsibilities and its policies regarding the treatment of older employees. The first-line supervisor is on the firing line when applying such policies, and therefore the quality of the supervisor's leadership is critical.

We are increasingly realizing that worker productivity in our "knowledge society," where output is not easily measured, is often determined by how employees feel about the job, their employer, their co-workers, and so on—in short, their level of morale and motivation. As we have seen earlier, the supervisor's behavior is primary in these areas.

The Paradox of Special Groups

Ample evidence indicates that most older people want to be treated as an important part of their work or peer group, they want to contribute and be accepted, and they want to feel secure and to be treated fairly. At the same time, it should come as no surprise that they want to be recognized for their experience and past accomplishments, they want interesting work that is within their capabilities (realistic challenges), and they want to be listened to when they have a problem or a suggestion. As people age, they may come to expect less from the workplace, but that does not mean that they *want* less.

An effective supervisor treats employees similarly when it comes to the issues of fairness, equality of opportunity, and the application of important rules and procedures. However, quality supervision also takes into account the special needs of each employee, his or her unique strengths and special situational factors, as they arise.

A supervisor would expect to spend extra time with a young new employee to provide guidance and information regarding orientation, organizational expectations, policies, job duties, socialization, and training—all to make that person more effective. Similarly, if a middle-aged person developed a problem with alcohol, encountered a personal tragedy, experienced a grievous family problem, developed a severe illness, or experienced the now recognized midlife crisis, it would be considered proper for the supervisor to expend some extra effort to help that person get back on the road to productive participation in the work group. The same kind of help might reasonably be expected by older employees when they have special needs. Successful supervisors characteristically pay enough attention to each subordinate to recognize special problems and needs and invest considerable time and effort to help employees resolve their difficulties, no matter what their age.

Getting the Job Done

Excellent supervisors, especially today, are sensitive to the needs, talents, experience, and ideas of their subordinates. They are not just paper pushers or administrators or overseers. Top-notch leaders are alert to any special knowledge, skills, and abilities that an employee possesses and integrate those contributions into the work of the group. They also strive to discover and develop an employee's special talents. They maximize each person's contributions over both the short and the long term.

Unfortunately, the immediacy of the first-line supervisor's responsibilities—that is, the concern for today's output, keeping on schedule, and getting a myriad of things accomplished—often leads to a kind of myopia that can be injurious to older employees' long-term needs. Consequently, many supervisors ignore older employees and fail to foster their long-term development. Assuming other employee factors to be equal, the antidote to such oversight can be a series of questions such as these: If I have a challenging project or assignment coming up that could lead to considerable new learning for a person, would I give it to a younger or an older employee? If an opportunity for advancement arose in another department and I were asked to recommend a suitable employee, would I tend to give the nod to a younger person because I assume that he or she will be around longer? If an opportunity arose for one of my employees to attend an advanced seminar, would I be tempted to send a twenty-eight-year-old person rather than one over sixty-five, even though their expertise and output levels were comparable? Your answers to these questions might not cause you any great concern, but the research clearly indicates that a great many supervisors would tend to favor the younger person, not only because of age prejudice and stereotyping but also because they felt that they were doing the right things for the organization and for themselves. This attitude not only is quite risky but has already produced a generation of older employees who see their future as dead-ended, their jobs as boring and repetitious, and their opportunities as truncated.

An effective supervisor concerned about group output would balance fairly the distribution of opportunities and would help older employees to rekindle their interest in self-development, believe again that their future holds promise, and experience job-related variety and excitement.

The Critical Link

First-line supervisors also provide the first line of fairness between the employee and the organization. They are the critical link in representing the company to its employees and the employees to the company. To many workers, their supervisor *is* the organization, and nothing much happens in the workforce until organizational goals and policies are implemented by the first-line supervisor. This linking relationship implies that the supervisor needs to know a great deal about organizational policies and intent so that these can be conveyed to the employees. Since we are moving rapidly toward an information-based technological society, it is clear that employees will make more and more job-related decisions. Therefore, they need clear guidelines and greater understanding of where their jobs fit in so that they can make correct decisions in the clear context of organizational goals. Supervisors will increasingly have to provide the knowledge and rationale needed by worker–decision makers. Thus, the supervisor must truly represent the organization to the employees in all of its manifestations, not just in relation to the performance of tasks.

The job of the supervisor as defender against age-bias suits rests not only on carrying out organizational policies on nondiscrimination but also on carefully documenting disciplinary actions, being reasoned and fair in conducting performance appraisal, and handling personnel actions on everything from employee training and sick leave to transfers and promotions. "No need to worry," you might respond. "I'm not prejudiced about age." Such might well be the case. One survey of management personnel indicated that few considered themselves in any way biased with respect to age. But as one authority said in discussing an age-discrimination case, "I'm not sure that I, for one, understand how you would teach that person that he was discriminating. We all know that discrimination goes on all the time, yet I wonder how many of you sophisticated . . . people, can stop and think of a time when you have been discriminatory against someone else. It is very hard because you rationalize beautifully. We all do" (Yolles, Krinsky, Kieffer, and Carone, 1984, p. 53).

The difficulty that any supervisor faces is clear. While managers have many sound standards for making personnel decisions, such as technical competence, skills, and experience, research by Rosen, Jerdee, and Lunn (1981, p. 518) (described in Chapter Three) suggests that some managers are also using an *unconscious* standard in making such decisions—that of the employees' age. This standard is often outside the managers' awareness, but it is grounded in beliefs about the inability of older people to perform as well as younger employees in jobs that demand flexibility, creativity, and a high degree of motivation.

One of the most powerful aspects of this research is that when participants were asked directly for their opinions on organizational policies regarding older employees, they favored greater affirmative action goals, including eliminating mandatory retirement and vesting pensions completely. These results suggest that the differential treatment of older and younger employees was not conscious discrimination but the result of unconscious stereotypes. Stereotyping is a much harder nut to crack than discrimination, because it is not visible as such and operates at a subconscious, unaware level.

Finally, it may at times be necessary for the supervisor to confront higher-level managers when their behavior or direction is contrary to the organization's responsibilities—risky as that confrontation may be. In age-discrimination lawsuits, the supervisor may become as involved as the organization.

A Safe and Productive Workplace

The individual supervisor generally knows more about the state of the workplace than any other member of management. Consequently, each supervisor has a particular responsibility for the safety and welfare of older employees and for maintaining a safe workplace. Supervisors, of course, have that responsibility toward all their employees, but here a knowledge of the special risks of older employees can be helpful.

Root (1981) reports that data collected by the U.S. Bureau of Labor Statistics from more than a million workers' compensation records of agencies in thirty states provide clear evidence that occupational injuries occur at a lower rate among older workers than among younger ones. It was clear that "the frequency of occupational injuries declines steadily up to age 64 and then drops even more sharply for workers age 65 and over. The data indicate the positive effect of experience in avoiding injuries" (pp. 30-31). The author even goes so far as to suggest serious preventive training for new young workers to reduce the incidence of workplace injuries.

Older workers do get hurt, and most often these accidents result from workplace hazards that affect all types of employees. However, Root noted that physical declines in some older employees increased the hazards to them. For example, those experiencing declining physical coordination may experience a greater number of injuries from falls on floors and other working surfaces. He also noted that such falls might more likely produce bone fractures in an older person than in a twenty-year-old. Also, such older workers' injuries might be more severe and more costly to the organization in lost time and compensation payments.

Five categories of injuries accounted for 75 percent of all such accidents: sprains and strains, cuts and lacerations, contusions and bruises, fractures, and burns. However, fractures, hernias, and heart attacks were markedly more frequent among older employees than among workers as a whole. Consequently, a supervisor might factor such possibilities into job assignments that involve severe pressure, stress or very long working hours, lifting heavy loads, or awkward positions or slippery surfaces. Such considerations involve an assessment of probability on the supervisor's part and an appraisal of individual capabilities rather than solely a person's age.

Consideration of such factors does not in itself imply favoritism but rather reflects sound management and the conservation of a supervisor's human resources. Root found evidence that this type of common sense was already operating in statistics that demonstrated that workers over sixty-five and teenagers were less frequently injured than all other workers. Root also notes that these two groups have fewer back injuries, because they are less likely to have jobs requiring heavy lifting. Such facts can tell supervisors where to look for potential health and safety problems so that they can concentrate on dealing with such problems rather than basing their decisions on an age category.

The same kind of reasoning can be applied to other age

groups as well. For example, "Being struck by and against, and caught in, under or between things, accounted for more than 50 percent of injuries to teenage workers, but the percentage steadily declined for older workers. Conversely, falls, particularly falls on the same level, became an increasingly serious problem with advancing age. For workers age 65 and over, falls produce nearly one-third of injuries compared with about 13 percent for teenagers" (p. 34). Thus, an effective manager might well provide extra training and careful monitoring of behavior of any age group to reduce the likelihood of the type of accidents that that group is prone to experience. For older employees, special attention should be given to slippery floors or other work surfaces.

It can be argued that supervisors should watch out for all of these things anyway, no matter who is in the work group. But like all absolutes, "*all* of these things" ignores the fact that a supervisor simply cannot monitor everything, all the time. Being sensitive to and aware of the special needs of some individuals or groups enables the supervisor to apply time and effort where the payoff in group health and safety will be greatest. And lest a supervisor avoid his or her responsibility for workplace safety (as some apparently do) by saying, "but we don't work in a factory, we have a nice, clean, safe environment here," Root says that "the age-specific patterns of injury characteristics were *similar across industry and occupational groups*" (p. 34) [emphasis mine]. Slipping in front of the copy machine or stumbling on a tab of carpet can hurt just as much as falling on a factory floor.

Problems in Perception

It is surprising how often a worker or supervisor who is having difficulty with an older employee attributes such behaviors as resistance to change, slowness, indecisiveness, talkativeness, insensitivity, or abruptness to the person's age. Yet Hagen (1983, p. 7) states that "with a few exceptions it is impossible to generalize about older employees—their individual differences are at least as great as those of any other age group . . . they include the wise and the foolish, the bitter and the cheerful, the dedicated and the clockwatchers, the slipshod and the careful workers." He further suggests that the

"Pareto principle"—that is, 20 percent of the employees create 80 percent of the problems in an organization—applies to this age group as well as to any other.

Hagen does not argue that older people in general do not develop a few distinctive characteristics that we can generalize about, such as reduced tendencies to take risks. However, he does point out that most of the negative generalizations that people use against the elderly have little to do with being old. The gossip has probably been practicing his art for half a century, the pompous old woman was a self-important young person, and the talkative individual has had a lifetime of such experience. He suggests that most of us have formed our impression of older workers (or older people in general) on the basis of a very limited sample. As with all such subjective samples, the extreme cases tend to make the greatest impression.

As we have noticed when we are upset with another person, we tend to grasp any negative generalizations that might strengthen our position and classify that person with an undesirable stereotype, such as "He's cranky, but I guess you have to expect that from someone that old." Therefore, the focus shifts from why he is cranky to the fact that he is old (an unsolvable problem), which may free the supervisor from responsibility for trying to deal with the behavior—crankiness. This tendency to cloud interpersonal conflict and performance problems with issues of age makes the problem difficult to solve and dangerous. Unresolved issues and continuing annoyances can lead to impulsive behavior by supervisors and impair their judgment.

Several writers have suggested that age prejudice, though often difficult to detect, may be more prevalent today in employment situations than race or gender bias. In a 1977 study of factors in employer selection of the disadvantaged, Haefner (1977, p. 201) found that race was often not as important a factor in hiring decisions as age, because of successful equal employment opportunity (EEO) training of supervisors and affirmative action programs. In his study of 286 employees in the state of Illinois to determine their assessment of hypothetical job candidates, twenty-five-year-old candidates were greatly preferred over fifty-five-year-olds even when all the candidates were highly competent. Few supervisors, it seems, have been well trained on issues of age discrimination, even today.

The issue of *generation* may have an influence even in the absence of specific ageism. There are some discernible differences that do *tend* to occur in groupings of people as they age. Though we should not assume that particular values, viewpoints, and physical conditions are characteristic of any particular individual, tendencies in such areas can provide clues for a supervisor's consideration of performance problems or planning of remedial action in some cases. Some of these characteristics are related to societal acculturation and may modify the workforce in general as our younger populations age. However, while such generalizations can be useful in understanding *some* older people and in solving *some* problems, when we assume that a specific individual falls into a particular category and should be treated accordingly, we run into trouble.

Harmonious Motivation

While motivation is an inner process, the supervisor is not helpless to influence it; she or he can offer incentives, recognize and reward performance achievement, listen to employees talk about their problems, provide help and assistance when needed and feasible, create opportunities, use employee suggestions, and share information with employees. These benefits should be offered to all employees regardless of age. Yet motivation flourishes best when the choices and behaviors mesh well with the individual's value system.

When it comes to the work situations of older employees, there are some generalizations, outlined below, that can guide supervisors—as long as they recognize that particular individuals may vary from the norm. Supervisors need to discover these variations and adapt their approach accordingly.

Older employees may not get as much positive reinforcement, encouragement, and recognition as others. Yet this type of "stroking" is a basic human need and is valued and required at any age for a good self-image and mental health. Older employees may have a greater than average need for praise and recognition because their personal lives may provide a diminishing supply of friends and family. A study of burnout and lack of interest among older employees (Shea, 1981) established that a relative absence of praise (being taken for granted) is one of their principal complaints.

Older employees value opportunity and challenge as much as anyone else if they believe that they are prepared for them and can handle them. They also need to keep their skills up to date; if they do not, their sense of self and of mastery of their work will suffer. Older employees tend to place the highest value on job satisfaction and feeling useful.

Older employees have a particular problem with an innate need for achievement that is often suppressed. Helping older employees to see themselves as more potent through achievement motivation training can release this desire. Smith (1970, p. 176) concludes that there is little systematic difference in achievement motivation among people of different ages. Therefore, the observed decrement is likely to be reversible if a supervisor tries to help. According to research by Cherrington, Condie, and England (1979, p. 622), "older employees placed greater importance on *the moral importance of work* and *pride in craftsmanship*" than did younger employees.

With the loosening of traditional family ties, some older employees may be less inclined to give up the social aspects of their job, a loss that might come from retirement. A worker's satisfaction with pay is likely to increase with age, since income may increase with age, and financial obligations are likely to decrease. However, research by Churchill, Ford, and Walker (1979, pp. 29, 46) showed that older salespeople have an increased desire for financial rewards, partly because their jobs fail to satisfy higher-level needs, such as recognition or advancement, and they often see money as a form of recognition or confirmation of personal worth.

The mid-career or midlife crisis may entail a shift in values. As people increasingly perceive more options in their work lives, these personal crises seem to be more common. Restlessness, fatigue, irritability, and depression may be clues. Without challenge, job rotation, or continued self-investment, people may see themselves as stuck or plateaued and may become less productive and develop negative behaviors that affect others as well as themselves.

Rethinking one's definition of success may be important.

Constandse (1972, p. 133) points out that many people consider wealth the only yardstick for success. Yet, he says, "People rarely resign for financial reasons. There are factors more important than money [for some], the power to *make* instead of *execute* policy, or the opportunity to give rather than take orders." If new values tend to emerge in midlife, motivation and morale will certainly be affected. Since the midlife or mid-career problem often occurs as people approach the age at which they would be considered older (forty), resolution of this crisis may be critical to preventing older employees of the future from becoming problem employees and of less value to themselves as well.

Problems of the Younger Supervisor

Most of us have been raised to expect that older people will have some authority over us, and many of us have been brought up with very well defined notions of our roles with respect to older people. The results of this early programming range from a sense of devotion and respect to a rather general notion that older people have some advantages that we cannot yet claim. The expected compensation is often that "some day we'll be big, and then the world will be ours." Of course, even when we grow up, the feelings of deference to age may continue. Sometimes this conditioning and the feelings it evokes cause the supervisor to be uncomfortable giving directions to an older employee. Some of this discomfort can be overcome by focusing on the person's performance rather than on the person.

These age problems can involve goals, values, and ideals as well as operating styles. For some younger supervisors, appraising the work of their seniors and communicating performance deficiencies to an older person become very difficult. Also, some sociologists claim that how we interact with another person depends on how we perceive that other person's status relative to our own. In an organization, this status conflict involves not only age but also seniority on the job, level of accomplishment and position, and even relative incomes.

Rosen and Jerdee (1985) again offer us some helpful approaches to resolving this age difference dilemma. They point out that supervisors can learn to take less threatening approaches to confrontation, to listen nonevaluatively, and to creatively solve performance problems with the older employee so as to achieve goals that both desire. However, this may require that the supervisor see the older employee as a needful person rather than simply as one who is older. The older employee may need appreciation for good work, factual data on deficiencies, and the possibility of achievement. Effective feedback, even if it is negative, is often better than no feedback. Once the problem is defined, mutual problem solving can start. But more than this may be needed. In performance feedback, most if not all employees need information rather than evaluation. Rather than "constructive criticism," people need factual data about the discrepancy between standards and performance—that is, a description of what is needed by management in contrast to what has been received.

Criticism is evaluative and judgmental and as such is threatening. It therefore evokes instinctive resistance rather than cooperation, since our primary human needs include survival and security. Criticism is particularly threatening to someone who may feel bypassed by events and who is not highly regarded. Information, on the other hand, is merely factual, and though it may be interpreted any way the receiver chooses, it is far less likely to be threatening, especially if the person is then offered assistance in closing the gap between what is needed and what has been given. This cooperative problem-solving approach means being forward looking rather than wallowing in what is past and cannot be changed anyway. Older employees often need the supervisor's help in looking toward a more hopeful future. This is what supervisory leadership is all about.

Chapter 11

Developing Productive Work Teams

Supervisors and managers in business, government, and institutions have long talked about "my team," "team effort," and "team players," but off the athletic field, real team play seems scarce and elusive. The traditional hierarchical structure with its lines of authority and chain of command still dominates the thinking and behavior of most managers. Culturally, we still see boxes on our organizational charts, with lines running to sub-sub boxes, and so on. This mental model of how organizations function is so pervasive that even when we consciously set out to build teams and teamwork, we often do it badly. William Dyer (1987, p. 10) reports on a research study of top management groups that found that 85 percent of the communication within the groups took place between individual members and their supervisors (up and down) and only 15 percent laterally between group members. Yet it appears certain that in our society we will increasingly need to work in teams of various sorts. As workplace problems become more technologically complex and interdisciplinary and as the various kinds of knowledge and expertise possessed by individuals need to be integrated creatively, we must focus more effectively on team efforts. However, it is exactly here that older employees in general present both a serious obstacle to team development and an unparalleled opportunity.

The teams of tomorrow will not be just collections of people reporting to their supervisors or the occasional committees of the past. Three or four decades ago, the hierarchical structure began to crumble in the high-tech industries, with informal networking, task-force teams, and ad hoc groups being used to solve problems where answers were needed more quickly than the traditional organization could provide them.

New and more complex forms of work teams are increasingly appearing. The use of quality circles, interdisciplinary study teams, matrix management, self-directed work groups, task forces, participative decision-making efforts, and new types of committees is shifting much of the focus in organizations from individual contribution to group activity. In fact, many of the competitive accomplishments in manufacturing for international trade credited to the Japanese have been ascribed to their superior use of on-the-job work teams. The question before us then is this: Does age make a difference in meeting our need for cooperative work-group effort, and if so, how can we maximize the contribution of older employees?

Age and Group Work

As early as 1974, research reported by Ross Webber (1974) of the University of Pennsylvania indicated that there was at least a generational problem for older employees in performing some types of work in groups. But he concluded that this problem could probably be compensated for if supervisors and managers cared to make the effort. The project was designed to explore a heretofore largely unexamined aspect of group performance, the effect of member age on the work of homogeneous age groups. Webber noted that several studies and reports indicate that cooperative behavior in groups produces more effective performance than individual effort. He tied this with another common observation: that young people today tend to be more cooperative and less competitive than earlier generations. Therefore, the study's aim was to determine whether groups of older or younger people perform best.

The study participants were given a task to perform individually and then put into homogeneous age- and status-related groups and asked to perform a pretested second task, of equal complexity and difficulty, in the group setting. The results bore out earlier findings that groups scored more highly than individuals. But more important here was the finding that younger groups scored better than older groups and did so because they were better able to draw on the performance of their "best" (or most able or knowledgeable) individuals.

Perhaps of even greater significance was the fact that younger groups, by utilizing the abilities of their best individuals, were even more likely to show superior *average member performance*. That is, group scores of younger groups most often outranked the average of the individual scores in their own group *and* the score of the *best* individual in the group. Therefore, relying on one "expert" does not always produce the best score—relying on the group most often will. In short, younger groups tended to more effectively discover and use their people resources. One factor seemed to be their flexibility in shifting leadership on each decision to a member who seemed to be best able to handle that item. In groups composed of older men, it appeared that the individual members were more interested in preserving status, exercising (or avoiding) leadership, and avoiding looking bad to their peers. Consequently, such individuals tended not to contribute as much to group discussion.

Many studies support the notion that group trust and familiarity with group problem-solving processes are critical in determining group effectiveness. Webber suggests that the "habits of managerial office" may have undermined older group performance. This tendency of many older managers to dictate decisions may be an age-related cultural phenomenon and the result of "learned expectations" that decisions are best made solo. Webber's study, as well as much empirical research conducted by myself, indicates that the tendency of older individuals to rely on one expert may not be as useful as it was once perceived to be. Webber and others also suggest that younger people may have far more experience (beginning with their academic studies) in group-process work and group decision making than older people do. They may be less concerned with status and control, less competitive in a group setting, and more able to focus on achieving optimum results than older individuals.

The foregoing discussion clearly indicates that where older employees are expected to increasingly operate in and contribute to group activities, they need to be trained or counseled in how to become more effective group contributors. Since the differences in group performance seem to be generational—that is, attributable to the way each was raised, educated, and socialized in the workplace—there should be no inherent reason why some of these habits cannot be overcome. While some individuals may be resistant, most people of any age can and will change their behavior if they find it desirable or advantageous to do so. Similarly, interviews and follow-up discussions I have conducted with 242 older (over 55 years old) first-line supervisors and mid-level managers (divided about equally between government and private industry) concerning obstacles to developing teamwork have indicated the following facts about many older managers:

- They were not used to working in teams except in competitive situations.
- They believed that informal teams were generally viewed as cliques and were to be avoided.
- They saw work on the job as usually organized for individual contribution so that group activity was not possible or at least was discouraged.
- They did not know very much about working cooperatively—cooperation was seen largely as meaning not making waves, not getting in someone else's way, and giving help only when it was asked for.
- They saw "a team player" as one who goes along with the coach (decision maker), does not dissent, and plays his or her assigned role.
- They viewed volunteering help as taboo, an insult, or something to be treated with suspicion.
- They had often been raised in the autocratic model of manage-

ment and saw asking for or accepting help as a sign of weakness or dependent status.

- They were in the habit of relying on "experts," which tended to make them passive in the presence of such people.
- They tended to see teamwork as any meeting where they agreed that a problem was solved, regardless of the methods used ("going along to get along" was considered acceptable behavior).
- Even when intellectually committed to teamwork, they lacked the skills to make it work.

A few older participants went so far as to suggest that they might be socially out of date and need training in how to work more cooperatively in groups. Some suggested that perhaps the reason the quality circles concept failed as often as it succeeded when it was introduced in this country a few years ago was this same difficulty in being able to cooperate. These older people often said that they (and other older employees who worked for them) had much to contribute to group problem solving but frequently did not feel comfortable doing so.

Additional Sources of Work-Group Conflict

The literature on older workers cites several other sources of work-group conflict that may affect older employee participation and therefore should be of concern to supervisors and managers.

Generational Conflicts. A decade or more ago, it was common to hear talk about a "generation gap" in values. However, research about that time supported the conclusion that many features of the generation gap were contrived rather than real. Perhaps this is why we hear so much less about that notion today. But there is still a problem here. Virtually all age groups tend to believe that the values and even the personalities of other generations are different from their own. A study by Ahammer and Baltes (1972) compared perceived and actual differences in some personality dimensions across a broad age range. In contrast to the method of some earlier studies, both the age of the perceiving group and the ages of the perceived groups varied.

The study demonstrated that, even though the various groups acted in similar ways, each group believed that the other groups were different from itself. In part, this seemed to be the result of differences in style—how they went about doing things—rather than differences in substance. For instance, two generational groups may both value work, but each may see it as a road to different kinds of reward, depending on their age. The generation difference between them, however, may be used as evidence that the other group does not value work per se rather than as a way for them to appreciate their commonalities.

Supervisors encounter the generation gap most commonly when a person makes negative generalizations about another person on the basis of assumptions about the values of the other person's age group. These generalizations can usually be detected by the use of absolutes, stated or implied, such as "all you kids think of . . ." or "all you old folks act like . . ." or the use of derogatory terms. For good group operating processes to be maintained, such "putdowns" should be confronted effectively and not allowed to pass unless they are used in a genuinely humorous sense.

Resentment of Seniority. Older workers are the most likely to be advantaged by seniority rules and agreements. Employees of organizations where seniority counts for job security usually buy into the system to the degree to which they gain seniority with the passing years. Therefore, resentment over seniority is not likely to be overt, but when there is a threat of layoffs or an economic downturn, it is not uncommon for spontaneous bickering, indirect negative behaviors, or snide remarks to unsettle an organization or group as tensions mount.

Blocking Advancement of Younger Employees. As the baby-boom bubble moves toward the older end of the life scale and older employees can stay longer on the job, it is expected that generational strife may increase. Though such a sentiment may be observable only occasionally, an increasing number of younger people may be wishing that older employees would move out of the workforce and give them a chance. This problem often flares when a younger person believes that the "old-timers" are holding jobs that they do not need. A supervisor might confront this attitude, which is often based on the assumption that the only needs for work are economic, by discussing among employees what work means to different people and why a person may want to hold on to a job long after his or her basic needs for sustenance could be met by the retirement program.

Competition from Women and Minorities. There is occasional mention in management literature of resentment toward older employees by other protected classes of employees, such as (presumably younger) women and minorities. Since ADEA legislation was passed, some older employees have been placed in direct competition with some other people covered by affirmative action plans when personnel actions are contemplated. Since some older employees also fall into one or more of these other categories as well, the situation can become very complicated. Supervisors should be alert to this type of potential conflict and possibly seek expert counsel if such problems arise.

Privilege and Status. In discussing flexible working hours arrangements, Elbing, Gadon, and Gordon (1974, p. 28) cited examples of professional staffs already operating on a flexible time basis that resented extension of that privilege to the rest of the organization because it eliminated a distinction that allowed them to see themselves as having higher status. The authors suggest that groups that are excluded when others gain or that see themselves as losing something need explanations in advance and a chance to talk through what is bothering them. If there is a union, its position may also have to be taken into consideration. Where older employees seem to gain or lose relative to other groups, reactions on both sides of the equation may have to be explored.

The Illness and Handicap Conflict. Although employers would have a difficult time preventing employees who have recovered from illness or injury or who would now be labeled handicapped from returning to work, some studies reported by Lipton (1979, pp. 60-65) indicate that other employees sometimes cause trouble for them. A study sponsored by the American Cancer Society found that fully recovered employees returning to their former jobs faced hostility, usually expressed by sarcastic remarks, shunning, and changes in assignments. They even found that, despite the law, 13 percent were denied reemployment because of their cancer history, and 35 percent perceived some form of discrimination after returning to work.

Studies have also shown that 30 to 40 percent of stroke victims who are later capable of full employment report resentment by supervisors and co-workers when they are able to return to the job. There seems at times to be almost a sense of embarrassment or resentment toward people who return to the workplace after a serious ailment. Therefore, despite the legal rights of elderly people, who are subject to some of these illnesses in greater proportion than other segments of the workforce, supervisors and managers do not appear always to be doing a good job in defusing conflicts arising from such illnesses. All of this indicates a deep need for conflict-resolution skills by supervisors and managers as well as an exceptional sensitivity to potential age-related conflicts.

Older Employees' Contributions to Work-Group Success

On the positive side of the ledger, examples are growing of organizations, teams, and work groups that combine the efforts of young and old for their mutual benefit. Sekiguchi (1980, p. 16) cites an example of a food industry corporation with a mandatory retirement age of fifty-five that, after having restricted the hiring of new production and marketing personnel for thirteen years, discovered that the average age of its employees was nearing fifty and extended the retirement age. However, the company's union opposed the notion that older workers should be separated or given special treatment. They argued that all employees can work in unison, with everyone enthusiastic about their work. They believed that younger workers, because of their youthfulness, should be used to rejuvenate the workplace.

The company consequently adopted a personnel management policy that encouraged older workers to fend off the feeling that they were too old to work or that they should resign or retire. Co-workers and colleagues were expected to provide emotional and other types of personal support to older employees. As a result, the company reported that older employee morale had risen noticeably and that the overall atmosphere was more vigorous even among younger employees.

Examples of youth-age cooperation in other industrial nations with rapidly rising older populations are also becoming more common. Kenny (1981) suggests that many companies should attempt to ensure that enclaves of older employees do not develop unless there is a very special reason for their existence. He argues that, while there may be much perceived security and mutual support within such an enclave, much of this support may be directed to setting unsatisfactory work standards and resisting change. In addition, the enclave group's relations with other departments or work groups can become strained. Thus, Kenny stresses the benefits of a balanced age structure within the organization and within its components. Information on decision making by younger and older individuals indicates ways that the strengths of each may be used to complement those of the other to produce superior results. Kenny found that younger managers are more willing to shift authority within the group, to listen to and accept the special expertise of another person, and to be flexible and tolerant of others. However, they also tend to more readily discount unpopular viewpoints and the inherent risks in a situation. Their self-confidence tends to lead them to overrate their abilities, and they have some tendency to be intolerant of details in an unfamiliar field. By contrast, older managers are better able to appraise the value of new information and tend to minimize risk by seeking more reliable direction from authority figures and expert opinion.

Given these types of findings, many researchers suggest that a balanced team of older and younger managers or professionals who respect the abilities and contribution of the other group members and who are sophisticated in the ways of team information processing, conflict resolution, and nonthreatening confrontation skills can produce superior results. The techniques of interpersonal problem solving that are available to the group and its members as well as the maturity of group members seem to be critical factors in group effectiveness.

Developing Informal Group Cooperation for Productivity

Almost all organizational units possess at least two identities. The most obvious is that of the *formal* organization, exemplified by the organizational chart, composed of the supervisor, line producers, and support staff. In this structure, the supervisor acts as leader and most often interacts with each subordinate on a one-to-one basis though sometimes organizing and directing team efforts. The *informal* organization is based on the often powerful and varied relationships among the team members themselves. The informal groups that arise from these relationships may be even more powerful than the formal structure. Such a group may have its own informal leaders to whom the members are more committed than they are to their formal supervisor. It may even be able to pull down the appointed supervisor through misdirection of action, formation of a union, or sabotage. Or it may support the supervisor and contribute greatly to that person's success.

Informal groups start by providing social interaction and support for each other. They teach newcomers the ropes (though not always what the supervisor would desire), provide comfort and often protection for each other, and may contribute greatly to an individual member's success or failure. These groups often link the group members to the grapevine and to other sources of knowledge and help throughout the organization.

Informal groups are usually loosely formed, and a given employee may actually be part of several of them: an informal information network in a car pool, a social group that regularly plays cards together at lunchtime, a women's network group, and the company bowling league. For many employees, it is membership in these informal groups that makes their job bearable. The informal group often has an important influence on whether a person retires or continues to work, both through its attitude about the alternatives and by the way that it communicates group values to its members. It can also make the job a home away from home or a living hell for an individual. Informal group members often provide the caring, pleasurable support system that a retiree misses after leaving the workplace.

Informal groups arise naturally in any social setting. Such

groups and their leaders often determine how much the work group produces. Despite the supervisory ego involved in the statement "A supervisor makes things happen," the supervisor may produce mediocre results if the work group decides that is what *it* wants. The protective conspiracy of "let's not do too much or they'll be expecting it all the time" characterizes the training of new employees in many organizations. Employee skills of foot dragging, goldbricking, sabotage, blowing the whistle on the boss, and staging accidents are well documented. Here the issue is that strong informal work groups often determine relationships, group norms, standards of behavior, and even output, in a very real sense.

The wise supervisor works with the informal group if possible, rather than against it. While the informal group greatly influences the social system and even solves its own "family problems," the aware supervisor can do much to help this type of organization work toward mutually beneficial ends. The wise supervisor will create innovative policies and methods within his or her sphere of freedom to do so that foster cooperative efforts (especially at the worker level, where there is more likely to be antiorganizational bias). Older employees often have inordinate influence in the informal group: if excluded from it, they are likely to leave the organization.

Training for Intergenerational Cooperation

Workshops that confront the stereotypes about aging and provide reality data about the physical, intellectual, and emotional aspects of the aging process are becoming increasingly common. Most often offered to supervisors and managers, these training programs aim at enhancing each participant's ability to maximize the contribution of each older employee. Victoria Kaminski (1983b, p. 22) has described such programs offered at the Lawrence Livermore National Laboratory, which train all the supervisors from one division or department at one time. "Since these supervisors create the organizational climate for their workers, it is helpful for them all to be dealing from the same information base."

Such training has often been justified by a set of assumptions that recognize that many older people do function or behave differently in many instances. When younger (not necessarily young) employees are ignorant of the realities of these differences (which may not be negative) and consequently believe the myths about older people, hold prejudices, or make unwarranted assumptions, it is likely to show in their words and actions. This can obviously hurt morale, produce conflict, and lessen team effectiveness. It has been suggested, therefore, that supervisory personnel should be given training that explains the peculiarities and realities of younger employees as well. This thought has been rejected by some, on the basis that all supervisors have at least experienced youth, whereas not all of them have as yet been old. However, such arguments miss the point that is relevant here. Companies can easily devise team-building training that includes the following:

- Information on the myths and realities about all age groups as they are related to group activities, problem solving, and decision making
- Information, exercises, or case studies on ways to resolve conflicts related to age differences
- Activities and exercises that make it easy for participants to try out new behaviors and attitudes related to age issues in an accepting and emotionally safe environment
- Team-building activities where the special contribution of each person is recognized and maximized and age differentials are discussed to see whether there are lingering problems.
- The latest skill-building techniques for nonthreatening confrontation, ways to improve team communication, and ways to improve group problem-solving skills
- A focus on maximizing team productivity, gaining harmony, recognizing individual contribution, enhancing cooperation, and building team spirit
- Provision for follow-up and individual counseling for individuals who appear to have a special problem when dealing with people of other ages or who find some types of cooperation difficult

The last item may seem strange to some readers, but individuals do have trouble freeing themselves from age stereotypes and adopting behaviors that encourage interactions with people of different age groups. Some of these individuals might benefit from being able to talk out their problems with an effective counselor.

In most cases, if older workers are to become an effective part of work teams, it will be necessary for the groups to engage in "skull practices" as do football teams, to talk over plans and strategies, review past actions, learn new methods, or consciously build team spirit and effectiveness. This frequent processing of team behavior in a healthy, positive fashion is essential to productive team development and high performance that allow employees of all ages to meet their needs for accomplishment.

Chapter 12

Overcoming Low Productivity

Low or declining productivity, or the "retirement-on-the-job" (ROTJ) syndrome, has sometimes been cavalierly assumed to be natural, expected, and inevitable in older employees. Before the days of age-discrimination laws, it was common to hear executives echo this belief and for some business writers to fall into the same trap. Because of the commonness and consequences of such a negative belief, we need to deal with the issue here.

Low productivity and "retirement on the job" conflict so completely with all that we know about human nature and human motivation that there must be a personal, interpersonal, or organizational malady at the root of such phenomena. It is simply not "natural" for people who can produce well (and usually have) to produce poorly. If we can identify, diagnose, and remedy the problem behind this strange behavior, their productivity should rise to very satisfactory levels.

This approach is analogous to the medical belief that if people are sound at birth and their physical and emotional needs are met, health rather than illness should be their natural condition. Illness has a cause that needs to be found. Therefore, if low output or goofing off occurs, it is the job of supervisors and managers to detect the motivational or other causes and assist the employee to overcome them. The employee also needs to see that quality work and productivity are the most healthy and personally satisfying working goals. The research on aging support this more positive view of older workers. For example, we have noted the following:

- Age-related changes in physical ability, cognitive performance, and personality have little effect on workers' output except in the most physically demanding tasks.
- Creative and intellectual achievements do not necessarily decline with age. For instance, the overall musical ability of musicians in general rises with age until their mid sixties and does not decline until they are eighty-five or older.
- Absenteeism drops as age increases.
- Older employees have less turnover.
- The work ethic is much stronger among older than among younger people.
- Older workers are more satisfied with their jobs, supervision, salary, and co-workers—and with their lives in general.
- If the methods are suitable, older people can be trained or retrained as effectively as anyone. Age-related physical and mental changes that influence abilities to learn tend to be minimal.
- Vocabulary, general information, and judgment either rise or do not fall before age sixty, and even then, they continue to develop in the majority of people.
- Senior workers, if treated with respect, show greater critical judgment, insight, and patience and in general are better able to come up with ideas that work.
- "Their greater experience and wisdom compensates for any declining speed in mental or physical effort" (Goddard, 1987, p. 34).

This list is not presented simply to rehash the virtues of older employees; it is intended as a clear cry to take the older person seriously when performance problems develop. A decline in an older employee's work quality or quantity or the onset of unsatisfactory performance should be taken as an *oddity,* not the norm. When a problem arises (or, more likely, is noticed), it in itself should be treated as a managerial challenge—a mystery to be solved.

The Core Problem

Older employees are obviously not the only people with problems of low productivity or even retirement on the job. Yet, the idea of a younger person being retired on the job seems incongruous to many managers. However, consider organizations such as police, fire fighters, and the military that offer twenty-year retirement programs. Some individuals who are in their late thirties may well spend a large part of their last few years on the job preparing for their subsequent career, lining up future job prospects, or trying to prove disability so that their retirement income will be enhanced. Similar behavior, or just goofing off, can also occur among tenured college professors (at perhaps a somewhat later age), in a factory with a strong union, or in a government agency where complex procedural requirements and lengthy personnel hearings intimidate or discourage supervisors from taking corrective action.

But there is another, generally more socially acceptable type of downgraded output and semiretirement, seen when people mentally withdraw from the job and concentrate their effort and energy on interests outside the workplace. They have given up on the job, and though they may "earn their keep," they are not contributing in full measure. This putting in time and doing enough to get by often leads to boredom, guilt, vague dissatisfaction, and burnout. This lassitude does not elevate people's spirits or bring joy to their daily lives.

It is often possible to trace low performance or taking it easy on the job to causes such as our enshrinement of retirement as a cultural goal (military personnel who can rack up two or three retirement plans during their work life are living the dream to the fullest); getting even for past wrongs (living well at the organization's expense is the best revenge); a reductive managerial style that reduces initiative and motivation, rather than a developmental approach that offers challenges and rewards achievement; an oppressive, regimented environment where thinking and creativity are discouraged; or our belief in perpetual advancement rather than the satisfaction derived from the work we do. Such situations may encourage those who see no further forward movement to withdraw from investing themselves in their work.

Even when such low output is socially acceptable (for example, "taking care of the old faithful retainer") or understood by everyone (as where it is customary for people to spend their last few years before retirement making contacts for their next job or to actively engage in proving job-related disability as a nest-feathering exercise), such customs damage the general image of older employees or, worse, enable other people to write off an older person's behavior as "just doing what comes naturally." To turn these attitudes and behaviors around, we need to recognize why some older employees behave as they do and effectively tackle such factors.

Responses to Discrimination

If older employees sense supervisory avoidance or discrimination, they have a limited number of ways to respond or deal with their frustration. The most common coping devices include giving up (but remaining on the job); leaving the environment—resigning or taking early retirement; detouring around the problem (avoiding it while getting their needs met in ways that are not helpful to the organization); getting angry and possibly "getting even" (including passive-aggressive behavior); and confrontation, which may lead to quarreling, lawsuits, and so on. Of course, the proper response of a supervisor is mutual problem solving, but that approach seems seldom to be used when an older employee is involved. Looking at these five typical responses, we can discover some interesting variations that have important consequences.

Giving Up. This does not always lead to unsatisfactory performance, ROTJ, or counteraction, but a price is always paid for it. A study done by the Long Lines Division of AT&T reported by Jacobs (1982, p. 21) revealed that when middle managers realized that their job goals were not going to be met, they "were not devastated. Family, hobbies and other interests became more important than work. They disengaged from work, didn't want transfers or promotions that interfered with their other interests. But they still yearned for autonomy." The author suggested offering such managers the power to make free, independent decisions in their area of expertise and lateral promotions with an enlarged job scope as ways of keeping such managers productive and interested. The same kind of approach could be applied to hourly workers as well.

Leaving the Environment. If an employee resigns to join another firm or seeks or accepts an early-retirement option, the company usually loses the skills, experience, or special company knowledge of a long-time employee. And the organization's proprietary know-how may migrate to a competitor. Yet Polaroid and Bankers Life found that a voluntary retirement plan (as opposed to mandatory retirement) was successful because "older workers who are not doing a good job, or who are unhappy, usually exercise self-selection and quit voluntarily" ("When Retirement . . .," 1978, p. 82). While to some managers and supervisors this voluntary migration may seem to resolve the issue, such departures usually represent a management failure to solve the problem rather than a "lucky break." And Floyd (1969, p. 22) found that when older employees "are forced into a state of atrophy, younger men learn from the status of older men and leave."

Sheppard (1972, p. 4) makes an interesting point on the issue of frustrated employees leaving: "Focusing on age variables in job changing versus non-age variables, generalizations such as 'low risk-taking' and 'conservative' are generated and sustained, whereas in truth older workers with high motivation and sound self-image are quite willing to change jobs in search of opportunity." Therefore, it is quite possible that when performance sags, for whatever reason, those who leave may be the very ones most able to regain their productivity if the problem were successfully resolved.

Detouring Around the Problem. Older employees and their managers often collaborate to avoid really dealing with low-performance problems. Mutually agreed upon transfers to other assignments or locations, sometimes including downgrading, may be seen as an acceptable way to solve the problem, but it may not be a truly creative or win-win one. In some cases, a change may restore output. However, for it to be really successful, the employee must *agree* to the change, rather than just accepting it, and this may be most likely if the employee develops the solution rather than having it handed down from above.

Curiously, considerable evidence suggests that whenever management develops and imposes a solution involving a protected class of employees, it is almost always a detour, since the employee is nearly always the only one who can really solve a reduced-performance problem (with perhaps some help from management).

Getting Angry and Getting Even. When employees spend long hours in daydreaming or goofing off or spend days in intense efforts to find another job or develop a supplemental source of income, such activity can be the moral equivalent of ROTJ. Weatherbee (1969, p. 33) states that "older employees have [often] learned how to negotiate a much closer correlation of contribution and compensation—outsmarting the system and taking more out of the system than they put in. Other employees do it often to prove something, rather than to get even."

Similarly, Dalton and Thompson (1971, p. 60) point out that often "When a man feels he is not highly valued in his own company, instead of looking for another company where his contributions might be more appreciated and his abilities more fully utilized, we found that he tends to cling more tightly to his present job and high salary, simultaneously angry and afraid." This suggests that the angry person, being also afraid, might well "go underground" and wage a passive form of guerrilla warfare against the offending supervisor or organization.

We have all probably known angry people who devote more time and energy to securing their sinecure, avoiding work, or filing grievances than it would take to do a good job. Therefore, doing the work is not the issue—something much more profound is operating here.

Confrontation and Fighting. When people are tenured, are protected by a union, or have a fully vested pension, they may feel secure enough to let their anger and frustration manifest itself in overt action against the employer. Incensed about what they perceive as unfair treatment, some will confront management overtly and battle to their fullest. Management usually feels forced to join the fray. At that point, both sides get locked into the seminonsense issues of who is right or wrong or who wins or loses. Such struggles are not productive and are costly in time, energy, and resources. The best that can come out of such conflict from the company's point of view is the confirmation of some principle or the avoidance of a defeat. This either-or type of orientation is not only unwholesome; it sets the stage for future struggles and often forces conflict underground so that no one really wins. Many modern managers are getting impatient with this unproductive adversarial strife and are learning better ways to resolve such conflict productively so that performance problems are really resolved.

Many older employees (and managers too) are unaware of the newer conflict-resolution skills that are proving so effective in restoring lost productivity and resolving other interpersonal problems in organizations today. Consequently, such conflicts may benefit from the assistance of a mediator or conciliator. Group training in these techniques may be even more valuable. As our workforce ages, basic conflict-resolution skills need to be taught to a greater spectrum of people in all organizations.

Resolving Productivity Problems as a Joint Venture

Many older employees feel trapped by their pension provisions (perceived as brass handcuffs, if not golden), family responsibilities, and perhaps twenty or more years of service. They may feel that they are left dangling, while they are culturally conditioned to prize advancement that they realize is unlikely to be achieved. Decades ago, Floyd (1969, p. 23) reported on three case studies that showed the odds against advancement after age forty-five as between 93 and 95 percent to one. And the older one gets, the higher the odds seem to be, except for the very highest level of executives in some industries. There does not appear to have been any great increase in the possibility of advancement for those over fifty-five since the passage of the ADEA, so the prospects for promotion of most older employees hardly seem rosy.

Advancement, however, is not the only way to increase job satisfaction. Research by Frederick Herzberg (1987, p. 112) indicates that "the work itself, increased responsibility, recognition and the chance to achieve can (as well as advancement) be powerful positive motivators for virtually any employee." Giving attention to these factors, such as providing incremental increases in decision-making authority or seeking and implementing older employees' suggestions, may be enough to regain their interest. To assume that a person is "just plain lazy" is certainly a lazy way to dismiss a problem and one's responsibility for doing anything about it. A "lazy" person is beyond redemption. Substituting the word *unmotivated* for *lazy* probably brings one closer to the truth, keeping open the possibility of redemption and inviting help and encouragement. Discussed below are some ways that supervisors and management have taken to gain a positive resolution of the ROTJ or low-output problems that they have had with older employees.

Effective Confrontation. When people are not pulling their weight, it does not always mean that they are unable to. However, to turn them around may take very careful, thought-through confrontation. Gordon suggests (1977, pp. 98–111) that failure to meet work standards, errors, or other performance problems should be stated as specifically and as descriptively (neutrally) as possible. The consequence of the person's behavior on the job and its effects on the supervisor and organization, now or in the future, should also be clearly stated, without threat or evaluation, and the degree of seriousness of the problem should be transmitted appropriately. This is called the "I message" approach to confrontation.

Effective Counseling. The anger, despair, or self deception that leads to ROTJ behavior is not healthy. It is stressful and can easily lead to low self-esteem, unhappiness, and illness. People with such problems should be offered help in getting on with their lives. In some cases, this type of help can be provided by supervisors or others who are trained or experienced in effective listening and counseling skills. Where the problem is deeper, professional counseling may be a good investment.

Problem Solving. Once the problem has been clarified, it is important to allow the employee time to respond fully, stating his or her own case, and for the counselor (especially if it is a supervisor or manager) to listen carefully to what the employee is saying. Argument at this point is futile. Each person's view is valid to him or her, and only by accepting each other's views as such can we progress to solving the problem. If a disagreement develops, determining who is right and who is wrong may not be very useful for changing behavior. An active two-way discussion of the problem and how to resolve it is critical. Both parties should search for new ways to cooperate if the issue is to be dealt with effectively.

Supervisory Support. The supervisor who can get beyond the failures of yesterday (since nothing can be done about what is past, anyway) may be in a position to help employees reevaluate their situation, set new, clear goals, develop a specific plan for productive change, and then inspire and support a sense of mutual winning within the relationship.

There is a strong tradition in some segments of our society that where managers are not specifically constrained by contract, legislation, or some similar factor, they expect to make one-sided decisions about operations, personnel, and even another person's future. And they expect no negative consequences to flow from this "management right." Despite the inherent human fallacy in this top-down approach, it is played out time and again because some of those affected also passively accept this tradition. But passive acceptance is not a sound basis for overcoming productivity problems. The notion of truly cooperative, mutual problem solving between employee and management, with both parties fully involved, still seems strange to some old-line managers.

A few years ago, in a classic study of Danish department store executives, Hedaa (1979, p. 25) hailed demotion as the best solution for older executives who have lost productivity or whose skills were obsolete. Employers were abolishing the fixed pensioning age, because early retirement was so expensive that it was an option only for large, prosperous companies and forced early retirement adversely affected the morale of others. When managers over fifty-five were given a choice of downgrade in title, responsibility, and salary or forced retirement, 28 percent said that they would accept downgrading without further question. However, some 13 percent said that they would work hard to reestablish their former position, 18 percent said that they would look for another job, 28 percent said that they would reduce their effort while accepting uncamouflaged downgrading, and the remainder opted for either camouflaged downgrading, such as transfer to the home office or downgrading of position without loss of title, or various forms of partial early retirement. I suspect that many who said that they would accept downgrading without question secretly expected to work less diligently than before. Frankly, there seemed to be relatively little effort to mutually try to restore the employees' productivity. Legal restraints would probably preclude such behavior in the United States.

A great many people know but do not behave as if they knew that when they arbitrarily decide on an answer to a problem that affects another party without real consultation or agreement, the other party will take compensatory actions and, as often as not, these countermoves will be negative. Where work standards are unclear or difficult to set, such compensatory behavior by employees may never be detected, especially if the employees are very experienced in manipulating the culture of an organization.

Individual Responsibility

Richard N. Bolles, author of the most popular job-hunting book of all time, *What Color Is Your Parachute?* (Bolles, 1988), describes in an article in *Modern Maturity* (Bolles, 1990) six general scenarios that people live out in the later working period of their lives. One of these, seeking or accepting early retirement, he considers rather risky. Another two—"coasting to retirement" and "surviving a difficult period"—he considers not to be viable in today's context.

Early retirement is personally risky because it is more unpredictable than most people realize; it involves possible idleness, social life changes, and loss of skills and meaningful work; and it tends to be a one-way street if you can't stand it. Risk in the other two areas is more complex.

People choose coasting to retirement when they feel that they have put in their time, worked hard in the past, and earned the right to enjoy the final years, while they simply collect their paychecks. The scenario of surviving a difficult period is played out when an employer faces difficult times ahead as a result of organizational downsizing, takeover, restructuring, and so on and employees hope to hunker down and hope that no one will notice them. To help us understand the risk involved in "coasting" and "surviving," Bolles offers the metaphor of the severe earthquake that struck the San Francisco Bay area in 1989. This devastating phenomenon is caused by the sudden shifting of huge earth plates twenty miles or more beneath the earth's surface. Today, our jobs stand on what Bolles calls "huge shifting work-plates" that can also move suddenly—with devastating consequences. Shifts caused by mergers and acquisitions occurring at an unparalleled rate, movement of our economy into the highly competitive world market, the transition from a primarily manufacturing economy to an information and service one, a large national deficit associated with a trade imbalance, the savings and loan scandal, and other factors are putting many jobs in danger of elimination. "Faced . . . with the bewildering discovery that suddenly they are competing with the world, U.S. employers since 1973 have assumed as their operating mottos 'be competitive,' 'cut costs,' 'downsize the operation' and 'eliminate deadwood' " (p. 44).

Not all companies experience these "workquakes" simultaneously. But when one "occurs unexpectedly beneath a particular company, the employer's question then becomes, 'Is there deadwood anywhere in my organization that I ought to get rid of and make our company more competitive in the dog-eat-dog world out there?' " (p. 44).

This leads to the high risks of the "coasters" and "survivors." And, Bolles says, "Employees who are 'on in years' have no immunity from the hunt for so-called deadwood—especially if they are costly. . . . Raised consciousness of age-discrimination lawsuits has only made management more clever in documenting its case and trying to subtly lure rather than to aggressively shove an unwanted employee out" (p. 44).

Because productive employees can usually demonstrate that they are not deadwood, it may well behoove the fed-up "coasters" and the hunkered-down "survivors" to take more active measures to ensure their continued employment. Early retirement is another option for some people, though even this can be risky, as Bolles has shown. But there are other, more personal reasons why individuals would want to avoid coasting, surviving, or the ROTJ syndrome as an alternative to trying to solve their productivity problems.

First, while surviving, as a commitment, may at first glance seem courageous, it is generally filled with fear and self-protecting activities. A person caught in this reaction is constantly waiting for the other shoe to drop. Stress is high, and the potential gain is far from certain. Second, while coasting can be rationalized, the self-justifying statements often serve as a buffer for guilt. If this were not true, such self-justifying statements and defenses would be unnecessary. Some researchers have suggested that beneath the rationalizing is the despair of ever getting the recognition or sense of achievement that has long been hungered for. Finally, the ROTJ syndrome may be similar to coasting except that it is often tinged with anger over past injustices or over having a mind-numbing, low-status, or demeaning job.

In all three situations, sadness, fear, anger, or a combination of them can be stressful and debilitating. This helps neither the individual nor the organization. People trapped in such a down-spinning cycle might well devote considerable thought and energy to how to break out of this self-defeating behavior. More important perhaps is that through change in the situation or in oneself, it is possible to gain the positive benefits that come from being productive. Though neither one's supervisor nor the company may ever acknowledge one's good work, an inner pride, self-recognition, and a sense of achievement must certainly be better than the negatives brought on by coasting, surviving, or the ROTJ syndrome.

Escaping the Productivity Crunch

An undue share of age discrimination in the past has rested on an expectation of later-life letdown in older employees. However, if such decline occurs at all in an individual, it usually starts much earlier in life. As Macleod (1983, p. 60) points out, "If a person misses even one promotion on schedule [or turns down an opportunity for whatever reason] it can be critical, especially in the latter half of their working life. They can be labeled mediocre and lose fast-track status and unfairly be labeled unpromotable [especially in the military services]. A person thus sidelined may ROTJ and so fulfill the prophecy of low productivity, lack of energy and no new ideas. This reinforces management's focus on youth and reinforces discrimination."

Bruce Jacobs (1982, p. 21) suggests that a "floor effect" may occur among dissatisfied workers, indicating that there is a limit to such dissatisfaction. He states that people must eventually adjust to basically negative situations in order to bring their sense of self into line. Thus, if older employees are dissatisfied, they tend to eventually bottom out but do what is necessary to get along. The literature on "balance theory" suggests that most people cannot stand personal disequilibrium or dissatisfaction for long periods of time. Mental and emotional withdrawal may be the answer for many older people. It may simply be that the ROTJ employee has gone further than co-workers in avoiding conflict, so that in poorly managed organizations, low productivity is the norm that protects everyone.

Some occupations face special problems. As more and more companies emerge in the service and information sectors of the economy and manufacturing declines, blue-collar workers remaining in a sea of white-collar workers tend to get lost, and their needs tend to be ignored. Macleod (1987) points out that such critical employees as maintenance workers (building and grounds), mailroom workers, and skilled craftspeople such as electricians and food-service workers, as well as their supervisors and related clerical personnel, are often overlooked. "They are relatively few in numbers and are scattered throughout the organization. They do not have the peer group support—or the clout—of the large numbers of blue-collar workers in manufacturing plants" (p. 233). "Blue-collar workers in white-collar companies may be particularly overlooked during increasingly common corporate upheavals, mergers, acquisitions, geographic moves, rapid technological change, or shifts in the nature of the companies' business" (pp. 233–234).

The young among these and other forgotten workers may

have some options, but older blue-collar employees in a white-collar company are often well along in their careers. They may find themselves in peripheral roles, unappreciated and badly outnumbered. Their response is often to simply hang on and maintain their living standards as well as they can. "It is not surprising that these workers try to understand what has happened and look for someone to blame—ill motives are ascribed to management and perhaps to all white-collar workers—they become 'enemies'" (p. 234). In this and other ways, Macleod suggests, they may become candidates for the ROTJ syndrome. However, in a broader sense, Macleod is suggesting that many organizations may contain identifiable pockets of employees who can be helped collectively to become more productive employees. "If management is to provide a working atmosphere in which employees feel good about their jobs and work productively, it must create that [responsive] atmosphere for all employees" (p. 236).

Effective Supervisory Actions

Some managers have been so unkind as to suggest that behind every ROTJ employee there is an ROTJ supervisor who has failed to solve the problem. While this may be unfair, since an employee's earlier supervisor may have caused the problem or allowed it to develop, there are certain bureaucratic approaches that encourage low productivity and retirement on the job. Those who depend on policies and procedures for guidance in virtually every job decision seldom develop the flexibility to work successfully with their subordinates to resolve deep-seated productivity problems. The fact that other supervisors all about them are successful in resolving such productivity problems just does not seem to register. When it comes to an older employee who is not producing, the courage to confront, the need for productive cooperation, and the win-win creative approach to problem solving are critical. Following are some guidelines that have been found to be useful to supervisors when considering an older person's productivity:

- Low productivity or ROTJ status may be of long standing. Try to discover the roots of it if you can (the person involved is usually the best source of such information).

- Short of discharge, older employees must correct their own productivity problems—but the supervisor can usually help.
- The person with the problem may be protected in some way other than through ADEA. Check this out.
- Do not generalize about low performance or use absolute terms to describe it; it may occur in only one or two areas of a person's job. Be specific when confronting.
- Confront—do not avoid the issue or seek easy outs. Also, be alert to developing productivity problems to catch them early.
- Arguing or trying to persuade generates resistance and keeps you from moving forward on the problem.
- Use employees' feelings as data. Feelings are the essence of motivation and need to be positively oriented to solve the problem.
- If employees are angry about past treatment, they need to freely express their anger in order to work through those feelings.
- A lot of low productivity results from a mismatch between the person and the job. A lack of needed training also may have produced the problem.
- ROTJ is usually *semiretirement*—ROTJ employees do come to work. They would usually prefer to do something worthwhile while there, unless they are "getting even."
- Some people have just given up on the idea of winning at work. Feelings of despair or fear may be fueling the problem. A low energy level or reticence to talk about the problem may be a clue.

Goddard (1987, p. 39) suggests that if people feel that they are not receiving adequate training, "A growing sense of despair or obsolescence may set in and may be especially pronounced among scientists, engineers and technicians who perceive themselves as less attractive resources in a corporate market that prizes state-of-the-art skills. Ensuing feelings of job entrapment compete with conflicting concerns for job security. One discernible symptom may be a lessened willingness to take chances." To the employer, however, this may appear to be a loss of ambition or motivation. "Sadly, when an employee is at a stage in their career where training or career redirection would have the greatest possible impact and value, management may decide that an employee is short-term. . . . In doing so, companies institutionalize misperceptions of human value and, in effect, create reality." Thus, organizations may be contributing to the very ROTJ syndrome that they fear.

Clearly, there is no single formula to explain how low-performing older employees became so. Though they are often called nonproducers, this can be dangerous and sloppy thinking, for they are usually producing something—ask what it is. However, older ROTJ employees usually consume management time and organizational resources, so supervisors should confront and not transfer them (or use some other method of sidetracking the problem). There are also high human costs to both sides. With the age cap on retirement largely removed, such a problem unresolved could be around for decades, so we need to deal with it, not avoid it.

When an older employee who has been around for a while performs inadequately, ask why. Do not accept the explanation that such employees are "at the top of their grade" or "they can't be motivated." Virtually all employees want to enjoy their jobs as much as possible. Help them to get on with it. When we begin to act as though we really believe the following six points, low productivity of both younger and older employees may cease to be a problem.

1. Expending physical and mental effort in useful work (on or off the job) is as natural as play or rest.
2. People will exercise self-direction and self-control in working toward objectives to which they are committed.
3. When rewards, including psychic ones (good feelings, recognition, a sense of achievement, satisfaction, and so on), are closely related to achievement of objectives, they build commitment to those objectives.
4. When conditions are supportive and rewarding, the average person learns to accept and even to seek responsibility.
5. Most people in any organization can contribute creative, innovative, and imaginative ideas to improving organizational operations and solving problems.
6. Today the intellectual potential of the average person is only partly used.

This modern restating of Douglas McGregor's (1960) Theory Y (optimistic) assumptions about human nature and human behavior is applicable to our whole working population, but particularly to older employees, who can add considerable experience, knowledge, and know-how to the equation.

Chapter 13

Leadership Techniques for Maximum Performance

"Be all you can be!" This army recruiting slogan might well express a lifelong pursuit of every person—especially those who choose to remain employed past middle age. In a very real sense, to "be all that you can be," a full lifetime might not be long enough. People who are motivated to stretch themselves reasonably and in varied ways sense their growth in personal power and ability. Such people tend to feel good about themselves, their job, their co-workers, their leaders, and their organization. Consequently, they are likely to give freely of themselves.

High performance does not mean superhuman output or consistently remarkable achievements. It does mean enthusiastically contributing whatever a person can at a particular time to a particular situation. High performance reflects people's level of training, their mastered skills, their special experience and insights, their imagination and ideas, special features of their personalities, and the power and energy that they are able to generate and use in the workplace. One measure of a leader is that person's ability to prepare, develop, and inspire his or her entire team to make high performance happen as an ongoing work-life experience, regardless of age.

To this point, I have discussed the older employee in the context of supervision or management, because that is the reality that most older employees have experienced. The supervisor-manager concept still represents the dominant model in enterprises, agencies, and institutions in our society, with some attention to the leadership aspect of those roles. However, many people today are finding the supervisor-manager role too confining and want to shift the emphasis to leadership—with supervising and managing reduced to supportive aspects of their jobs. Emerging workplace realities are reinforcing that shift in emphasis from managing to leading—in fact, they are making it imperative.

Workplace Developments

What will the workplace be like in ten, twenty, or thirty years? While we cannot be certain, there are enough fundamental changes occurring to ensure that older employees, if they are to remain in the workforce, will be living a quite different work experience than they are today. How will older employees fit in, and how might they even lead us into that future? Such a future can be fraught with challenges but also potentially very rewarding. Following are three examples of approaches being used today that point the way for more changes to come.

Self-Directed Work Teams. In 1989, I had an opportunity to observe the experience of General Electric (GE) with self-directed work groups (Shea, 1989). These self-managed teams are usually composed of five to a dozen employees who assemble, produce, or deliver a complete product or service unit rather than subunits or components. The teams assume broad supervisory and management responsibilities, including scheduling work and vacations, hiring new members, and introducing new technology. Members are generally trained to perform all the tasks of the group (cross-trained) and move from job to job with little or no supervision.

Such self-directed work groups have an impressive history.

As Hoerr (1989) reports, Procter & Gamble began using work teams in 1962, followed by Cummins Engine in 1973, General Motors in 1975, Digital Equipment and Ford in 1982, and Tektronix in 1983. All have experienced significant productivity gains as a result. Companies that have more recently adopted this approach, including Champion International, General Electric, and LTV Steel (all in 1985), Caterpillar (1986), Boeing (1987), and A. O. Smith (1987), are beginning to confirm high productivity gains. Many more companies are moving in this direction because it pays off.

So far, large gains in productivity and financial performance have kept participating companies interested. Increased worker security has done the same for the employees. But personal factors are important to workers as well. They no longer perceive themselves as machine cogs. They know that their contribution is a primary key to company success. Many high-producing managers believe that when automation is combined with new (revamped) systems and work teams, the result can be a 30 to 50 percent productivity improvement. There is abundant evidence to support their claim.

An MIT study (Hoerr, 1989) of sixty-five auto plants around the world reveals that the "human factor" is the critical element in making auto plants more competitive. When plants combined computer-based technology with innovative work reforms, they outperformed all the rest. When automated plants ignored employee involvement and motivation, they performed the worst. The "magic" of employee involvement seems to be a consequent release of tremendous energy, insight, and creativity as employees move from workplace passivity to positions of active influence over their own destinies. No longer are employee contributions stifled by oppressive management, burdensome bureaucracies, and the minute control of assembly-line thinking.

Workers themselves give very convincing endorsements. Interviews with workers at one plant revealed three themes: employees appreciate the opportunity to use their minds as well as their bodies; they welcome learning the social and job skills required to take on greater personal responsibility; and they feel an increased sense of dignity and self-worth as a result of greater involvement in decision making.

At General Electric, work-team participation is voluntary.

GE sees the work-team idea as driven not by theory but by need—the need to compete successfully in a global marketplace. While work-team approaches first flowered in manufacturing plants at GE, the movement is spreading to involve white-collar operations and even professionals in high-tech departments. GE managers believe that their use of work teams is made possible by the high quality of their workforce at all levels—their education, skills, and expectations. But GE's highly trained workforce is intently committed to social as well as technical training. For instance, a document entitled "The Vision," produced by the Motor Manufacturing Department, states, "To be world-class—progress in human relations must match progress in technology."

The key at GE, however, seems to be a massive cultural change from "control of the employee" to development of employee commitment. This includes cracking the hard nuts of building employee trust, team self-evaluation, and developing a sense of "ownership" decision making. Each member is responsible for the quality of his or her work habits, for personal productivity, and for working as part of the team. Workers also make inputs to the appraisal of their leaders and to team discipline. For some, this indeed seems to be "a world turned upside down" (Shea, 1989, pp. 1–3).

How does the older employee fit into this scheme of things? The focus on group-centered leadership meets workers' needs for autonomy, personal dignity, the respect of peers, and the ability to contribute from their large store of experience and knowledge. The teams also provide for anyone in the group to take the leader role (not to "take charge") whenever appropriate. This floating group leadership enables each person, old or young, to step forward when he or she has key knowledge, a fresh idea, or a special insight. Since self-directed work groups are highly practical, profit-producing activities, not simply the latest fad, they offer older employees a reason to stay on. Also, since the self-directed team needs every member, organizations can no longer discriminate in training opportunities or job assignments.

The Boundaryless Organization. As Sherman (1989) points out, when General Electric began to focus on establishing dominant market position in several key manufacturing areas and using self-directed work groups as a tool for doing this, it not surprisingly ran into situations where the bureaucracy of the firm (which is close to a century old) resisted. To provide an ongoing system of methods improvement and cost reduction, the company developed a technique called "work-out." The goal of "work-out" was to engage every employee in constantly reducing the work content of every job, procedure, and operation performed in the company. This would lead to continuously "right-sizing" (versus frequent "downsizing") the organization, ensure a competitive position in a global marketplace, and provide a solid economic base for employee job security.

Using "work-out" requires that employee-developed improvements be pursued wherever such opportunities lead—even across organizational boundaries, into the research laboratories, and beyond the organization itself to suppliers and dealers, including the movement of work across international boundaries. Managers, already beset by a decline in supervisory authority through the use of self-directed work groups, feared perpetual intrusions into their bailiwicks. No longer was their department, their chain of command, or even their geographical territory sacrosanct.

This crumbling of hierarchical power and authority in industry in general actually began at least as far back as the 1950s, when projects such as the Polaris missile program became so complex that individual managers could no longer keep track of the details to be integrated, and the chain of command was too slow in responding to changes. At that time, ad hoc groups to solve problems (task forces) and informal meetings between engineers (networking) were needed to solve problems as they arose.

Today, although many old-time managers still see these changes as a threat to supervisory and management power and authority, they actually represent more of a shift from position power and authority to empowerment of their employees. This democratization of power shifts the emphasis from *structural* authority (position in the hierarchy) to *expert* authority—what one knows about a given technology, problem, or situation. Consequently, leadership could now come from anywhere.

The boundaryless organization is not another fad but the inevitable result of the need for greater flexibility in an age of growing complexity and global competition. But international giants are not the only organizations that must adapt. My company recently prepared an emergency response manual for a state highway administration. This agency was looking very hard at problems such as evacuation of a crowded resort-filled barrier island in the event of a hurricane, the need for snow-removal crews to cross district, regional, and even state lines to keep local and interstate traffic flowing, and the integration of the emergency response activities of a variety of national, state, and local agencies in the event of a nuclear reactor leak, war, or some other national emergency. But the key issue was not the familiar one of old-fashioned interagency coordination. Rather, it was a call for creative leadership by people who were no longer constrained in their thinking by the boundaries of their organization chart, geographical districts, or even the formal description of their jobs.

This concept has a number of implications for older employees. First, the broad experience of some retired people who want to return to the workplace should not be discounted. In the boundaryless organization, we are no longer merely "filling slots." The more varied and different the experience of a senior person, the more likely it is that he or she is able to "think across boundaries." Second, since leadership will often be more situational—that is, more dependent on the task at hand or the problem to be solved—than a matter of a person's location on the organizational chart, an older person's desire for autonomy, personal contribution, and respect from peers can be met without a concern for career climbing. Third, an older person's need for continued education, training, and development in the broadest sense becomes imperative. Fourth, some older workers may need assistance or training in synthesizing, generalizing, extrapolating, and applying general principles from their lifetime of experience in all aspects of their lives to the workplace. Finally, the opportunities to act as job coach and mentor to younger employees and to provide special knowledge and insights to groups across boundaries are likely to become legion.

This last point is particularly critical. In an emergency response activity, for example, where a command post has been established to coordinate the activities of police, fire, transportation, public health, and even military personnel, experience is vital. An older person often knows why something has been done a certain way, the hazards involved in proposed alternatives, and what to contribute to innovative solutions that will meet the responsibilities and needs of the component organizations. Developing leadership, team play, respect for the needs of others, and the ability to think across boundaries may require training for older employees, but the trainee's "data base" is likely to be rich and fruitful. We have come a long way in the development of employees from the notion of "the leader" toward "everyone a leader."

The Learning Organization. In an article in the *Sloan Management Review,* Peter Senge (1990) discusses the concept of the Learning Organization. He points out that except for very small organizations, companies cannot rely on the learning of exceptional individuals such as Thomas Watson, Sr., Alfred Sloan, or Henry Ford to do the principal learning for the organization. Virtually everyone at every level and in every job needs to be involved in learning for the organization—change is too fast and dangerous to do otherwise. "The old model, 'the top thinks and the local acts' must now give way to integrating thinking and acting at all levels" (p. 7).

Senge offers a fascinating analogy of what the learning organization requires: a holographic approach to employee development. We have all seen pictures of work groups where the implication is that the individuals are working as a team. If we were to tear the picture apart, being careful to preserve each individual's identity, we would have a collection of individuals. However, if we were to take a hologram (a three-dimensional projection of the same picture created by interacting light sources) and divide it, each part (regardless of its size) would be a total, intact replication of the whole image. Senge suggests that for an organization to have adequate knowledge of itself, each member should have a total and undistorted vision of organizational goals, data base, and resources from his or her own perspective. With that harmony of vision, cooperation can flower. But, each component piece of the hologram is not identical; each exists from its own perspective. While each person's vision would be shared, each person's contribution to the success of that vision would also be unique. The concepts that

Senge suggests contrast greatly with the fragmented, unfocused, and often contradictory views of employees in many organizations. Learning to work knowledgeably toward a shared organizational image is a great challenge.

The learning organization is already a reality in a few highly successful firms, and others are rapidly following suit. At Nissan USA, I recently interviewed an employee who said, "Here we are learning virtually all the time. Every problem becomes a learning experience. When something goes wrong, we don't much care who caused the problem—we want to learn what happened and fix it. We are all cross-trained, able to fill in for each other, and no one hoards knowledge—sharing what you know is the name of the game. We learn from our [Japanese] technical advisors and they from us. Here you can be trained in almost anything you want or need to know" (Shea, 1991).

A mid-level engineering manager said, "We don't have to launch special campaigns such as Total Quality Management [TQM], good as that is for some people, because we already live it. I see TQM as three things: first, the acceptance of the idea that people can produce reliable, nearly perfect products, and the expectation that that's what they'll deliver; second, providing ways to solve the people problems that will arise in a win-win fashion; and, third, that we have personal and organizational integrity—we will deliver what we promised—quality, reliability, and consistency. To do that requires that our knowledge base is being constantly updated—forever."

Nissan USA is "an American company that just happens to be owned by the Japanese." Through a blending of American and Japanese cultures, the company has the adaptability to adjust successfully to the pressures of global competition. But what does this mean to its older employees? First, employees are not going to be bypassed in educational and developmental activities no matter what their age. Second, the excitement of "being in on things" generates the energy, enthusiasm, interest, and involvement that can carry people to the end of their working days. And, third, staying current means that there is no need to expect decline. In other organizations dependent on older employees, it means that a massive remedial effort will be necessary, one that goes far beyond the mere acquisition of high-tech skills and knowledge. Older employees will have to become team players on wholly new types of teams.

A Solid Foundation for Older Leaders

In the future, a greater part of our older workforce is likely to be less dependent and passive. Their professional status and, hence, job mobility will be greater; they will probably have greater economic independence with IRAs, transferable pensions, and investment income; and many will be able to retire but continue to work because they find it rewarding. Such a new breed of older worker, better educated, possessing a greater sense of self, and knowing more about the world and the possibilities that it offers, is already in the workforce, covered under the ADEA, and its numbers are growing rapidly. Because of their greater self-confidence, options, and awakened drives, such employees will be far less willing to put up with mediocre supervisors or uninspired management. They will increasingly demand better treatment, more satisfying work, and greater challenge from the organizations that employ them. What can leaders do to successfully meet this challenge?

For many years, I have been asking supervisors and managers—several thousands of them—a basic question and soliciting their responses. I ask that they think of the best leader (of any type) that they have ever worked for and to list one specific thing that that person did or said that indicated that he or she was a good leader. The results of this survey have produced a powerful but remarkably short list of things that these "best" leaders did. In general order of frequency, they are:

1. Told me what was needed and gave me the freedom to do it my own way (that is, effectively delegated authority).
2. Listened to my problems, personal and job-related.
3. Explained the job to be done and then solicited my ideas and used them when appropriate.
4. Backed me up.
5. Encouraged me to improve myself.
6. Gave me credit and praise when I did well.

7. Treated me with respect (didn't chew me out in public, talked to me as an adult, reprimanded without harshness or anger).
8. Was accepting of me. It was comfortable to go to him or her with a problem.
9. Understood the work well enough to set high standards, explained what was needed, and helped us to meet those standards.
10. Kept his or her word or let me know if he or she couldn't keep a promise and why—was straight with me.
11. Divided the work fairly, so that everyone got some of the interesting and good stuff.
12. Was well organized and knew what he or she was after.
13. Let me know about changes that affected me as soon as possible.
14. Was constantly searching for better, simpler, faster ways to do the job (and cut costs).
15. Structured (laid out) and explained the work carefully (some people need a high level of structure on the job).

Are these things so difficult to do? Apparently they are, if these behaviors are the premier ones that people remember, often years later, about the *best* leader they ever worked for. These fifteen items might be listed on a card affixed to a supervisor's desk as a self-training device or serve as a checklist for daily self-improvement and decision making.

High performance in the work group naturally flows from the consistent application of these behaviors with any employee, but what of older employees? The items on this list are all applicable. Items 1, 3, 9, 11, and 14 involve respecting older employees and their interest in fairness on the job. Items 2, 5, 6, 7, and 8 are ways to overcome the shunting aside, isolation, and lack of respect and dignity that older employees (and often older people in general) sometimes experience. Items 4, 10, 12, 13, and 15 clearly meet the need for structure, certainty, and the sense of security sought by some older people. Items 5, 9, 12, and 14 also indicate a personal interest in older employees, deal with their uncommon interest in the job, and help them focus on their future. Additional correlations also are possible.

You may do many of these things quite well already, so that improvement is mostly a matter of self-expansion. But how does a person who wants to maximize the potential and performance of each older employee solidify these behaviors into a pattern that quite automatically functions as it should—that is, operates as a habit? We often need a rational basis for the acceptance of new behaviors and an attitude that facilitates and reinforces their adoption. It is frequently argued that if new behaviors are practiced and found rewarding, the facilitating attitudes and rational acceptance will follow. But since we know that the fifteen behaviors listed above are what people want and that they encourage productivity (and have the rational and attitudinal underpinnings as well), why not use both approaches?

In the future, we must consider leadership and high performance as synonymous with high value if we are to fairly assess the older employee's contribution to organizational productivity.

Chapter 14

Creating Alternative Work Programs

While it appears that most employers are indifferent to the needs of older people for at least part-time work, there are some outstanding exceptions. The following well-documented examples of what creative people, organizations, and companies are doing to encourage older people to keep producing are drawn from dozens of sources and represent some of the best efforts that others can emulate.

Though the Conference Board reports that barely one company in a hundred has any type of retirement transition program, there is a growing number of innovative programs around the country that offer hope and productive models. A few examples of these are documented by Ramirez (1989).

Varian Associates, a $1-billion-a-year high-tech equipment maker, offers a retirement transition program that permits employees fifty-five and older to work twenty to thirty-two hours a week as long as they and the company wish. Such employees "get proportional benefits, partial medical and dental insurance, vacation, sick leave, even in some cases stock options and profit sharing.

Employees already retired can resume work through the program" (p. 180).

Corning Glass Works in Corning, New York, has for twenty years had a program for recognizing superior performance, which the company believes is "an important inducement for getting people to stay on. . . . About 100 employees have the title of 'Senior Associates' " (p. 184). These employees often serve as advisers, mentors, troubleshooters, and backup in managerial and technical fields. Senior associates also receive extra pay with these titles (8-10 percent increases are not uncommon), and many are reluctant to part with these benefits to retire.

Builders Emporium, a chain of 121 California-based home centers, has taken to redesigning jobs to "accommodate older workers" and "encourages their continued loyalty and presence." They "recast the job of store clerk, which makes up about two thirds of its 7,900 jobs. The company eliminated heavy lifting by assigning night crews to replenish shelves and emphasized salesmanship instead—as a rule the older staff know the merchandise better and have more experience dealing with people (p. 184). By focusing on senior employees, the company also reduced the turnover rate substantially.

Wells Fargo has come up with imaginative programs to forestall burnout. A sabbatical program called "personal growth leave" allows "employees with ten or more years of service . . . to take up to three months fully paid leave to pursue a project of their choice" (p. 184).

Instron, a $100-million-a-year maker of materials-testing equipment based in Cambridge, Massachusetts, uses retired workers in its "sales emeritus programs" to coach younger salespeople, "often with quick and substantial results" (p. 186). Sharing their experience in developing people skills often keeps down the "learning by mistakes" costs of younger salespeople.

Goddard (1987, p. 37) reports further examples of successful programs: *Chicago Title Insurance Company* employs older employees in job-sharing teams "as interoffice messengers who work alternate months, an option that attracts retirees from other companies." *Texas Refinery Corporation* has 500 part-time salespeople in their sixties, seventies, and eighties who work as independent contractors. *The Travelers'* Office of Consumer Information "is entirely staffed by 16 retired employees who job-share four positions and field 36,000 calls per year." *Continental Illinois Bank and Trust* offers retirees clerical work one or two days a week with "other work schedules periodically available for specific positions in specific divisions: three eight-hour days per week, flexible short hours five days a week, 12 eight-hour days per month and flexible hours on Saturday and Sunday."

To strengthen job security for their older employees, many companies are engaged in new career training. *McDonald's Corporation* created its McMasters Program to train and place people over age fifty-five. *Sterile Design* "uses minishifts to accommodate those interested in working less than full time." At *Polaroid,* one of the most versatile of employers of older workers, "flexible work alternatives, which have encouraged 30 percent of people over 65 to stay on the job, include rehearsal retirement, tapering off, temporary or permanent part time work, job sharing, flex time, consulting contracts and a retiree pool for work during peak periods." *Aerospace Corporation* of southern California saw the loss of highly skilled employees to retirement as a competitive disadvantage, so it launched a program called "casual employment." Under this program, an employee can work 1,000 hours a year (approximately half time) without his or her pension benefits being affected. Such companies want to keep producers.

None of these programs is aimed at favoring older workers over younger ones; rather, they represent a coming to grips with workforce realities. As Stephen Enna, personnel director of Wells Fargo Bank, says, "The workforce of today is going to be the workforce of tomorrow" (Ramirez, 1989, p. 179). The retiree job banks established by such socially responsible firms as Travelers Insurance, Wells Fargo Bank, Combustion Engineering, and the Grumman Corporation provide part-time or full-time work in their own facilities as well as referring retirees to other firms in their area seeking older workers. Even temporary-help agencies are looking hard for older people. Kelly Services has a program called "Encore" for workers over fifty-five. At Manpower, Inc., the largest temporary agency in the world, senior workers constitute more than 25 percent of the 700,000 people in the worldwide workforce. Manpower contracts with clients for both short- and long-term (up to several years) assignments for its older employees. Eric Lindberg, president of MS International, a large personnel services firm, estimates that 15 percent of the company's temporary employees are over sixty years of age.

Daniel Knowles, vice-president for human resources at Grumman Corporation and a board member of the National Council on Aging, says that "Most companies treat older workers with benign neglect. There is a type of discrimination going on that's very, very subtle. In fact, those who discriminate usually aren't aware they are doing it. Ironically, they are generally middle-aged themselves" (Stackel, 1988, p. 72). Knowles contends that it is up to the private sector to take creative and positive steps to encourage new or continuing employment for older workers. Grumman, for instance, established a "temporary/part time/on call" pool of Grumman retirees when a survey revealed that 50 percent of its retirees indicated that they would like such a pool. This, Knowles claims, "Is partly in response to the continuing respect . . . employees know the company has for its older staffers." Further, Knowles claims, "We show in dozens of ways that we value our senior employees." This positive note contrasts sharply with the "benign neglect" that Knowles refers to. Grumman's Job Bank, incidentally, now fills nearly 60 percent of the company's temporary employment needs.

Whether we are retirees ourselves, people with a vested interest in the soundness of the Social Security system, or young people paying taxes, each of us has an investment in finding ways to ensure that older employees can continue to work if they wish to.

Sources of Help

Denise Loft, manager of the Workforce Education Center at AARP, says that "Demographically people could live a quarter to a third of their lives in retirement if they retire early, as so many people are doing" (Watts, 1987, p. 32). Knowing that many people prefer continued work to retirement, AARP offers a workbook for conducting preretirement seminars, which includes a section on work alternatives and focuses on why people work and the advantages of doing so. It encourages companies to bring employees into "life-planning" programs as early as possible (often at age fifty or earlier) and offers suggestions on how to reenter the workforce by using self-assessment and a self-directed search method.

Some companies conduct "working-option sessions" as part of their retirement programs to explain the situation in their own company and how to participate in such work options. Travelers Insurance holds a special careers session to discuss the organization's "Unretired Program," under which employees who have experienced retirement for six months can come back and, if qualified, fill a part-time or full-time job—some for a full second career. Walt Disney Company uses a network system to invite retired employees back to work on an as-needed basis. Increasing efforts are being made by a few major firms to reverse the early-retirement trend through part-time and occasional options.

Amy L. Weiss, an associate editor at *Business Age* magazine, points out that "Many companies are discovering that ability, not age, is the distinguishing factor of quality employees" and the "lack of entrants into the job market is forcing businesses to reevaluate their policies regarding retirement" (Weiss, 1989, p. 38). But how does an employer do that? Weiss mentions three sources of help. First, "AARP maintains the National Older Workers Information System (NOWIS), a data base containing over 100 programs on retaining and retraining older employees." Second, Days Inn of America sponsors "Senior Power National Job Fairs" which have been held in sixty-six cities across the nation. In 1989, more than 7,000 senior citizens attended these fairs, which were sponsored by more than 1,000 national and local businesses that joined together to target older workers for employment. Third, the Business Partnerships, Worker Equity department of AARP (located at 1909 K Street, N.W., Washington, D.C. 20049) offers considerable information on how older employees can contribute to a particular organization.

In our age of global trade, examining models from outside the United States may also be fruitful. One way to enable older people to keep working is through gradual retirement programs, whereby workers continue to work part-time while drawing part of their pension. The need for gradual retirement options has often been voiced by many industrial gerontologists. One of them, Philip

L. Rones (1978, p. 5), has pointed out that "When older workers no longer wish, or are unable to work full time, few options short of total retirement are available. Part time 'phased retirement' is rarely offered and those jobs that are open to retirees tend to be of the low skill, low pay variety."

However, "Because there is so little domestic experience to draw on," Helen Ginsburg (1985, p. 33) studied the effects of gradual retirement programs in Sweden and Norway. She found that the partial pension has had a positive effect on its recipients. Partial pensioners value their increased leisure, and many report that they are more rested. Their health seems to improve, and absenteeism declines. These factors account for a feeling among employers that partial pensioners produce more per hour than full-time workers. They are also less likely than full-time workers of the same age to become disabled or unemployed.

While rare in the United States (John Deere Corporation is a notable exception), partial retirement is sometimes used as a form of work sharing. Ginsburg reports that the partial pension has been found to work against the tendency for early retirement. The common use of partial retirement in Sweden is considered one reason why Swedes stay in the workforce longer than Americans. Though Swedes ages sixty to sixty-four can rather easily receive generous disability or other retirement pensions, they are much more likely to remain in the workforce than Americans. Ginsburg further reports that "In 1982 57 percent of 60 to 64 year-old Swedes were in the labor force compared to 44 percent of Americans that age. Participation among 55 to 59 year-olds [was] also higher in Sweden (p. 40). Since then, the gap seems to have widened, thereby depriving the United States of an even larger percentage of its productivity.

Win-Win Work Options

In addition to the programs discussed above, some organizations are experimenting with a variety of work arrangements that can meet the needs of employee, supervision, and management at the same time. Researchers are discovering that many people would be quite interested in postretirement work or putting off retirement if they were allowed such options as the following:

- More flexible scheduling (flextime)
- Job sharing
- Part-time employment (usually less than thirty hours per week)
- Consulting
- Seasonal work
- Compressed work week: twenty to forty hours in two to four days
- Short-term projects
- Reduced hours (even with reduced pay)
- Special assignments
- Job rotation—flexible shifts
- A chance to do company work at home (a high-tech type of cottage industry)
- Contracted work
- The standard forty-hour work week

Ginsburg says, "Sweden's experience with the partial pension plan demonstrates that reductions in hours can be implemented in a wider variety of ways and in more occupations than the conventional wisdom suggests, especially when management is cooperative." Ken Dychtwald, a recognized authority on aging workers, reports that "As people grow older they might want to work less or less frequently rather than to stop working. They don't want to work as often or perhaps as hard" (Dychtwald and Flower, 1990, p. 174). He believes that the lines between working and nonworking will blur. He points out that Sun Oil, Arco, and Travelers now have retiree-relations directors, and many other companies are beginning to build older worker expertise within their human resources departments.

At-home work or projects that allow a person's expertise to be used only as needed can create substantial cost savings to the organization. Many of these new forms of work arrangements can reduce on-the-job idleness by using people's services only when required, rather than having them on the payroll or laying them off when work is slow. Not incurring the fringe benefits and other overhead involved when people are not on the payroll full-time sometimes makes it possible for the organization to pay the part-time employee higher rates. With many of these working arrangements, it is also sometimes easier to judge the value of the work performed rather than assume that the real value is a function of the number of hours invested.

Flexible work policies tend to pay off by allowing people to continue to willingly contribute to our national wealth, to the organization, and to their own income, health, and sense of well-being. Employers who maintain options for their employees to continue working obviously gain from the process; the others have only their fears, questionable assumptions, and indifference to deal with.

A 1989 survey by Catalyst, a research group promoting women's issues in business, found that for 70 percent of the managers interviewed, retention of an experienced employee was the primary reason for offering a flexible work schedule in the fifty companies studied. Thus, flexible work options tended to be an individual decision rather than a general company policy. This research also revealed that only four out of the fifty companies knew how well their flexible work plans were actually operating. About one-third of the companies studied (32 percent) allowed job sharing; those that supported it felt that job sharing retained experienced employees, improved return ratios of people on elder care or maternity leave, and boosted the company's image in the community.

According to Walsh and Lloyd (1984, p. 51), phased retirement plans, by slowly reducing the number of hours worked each week, allow the employer to retain the services of a valued, trained employee for a longer period of time, while often making the employee's adjustment to retirement less traumatic. Even a one-time reduction to part-time employment permits a compromise between a worker's desire to slow down and the employer's need for a skilled staff.

Phased retirement, redesigned jobs to deemphasize physical labor, arranged paid sabbaticals, and new, more prestigious job titles for those who voluntarily accept downgrading because of personal infirmities are only a few of the ways in which older employees' productivity is being recaptured. These efforts to stabilize an organization's workforce, reduce turnover, save on training costs, and ensure continuity of policies for those organizations wise enough to conserve older employee resources.

Job sharing is one very viable option for resolving employee shortages if it is done right. For instance, jobs that are boring, tedious, and stressful, physically or mentally, are usually very suitable for job sharing. Job sharing is a viable option when a full-time opening cannot be filled because the skills needed are in short supply or there is a general labor shortage; employees (or applicants) need to do something else part of the time, such as attend college or care for children or older relatives; an employer wants to avoid layoffs during an economic downturn; a full-time employee needs or wants to reduce work hours and is willing to split his or her job with someone else; or when a company is growing and new jobs are being created. Many organizations fill a slot with a full-time person when only a part-time person is needed, and Parkinson's law (that the work tends to expand to fill the time available) takes over—perhaps forever. A half-time person may obviate the need for sharing.

The expense and time required to plan and administer a job share arrangement are usually more than compensated for by the gains from the process, which often include retention of talented and experienced older employees who otherwise might leave; options for coverage—when one person is ill or absent, the other can often fill in for him or her; reduced absenteeism when one "partner" is faced with a family or other crisis; increased quality (where the job is boring and/or fatiguing, errors may decline); and greater productivity—you may double the ideas, creativity, and energy available on a shared job.

Travelers, for instance, has largely gained such benefits, as each week several hundred retirees work throughout the company in professional, clerical, and secretarial positions. Ranging in age from the late fifties to the mid-eighties, they also fill in during peak work times and when other employees are absent or on vacation. An older employee who decides against retirement is immediately available, able to contribute to the organization at once without needing to learn anything about the organization's culture, rules and regulations, policies or procedures, or traditions or work ethics. An older employee knows the job to be done and does it. Contrast this with hiring a new person for the job if the older person had opted for retirement.

Many employee-benefit experts believe that flexible work arrangements produce a competitive advantage only when such policies are formal, publicly supported, and closely monitored. Tracking and encouraging such practices throughout the organization seem critical.

Aetna Life and Casualty, for example, which has instituted programs to offer part-time work, job sharing, at-home work, flexible schedules, family leaves (which include up to six months of unpaid leave for family emergencies), and referral services to locate help for care of elderly relatives or children, has been a successful part of a wider program to recruit and retain the best people available. When properly managed, such programs definitely pay us back many times over for the time and resources expended. Such enlightened management is bound to improve America's competitive advantage.

Chapter 15

Keeping Pace with Changes in the Workforce

The challenges of managing older workers decently and productively do not lend themselves to neat packaging. Rather, they emerge from the fabric of our society in at least seven broad themes. These quite complex themes are so interwoven that it is difficult to perceive the patterns that they form if we stand too close. In addition, the weaving continues moment by moment, so it is difficult to predict what the tapestry will look like in the years to come. These themes are by no means settled. Each contains explosive elements that could erupt in the next decade or two and invalidate much of the corrective action that we might take to resolve these issues and problems. The seven primary themes are as follows:

1. *A medical revolution may climax with far more older candidates for work than we anticipate.* The statistics on older workers wanting (even demanding) gainful employment may burgeon beyond our wildest dreams; if certain medical research projects pay off in the next ten to fifteen years, they will create a mass of people

who are physically and mentally more capable than ever before to the very ends of their longer lives.

2. *Public policy and our needs for a balanced and fair society will be severely challenged.* Political power will certainly shift more clearly to our older population. Therefore, the necessity of reconciling competing needs of various age and interest groups will intensify. Consequently, greater personal maturity, ethical wisdom, long-term vision, and creative skills will be sorely needed by all of us.

3. *Our workforce must reconcile a need for internal organizational harmony with the ability to compete externally.* The lines between management and labor seem to be blurring, with work groups becoming more self-directed and management more dependent on the expertise of employees. Dissonance between the two is increasingly shifting to creative tension that allows for greater individual contribution and cooperation. Managers and workers who do not adapt to this changing workplace may have difficulty contributing to the more advanced and successful organizations.

4. *Personal change, self-investment, and individual growth will be the mark of tomorrow's successful employee.* The old idea of the way to survive (and possibly succeed) on the job—to hunker down, keep your mouth shut, and do what you are told—has died but is not yet buried in many organizations. By contrast, career climbers will often find the organizational ladder truncated and more crowded as the effects of downsizing and restructuring set in. Practically, this will mean more self-investment in education and training in a wider range of skills and knowledge and a demand for greater professionalism on the job.

5. *Organizations need to create an environment that will encourage employees to stay longer.* This will mean for many, many managers and managements a change in style and substance. Changes in policies allowing for greater variety in work options and career moves will be helpful, but they alone will not do the job. Older employees will be less dependent on their employers, more demanding of satisfying work and a quality environment, and expecting higher levels of managerial leadership and performance.

6. *Acts of age bias and age discrimination must be made*

visible, measured, and managed well enough to curtail their negative effects on employment. Though bias and discrimination will still exist, they can be controlled so as to be rare rather than common, discouraged rather than tolerated, and made conscious rather than hidden in the minds of the perpetrators, thereby moderating their effects.

7. *Societally, we need to broaden our concept of work and regard it as a healthy force in our lives.* This will require a major cultural shift away from the negative reservations about work that were cast in the early days of the Industrial Revolution and reinforced by the era of "scientific management." It will also require a new era of exceptional leadership at every level of our organizations and integration of such notions into a comprehensive social philosophy great enough to crowd out competing visions of work.

If these seven themes prevail, employers may be overwhelmed by an embarrassment of riches in the quality and quantity of our older workforce and a consequent surge in national wealth. The power behind these possibilities is foreshadowed by current research and social developments already under way. Since predicting the future is bound to be imprecise, we will let these developments, projects, and trends speak for themselves.

The Medical Revolution

Several current medical research projects could toss all our statistical projections about our older employee workforce into a cocked hat. Without any lengthening of the human life-span, we may find that virtually everyone is well and physically and mentally able as long as he or she lives.

Here we are not talking about the *average* life expectancy of people (which by the year 2030, without any great changes in medical knowledge or practices, should be about 75 for men and almost 83 for women). Nor are we discussing the limits of human life, which some scientists think is fairly fixed at between 110 and 120 years unless some radical new knowledge or techniques are discovered. What we can infer from the current findings of this research is that far higher percentages of our population will live out their full span of years and be mentally and physically vigorous to the end of those years.

Average life expectancy could pass the century mark in twenty years if this research bears expected fruit. Further, there will be a host of new therapeutic drugs, medical procedures, and devices that could even accelerate these possibilities. Some of these new areas of research and treatment are discussed below.

Cracking the Body's Genetic Code. As we approach the twenty-first century, genetics promises to revolutionize medical treatment. The federal government is currently engaged in a fifteen-year research effort to locate every one of the 50,000 to 100,000 genes in the human body through its "human genome project." Congress and the administration have agreed to spend $3 billion to help physicians control nearly every disease, from the approximately 4,000 inherited illnesses to the more common heart disease and cancer. When researchers have developed a complete map of all human genes, "they will be in a position to cure many diseases by *altering* genes" (Miller, 1986, p. 396), a system of treatment unknown until now.

Growth Hormones. A decade-long study is under way to determine the effects of growth hormones on older people who have stopped producing this substance naturally. So far, there are indications that adding this hormone to the system retards, stops, or perhaps even reverses the aging process. The study's principal researcher, Daniel Rudman of the Medical College of Wisconsin, reports that the use of a "synthetic human growth hormone can reverse some effects of aging in some people. Tests showed the hormone enhanced the size and efficiency of some organs such as the kidneys" that usually decline as a person gets older (Stephens, 1990, p. 10).

The original experiments involved twenty-one healthy men ages sixty-one through eighty-one who were deficient in the human growth hormone. At the end of six months, patients who were given a placebo showed no changes in body composition, but those who got the hormone "gained almost 9 percent in lean body mass and dropped nearly 15 percent in body fat and increased skin thickness by 7 percent. X-rays revealed some increase in muscle size and some participants reported that they no longer 'tired as easily.' This," said the scientists involved in the study, "was a reversal of physical changes incurred during 10–20 years of aging." However, this treatment will probably be of use only to the one-third of our population over sixty-five who are deficient in growth hormone.

While it is unlikely that this therapy will be a fountain of youth, it does seem to firm up muscles and help the body recover functions lost through the aging process. However, the use of such hormones could possibly lead to serious side effects. By the end of the century, we will know much more about selective ways to preserve or restore vigor and health in many members of our older population.

Gene Replacement Therapy. Many once-incurable diseases or marginally effective treatments will be solved by gene replacement therapy, according to William R. Miller (1986), vice-chairman of Bristol Myers Company. These techniques will also "be able to alter immune systems, preventing rejection of grafts or transplants" (p. 398). Similar advances "should lead to the creation of a whole new catalogue of hormones, enzymes and other physiological materials to use as replacements for the system's essential regulators before they finally wear out. For the elderly, that could even mean replacing weakened neurotransmitter systems in the brain—including [conquering] Alzheimer's disease" (p. 397).

Naturally Replacing Body Parts. Miller also states that "By the early 21st century, we should be able to induce injured nerve cells in the brain and spinal cord to grow back. Bone growth hormones to stimulate the body's repair of itself also seem likely" (p. 397). This type of development in replacing body parts will carry us "beyond the skin, bones and the occasional vital organs [that we replace now] to the replacement of blood vessels, nerve cells, hormone-producing cells, even brain cells."

Drugs and New Classes of Therapies. New classes of psychotherapeutic drugs are on the way, particularly some that "can be expected to bring significant new benefits to victims of senility by moderating anxiety, depression and other behavioral abnormalities—this without compromising the individual's ability to perform normal tasks and without the risk of addiction or dependence. . . . Among them will be effective cognition enhancers to restore memory" (Miller, 1986, p. 397).

Other psychotherapeutic drugs will do much the same for victims of schizophrenia, depression, and Parkinson's disease. "More generally we can expect nearly all drugs . . . to be far more predictable and specific in their actions than what we're accustomed to . . . and that dosages will more precisely reflect the needs and respond to the metabolism of the individual patient," thus enhancing their safety.

Miller calls these new therapies and drugs *probabilities* rather than possibilities. While he warns us to be wary about overstatements in the media about these advances, they are likely to creep one by one, without great fanfare, into common usage by the medical profession to enhance our lives. Considering our current scientific and technological base, such advances are no more startling than what has occurred in the last twenty to thirty years, given the knowledge base of those years.

What does all of this mean for older workers and their employers? It means that a lot more people will be a lot older and a lot more able to work to a lot later age. This healthier, more able workforce will increasingly demand outlets for its energies, abilities, and talents. The scope of the opportunity for effective use of this human capital is almost beyond belief.

Public Policies and a Fair and Balanced Society

Daily, the political and economic power of older citizens increases, as does their awareness of it. So far, most of this power has been used to redress grievances and achieve fairness for older people. However, some of us worry that this growing clout could be used to gain advantages for older people at the expense of the needs of other segments of our population.

The art of government in a democracy is a public effort to ensure that we govern our society so that *all* its segments are healthy and productive. This cannot be achieved when some are disadvantaged by the unfair gain of others. Consequently, each of us needs to carefully study each policy and law to ensure that it will strengthen all of our society, not just the segments to which we belong.

For example, James E. Duggan (1984, p. 429) of the Bureau of Labor Statistics reports on an elaborate study of the decisions of people over fifty-four years of age to participate in the labor force. He states that "Over time . . . changes in public policy will have a dramatic effect on the labor supply of older persons. For example, expanding the scope and the generosity of the Social Security Insurance program would lead to a decline in the labor force participation of older persons. On the other hand, raising the age-eligibility limit for full social security benefits would result in an increase in the labor force participation of older workers."

While Duggan acknowledges that payment increases would be popular with annuitants while raising the age eligibility limits would not, he suggests that "Any changes in the benefits or requirements of these programs should account for the anticipated effects of each program as well as the potential effect that may arise from the interaction of all of them [on the workforce of the future]." Public policies must be carefully drawn and ably administered lest they have negative side effects or counter their own intent.

But the problem goes deeper than that when we consider the needs of working and nonworking older people. Fully retired people are dependent people—dependent on Social Security, their pension funds, their savings, their investments. Whether we are talking about tax policies, amendments to the Social Security system, or the savings and loan scandal, public moves to alter the status quo or correct problems can be threatening to people dependent for their living on external forces that are working in society. When we feel so threatened, we are all likely to lash out and support policies that appeal to our need for security (and even our perceived survival needs) without much consideration of their overall long-term effects on others. Older workers are not immune to such pressures or concerns, but they are earning money now and, if eligible, can fall back on Social Security or other financial options and possibly on other jobs.

Fully retired people tend to find their options narrowing the longer they hold that status. Working people tend to retain the options that they have always had and even gain additional ones as time goes on. They tend to be more in contact with other segments of society, more involved with and aware of the needs of other workers because of their daily contacts, and more self-confident because of their daily demonstrated ability to take care of themselves. They may therefore find it easier to develop a measured response to controversial public policies that affect them. The greater the percentage of Americans who are gainfully employed, the more likely to occur this balanced approach to public policies is.

Creating a New Competitive Workforce

The evolution of workplace changes such as self-directed work groups, boundaryless organizations, and learning organizations can lead to the development of workers who are quite unlike what we have seen in the past. These paeans to ultimate human responsibility, maturity, and self-actualization should sound loud and clear to older employees, especially those who have seen enough of passivity, dependence, and often second-class citizenship in the workplace.

To participate effectively in this new workforce requires training in skills seldom previously offered to older employees, even when they were part of management. These often include rather new interpersonal skills, such as nonthreatening confrontation techniques, conflict-resolution skills, active listening, creative problem-solving methods, cooperative decision making, ways to request help, giving feedback to help others, positive responses to negative situations, dealing with changes, getting your point across, and effectively participating in group meetings.

But, as the lines between workers and management blur, most workers are becoming more professional, and management is increasingly dependent on the special know-how and skills of its workers. Consequently, we need workers who are more self-confident, adaptable, and socially competent. At every level, we need leaders who are more visionary, collegial in behavior, and, again, adaptable. This is the new ball game in which older employees will increasingly be playing.

Nathan Keyfitz (1984, p. 229) offers an interesting idea on

changing technology and the future of our workforce: "The very efficiency of computers limits the number of individuals who will earn their living by making, repairing, operating or programming who will be directly involved with either hardware or software. The activities that have expanded are in the fields of travel, entertainment, selling, local government [and so on]. Such jobs will demand a certain level of culture and literacy, and perhaps this will encourage a return to liberal education so neglected today. It could be that liberal arts will be the dominant vocational training of the 1990s."

Keyfitz continues, "The most effective retraining of workers is not enough. They cannot be useful without managers and enterprisers. The training of enterprisers is even more elusive than the training of workers, but we have to find some way to produce and encourage them. The new situation will call for the retraining of people to keep up with new methods and equipment. A man or woman of 45, compositor or toolmaker rendered obsolete by the computer will need two or three years to be reeducated, not in another equally narrow skill, but in some occupation consonant with the times." He even suggests that we allow people to draw one or more years of their pension in advance to accomplish this occupational recycling. This investment would repay the equivalent in years of delay in retirement and enhance the employer's competitive stance.

Self-Investment. Neither government programs nor employer assistance in updating employee skills and knowledge will amount to much without the dedicated involvement of older employees themselves. We must all develop the habit of self-investment as early in life as we can to ensure that we optimize our mutual future. Our society has a long history of personal passivity, where things were done to us or for us for long periods of our lives without many of us having to make personal decisions to ensure our future. If we simply did our job adequately, things tended to take care of themselves.

Now this is changing. Increasingly, it will be up to each individual to decide how much and what type of ongoing education and developmental activities he or she will engage in. Obsolescence results from a type of mental lethargy that we can no longer afford.

In this regard, human involvement in work tends to be total, in the sense that an employee on the job is always involved physically, mentally (cognitively), and interpersonally to some extent. And even when a person is only marginally involved in one or more of these ways, the potential for such involvement "can be just as important to total performance as major involvement" when we consider a worker's suitability for a career.

For example, in the 1930s, Allan Mogensen (Mogensen, 1963), the father of work-simplification training, said that the worker closest to the job is best suited to improving it, since he or she knows most about it. Since then, literally millions of systematically developed job improvements suggested by workers have greatly benefited their organizations. However, if a supervisor wastes this human potential by prescribing the job methods too narrowly, discouraging suggestions, and punishing innovation, as some supervisors do, that supervisor is also discouraging workplace growth for the employee. I have heard many employees say, "Why bother if all you're going to get is a lot of hassle for your suggestions?"

Consequently, it is often the supervisor and the organization that is getting obsolete, rather than the employee. They have failed to see the cognitive (mental) component of the job or undervalued it, thereby wasting potential. If, however, an experienced older machinist were to be transferred to the methods department, made a part of a problem-solving team, or given a special assignment to improve an operation, all of which involve valuing ideas and experience (largely the mental part of the job), intellectual development would be ensured, just as jogging leads to physical strengthening of the body.

Learning on the job and using that learning are a natural need, since our work consumes so much of our time. But learning and application can also be a habit—one that may wither and die if not encouraged. People tend to become obsolescent because they use only a small part of their natural abilities.

Employer Encouragement. In *The Future of Older Workers in America,* Rosow and Zager (1980, p. 98) point out that "since developmental programs will have to stretch over a greater age span, concepts of training and development will have to become more elastic." They also maintain that "present career paths are too narrow, vertical, and compartmented to prepare employees for unforeseeable future demands." Further, "When functional and organizational specialization are grafted onto occupational skills, major business functions become walled fiefdoms," and "overspecialization shrinks opportunity, confines competition within the borders of one organizational or functional arena and raises unnecessary barriers to promotion from within."

They boldly state that the "rigid definition of careers is a root cause of mid-career crisis" and "when the middle aged worker must get a special dispensation to cross over into new functional territory, opportunities for management development, reassignment, and new career paths are choked off." Additionally, the same organizational rigidity that creates the mid-career crisis makes it difficult for people at later stages of their working lives to resolve the crisis in a constructive way without leaving the organization. For those who stay but feel forced to give up their hopes and dreams, the result of the unresolved crisis may be apathy, boredom, or resentment—certainly not the ingredients for high performance. And curiously, the mid-career crisis and its aftermath often occur at the very time when people are best suited to explore new career paths and broaden their perspectives.

The mid-career crisis can hit at any time between ages thirty and fifty; it is generally during this period that people reach a reasonable level of maturity, master their trade, gain substantial contact with their peers in other disciplines, and come to appreciate the contribution of the various professions to the success of the organization. If people were offered an opportunity to reexamine their life goals, delve into another area of work, and explore the sources of their work satisfactions in a friendly, supportive environment, the rest of their working lives might be more productive and rewarding. But how often is an engineer expected to consider personnel work or a millwright a career in plant security without some eyebrows being raised or even negative sanctions being imposed? The cry rings out: "But they don't know that other trade!" "They aren't trained to do that work!" Surprisingly, the answer to that outcry in many cases is simply a bored, "So what?"

Intuitively and by checking our own work experience and that of others, we know that serious employee development programs stripped of their "nice-to-know" frills can often lead to mastery of the basics of most fields in a matter of weeks or months; that updating in many a career field is something that goes on continuously (such as in in-service training) and consequently people drop into the stream of learning at any point (and do not have to catch up by swimming the whole river); and, most importantly, that mid-career employees, especially those past fifty, have often reached a point in their career development where crossover to a new field should become easier, not more difficult.

This last point is an important one yet is often unappreciated. A young accountant just out of school is expected to labor in the vineyards doing strictly accounting work for many years. Gradually, if successful, he or she comes to do more complex work, being more integrative but also less specialized, and may come to work more with systems than with details. At this point, contacts with other departments and other professions become more significant, and accounting competence is more taken for granted as it becomes less used—others are doing the details. If the accountant is promoted several times, the specialization of skills and knowledge that got him or her the original job in the field becomes even less critical, especially if he or she is doing more conceptual or supervisory work. It is at this point, when the person is older, that a crossover to another field becomes most practical. He or she is no longer tied to the specialization and now possesses the broader picture. This phenomenon is not unusual; it is already going on every time a scientist, mechanic, or marketeer enters general management or starts his or her own business.

For many people, the notion of mature people seeking a career change late in life goes against the cultural grain. But if we are to have an effective, viable, motivated workforce, we may need to consider the possibility of more flexible careers more seriously. The alternative may well be that for many of our more productive older employees, limited opportunities to develop latent talents and interests may be a turnoff, leading to apathy and lowered output. For knowing that they are stuck in a job that they no longer find satisfying for another ten to twenty years can destroy self-esteem, optimism, and the joy of achievement. More to the point here is the fact that narrow and limited career paths are often a creation of limited imagination and to an incredible degree unnecessary. Also, since we know that broadly educated people are most adaptable and most able to master new subject matter or skills, this could be an argument for more liberal arts education.

Reducing Age Bias and Discrimination. Almost no one seems to believe that he or she is biased against the aged, and few would dream of discriminating against the elderly, yet both go on all the time. How can this be? Apparently, even some of us who *think* in ways that respect the rights and needs of older people have some deeply buried prejudice and feelings that pop out in unguarded moments. Our actions and thoughts may not be congruent, and when we are emotionally stressed, these negative beliefs may escape without our awareness. I have certainly caught myself being inconsistent in my response to an older person. In my teaching on managing older employees, I have uncovered a thousand different ways in which people express the dichotomy between their feelings and thoughts about elderly people even when they are old themselves.

I think that there is a broad need to publicize age bias and discrimination, our frequent personal participation in them (especially the subconscious aspects), and the varied forms that they take in our society. This type of consciousness raising might lead to the use of encounter groups and similar techniques to lessen the negative effects of such bias, as was done with racial and gender biases decades ago. Such activities certainly do not cure everyone's biases, but they have reduced discrimination and could help many to deal better with their own feelings and thoughts about the aged or about being aged.

I am not suggesting slavish adherence to rules, laws, or guidelines; rather, I encourage exhibiting a positive attitude and creating enthusiasm for making the most of the opportunities offered by older workers.

Modifying Concepts of Work and Productivity. Anyone past forty who is not very satisifed with the work that he or she is doing may need to reappraise why and how this state came about and what should be done about it. Personal productivity, at least that part that is not process determined (automated, computer controlled, and so on), largely hinges on how we feel about ourselves and our situation, the value that we attribute to our output, and the degree to which it sparks our interest.

When they were young, many people strove to get a "good" job that offered income, security, prestige, and perhaps a chance for advancement. Often, they never asked "Will I enjoy the work?" "Will what I'm doing strengthen my personal sense of worth?" "Will it help others?" Later, when boredom and a sense of purposelessness set in or the opportunities faded, some felt almost guilty asking, "Is this all there is to working?"

The alternative to job dissatisfaction is not an endless round of fun, though the best jobs usually offer some of it. The best jobs may offer satisfying social relationships, recognition, opportunities to achieve, and other satisfactions for a person's spirit. It often seems that most people assess a job on the basis of its external manifestations rather than considering whether they really want to do that work long run.

Fortunately, some people do focus on and find work that they enjoy and are able to shift to new, more pleasurable jobs if their enthusiasm for certain tasks wears thin. Some people want to use their pension in order to find more pleasurable work or to perform it under more satisfying conditions. Though most of us want "good work," many do not know how to find it, feel that their ability to perform it is limited, and may not even know that it exists for them. Below are some ideas concerning work that could be helpful in managing a society increasingly composed of older workers.

1. We need to see work (the time, energy, and other resources expended to achieve some good) as a natural, integral part of our lives—so natural that though people might want to vary their diet of work, they would no more end it than they would stop eating.

2. What we work at, where we work, how we work, and when we work should (within reason) be more of our own choosing.

3. More people, especially older employees, need to become better educated about themselves: their personalities, their feelings, their special talents, their occupational interests, their attitudes to-

ward work and people, and their general abilities. When considering new work, many people seem to be flying blind as far as understanding themselves is concerned. The use of self-assessment instruments and general counseling should become more common.

4. We may need more of a clear-cut split between how we earn our living and the work we choose to do. Einstein worked in the Swiss patent office at what he called "a shoemaker's job" that paid the bills while he developed his theory of relativity. This reality could keep us from losing sight of the discrepancy between one's job and one's purpose in life. While we want to gain congruence between ourselves and our work, this may be a long-term project as our years pass away.

As we settle down for working in the long run, there are several workplace developments occurring that could modify our concepts of work. First, more Americans are becoming independent consultants, trainers, and temporary workers, preferring to work for themselves rather than for a regular employer. These tend to be professional workers taking care of their own retirement needs. Many retired professionals also fall into this category. Second, "job" counselors are tending to become "work" counselors, focusing more on the person and his or her needs than on just what is being offered in the job market or the needs of the employer. Third, more flexible work arrangements seem certain. Fewer people will have a solid claim on their jobs, nor will their jobs have a claim on them. Portable pensions, flexible benefits, and work contract arrangements may lead individuals to form free-flowing temporary associations (that is, personal joint ventures between themselves and other people or organizations). Fourth, within their employing organization, more people will invent their own jobs—jobs that suit their own interests, needs, and personalities as well as those of their employers. Finally, the varieties of work to be done are likely to continue to expand, providing new opportunities for those with vision and special abilities. Thus, more people are likely to do more work of their own choosing.

Addressing the New Realities

As workers and the workplace change, those who treat older workers lightly or brush them aside today are damaging our nation's future.

Until the realities of our changing workforce and its demographics, primary educational level, and attitudinal characteristics really hit a company in its staffing efforts, they will be considered abstract and unimportant and remain ignored. But, in time, employers will have no choice but to address their new reality. Those that have effectively conserved their aged human resources will be far better equipped to meet tomorrow's challenges than those who have not. As Goldstein (1988, p. 42) says, "The trends influencing the close of the 20th century will compel companies to change—or collapse. In the arsenal of competition a productive quality workforce will take its place alongside new technology and restructuring." The choice is clear. If employers, management, and workers themselves do not solve the problems of older employees, all of us will suffer—not only through social and economic losses that we may never measure adequately but through the decrease in opportunities that we permit.

We have discussed many ways in which employers can encourage older individuals to work longer and more productively. However, a great deal of imagination will be needed if we are to gain the great potential offered by older employees working late in life. Many (if not most) older employees seek retirement because they are bored or otherwise dissatisfied with their work. Creating a work environment that stimulates interest in continuing may require a fresh look at careers and occupations for older employees. While more of the same old thing may not cut it, fresh ideas may do the trick.

Resource

Legal Aspects of Working with Older Employees

In recent decades, we have come to see a kind of warfare between employees and their employers that has been largely waged in the courts. These disputes may affect other people in the workplace and may, in some cases, threaten the future of the organization itself. Legal battles over age discrimination are mostly unnecessary and often self-defeating. Effective and fair management practices could eliminate most suits. The remainder, those initiated for some unrelated ulterior motive of the plaintiff, would be few and largely unsupportable. Yet because of misunderstandings and a tendency to handle adversarial situations in less than competent ways, age-discrimination battles are common.

Managers at all levels may flounder when dealing with age issues because they lack clear information on the laws related to age discrimination and how these laws are applied in the workplace. Here we provide a description of the laws, a quick reference guide to their essential aspects, information on how they are being applied, a perspective on the impact of key legal cases on employers, and guidelines for avoiding a charge of age discrimination.

According to Faley, Kleiman, and Lengnick-Hall (1984, p. 328), "Much of the sharp increase in the number of age discrimination complaints and lawsuits can be traced to age-biased stereotypes and innuendos [by supervisors and managers] as well as ignorance of the law by many organizations. Those problems are often attributable to misunderstandings of the nature of the relationship between age and work performance as well as the legal rights guaranteed older workers by Federal and state laws. Thus a better understanding of the age-related psychological and legal literatures is necessary before the problems their ignorance creates can be mitigated." The Age Discrimination in Employment Act (ADEA) aims to achieve age-neutral decisions by management and their organizations—that is, to ensure that hiring, promotion, training, education, and other personnel actions are not influenced by a person's age unless there is a "bona fide occupational qualification" (BFOQ) that overrides the age-neutral intent of the law.

The stated purpose of the ADEA as set out by Congress is "(1) to promote employment of older persons based on their ability rather than age; (2) to prohibit arbitrary age discrimination in employment; to (3) help employers and workers find ways of meeting problems arising from the impact of age on employment" (29 U.S.C. 621). The act was amended in 1978 and again in 1986, the second time to remove any mandatory age for retirement on most jobs. Currently, therefore, no employer covered by the law can arbitrarily force retirement on any covered employee (age forty and above) no matter what his or her age. Thus, the third stated purpose of the statute cited above takes on even greater significance.

There are two ways in which a plaintiff can establish a showing of discrimination. To prove *disparate treatment,* the plaintiff must show that the discrimination was intentional; that is, that the employer purposefully applied terms or conditions of employment that led to less favorable employment consequences for older workers. To prove *disparate impact,* "it is only necessary to show that the employment practice(s) in question had a differential effect on older workers regardless of employer motivation" (Faley, Kleiman, and Lengnick-Hall, 1984, p. 329).

A brief summary of federal laws and regulations is a good starting point for discussion of older employees' rights, whether one is an affected worker, a corporate policy setter, a first-line supervisor carrying out those policies, or an executive striving to chart a trouble-free future for his or her organization. A summary of the provisions of the ADEA is presented in Exhibit 1.

Exceptions and Their Defense

The exceptions to the act noted in Exhibit 1—"bona fide occupational qualification" (BFOQ), "reasonable factors other than age," "good cause," and the terms of a seniority system or benefit plan that is shown not to be a "subterfuge to evade the purposes" of the act—require further discussion.

When using the first defense, BFOQ, in an age-discrimination lawsuit, the employer must be able to make a specific factual showing that employees over age forty are no longer capable of performing the job in a manner that is "reasonably necessary to the normal operation of the particular business." The employer should not expect a court to simply accept, without proof, that a certain level of good health or physical strength is necessary to satisfactory performance of the job. Obviously, the employer has a much stronger case if it can demonstrate that the BFOQ is needed to protect the public. However, even in cases involving bus drivers and police personnel, the argument of public safety has not always overcome an unconvincing case. [See *EEOC* v. *KDM School Bus Co.,* 612 F. Supp. 369 (D.C.N.Y. 1985); *EEOC* v. *Commissioner of Pennsylvania,* 768 F.2d 514 (3d Cir. 1985)]. Snyder and Brandon (1983, p. 47) state that economic considerations also cannot be used to justify decisions based on age where age is not a BFOQ. The employer cannot exclude older workers from a position simply because doing so would be more cost-effective. However, when an employer is forced to reduce the workforce for reasons beyond its control—generally economic—the discharge of older employees will be considered to be due to "reasonable factors other than age" if the reduction is not primarily of such workers.

The "good cause" exception allows the employer to discharge or discipline an employee, despite the fact that he or she is part of a protected class, if it can be shown that age was not a determining factor in the decision. When using the "good cause"

Exhibit 1. Key Provisions of the Age Discrimination in Employment Act.

1. *Prohibitions*

The act was designed to apply to three entities: (1) employers, (2) employment agencies, and (3) labor organizations. For purposes of the act, *employer* is defined as any person or business engaged in industry that has "twenty or more employees for each working day in each of twenty or more calendar weeks in the current or preceding calendar year" (29 U.S.C. 630(b)).

Employers are prohibited from (1) refusing to hire or discharging any individual on the basis of his or her age, (2) depriving any employee of employment opportunities because of his or her age, and (3) reducing an older worker's wage rate (29 U.S.C. 623(a)). However, section 631(b)(1) of the act allows employers to mandate retirement of the executive who "for the 2-year period immediately before retirement . . . is entitled to an . . . annual retirement benefit . . . which equals, in the aggregate, at least $44,000." Tenured college professors and public safety officers are similarly exempted.

Employment agencies are prohibited from either failing to refer for employment or referring for employment any individual because of his or her age (29 U.S.C. 623(b)).

Finally, labor organizations cannot, on the basis of age, (1) expel or exclude any person from their membership, (2) refuse to refer a person for employment or in any other way deprive an individual of employment opportunities, or (3) cause an employer to discriminate against an employee (29 U.S.C. 623(c)).

It is unlawful for any advertisement published by an employer, employment agency, or labor organization to indicate any age preference (29 U.S.C. 623(e)).

2. *Exceptions*

The act contains three exceptions to the preceding prohibitions. Differentiation based on age is allowed where (1) age is a "bona fide occupational qualification (BFOQ) reasonably necessary to the normal operation of the particular business, or where differentiation is based on reasonable factors other than age," (2) the terms of a bona fide seniority system or any bona fide employee benefit plan, such as a retirement, pension, or insurance plan, are being observed, and these terms are not a "subterfuge to evade the purposes" of the act, or (3) a discharge or disciplinary action is taken for "good cause" (29 U.S.C. 623(f)).

3. *Legal Action*

The act creates a private right of suit, so that any person aggrieved may bring a civil action, provided that the EEOC does not first decide to file suit on behalf of the individual. The 1978 amendments added to this private right of action the right of the individual to a jury trial (29 U.S.C. 626 (c)).

Exhibit 1. Key Provisions of the Age Discrimination in Employment Act, Cont'd.

4. *Deadlines for Filing a Lawsuit*

No suit can be commenced until the plaintiff has given the EEOC not less than sixty days' notice of intent to file such an action. Such notice shall be filed (1) within 180 days after the alleged unlawful practice occurred or (2) in the event that legal proceedings are initiated under state law, within 300 days after the alleged unlawful practice occurred or within 30 days after receipt by the individual of notice of termination of proceedings under state law, whichever is earlier (29 U.S.C. 626(d)).

5. *Statute of Limitations*

The running of the time during which an action must be filed is stopped during the period when the EEOC is invoking its right to attempt "voluntary compliance with requirements of this chapter through informal methods of conciliation, conference, and persuasion . . . but in no event for a period in excess of one year" (29 U.S.C. 626(e)(2)).

6. *Posting of Age-Discrimination Notices*

The act requires that every employer, employment agency, and labor organization post, in conspicuous places, notices expressing the purpose of the act (29 U.S.C. 627).

7. *Civil Penalties*

The court, according to its discretion, can award the plaintiff "unpaid minimum wages or unpaid overtime compensation" (29 U.S.C. 626(b)), or, in the event that the defendant's violations of the act are deemed willful, the court can order the payment of liquidated damages. Liquidated damages are an amount equal to the plaintiff's award for back pay and fringe benefits; that is, a finding of willfulness results in doubling of the damages. In addition, the court can order "judgments compelling employment, reinstatement or promotion."

8. *Criminal Penalties*

The act authorizes the imposition of a fine and, where there has been a prior conviction under this statute, imprisonment for not more than one year where an individual impedes the enforcement of the act (29 U.S.C. 629).

---

exception as a defense in an age-discrimination lawsuit, the employer should be able to present evidence to demonstrate that the employee's performance has fallen below organizational standards that are themselves reasonable and clearly articulated.

Bakaly and Grossman (1984, p. 46) state that it is also important that the employer show that it followed the customary procedures, known to all employees, when taking disciplinary actions. The key here is consistency and fairness. If the jury finds that the employer's personnel decisions are arbitrarily and inconsistently applied, the case will be lost.

If the final exception is used as a defense, it requires an examination by the court of whether a seniority system or benefit plan is bona fide and not simply a means of evading the purposes of the act. At least one court has ruled that, with respect to pension plans, the plan that is considered bona fide—that is, it is "genuine" and pays adequate benefits—may still be held to be a subterfuge [*EEOC* v. *Home Insurance Co.,* 553 F. Supp. 704 (D.C.N.Y. 1982)]. Generally speaking, in order for a seniority system or benefit plan to constitute a subterfuge, it must treat its older workers in a manner that disadvantages them.

Legal Implications and Lawsuits

Efforts to extend protection to older people or to ensure that they have a fair opportunity to participate in the workforce are not likely to cease in the near future. Many management authorities expect that refinements in the laws related to age discrimination will continue to be made. For example, some current laws requiring older people to take a physical examination in order to remain employed while younger personnel are not so required will probably be outlawed in time; even people in their thirties can have heart attacks, and if the safety of other people is affected by an employee's physical condition, all employees should be examined.

In 1989, the AARP made a number of suggestions to the Bush administration on issues vital to older Americans. Among their recommendations were that the Equal Employment Opportunity Commission (EEOC) should rescind the present regulation that prevents older workers from being eligible for apprenticeship programs; include with its form EEO-1, used by the EEOC to ascertain whether certain legally protected groups are underrepresented, the requirement that employers must also list the age of their employees; and rescind the regulation that gives federal workers only 30 days to initiate the filing of age-discrimination charges (the

ADEA gives all private-sector workers at least 180 days). The AARP and other groups are likely to press for these and similar changes in the law as time goes on.

The number of age-discrimination suits has increased greatly in recent years, and since the basic law allows jury trials, some of the awards given to employees who prove their cases have been very substantial. This can place a great financial burden on organizations that lose.

The implications of the ADEA for the employer are clearly reflected by the case statistics. In 1979, 3,000 age-discrimination suits were filed. By 1980, that number had tripled to 9,000 (Snyder and Brandon, 1983, p. 41). In more recent years, the number of age-discrimination complaints has risen sharply. However, it is very difficult to develop accurate statistics because the battle against age bias is going forward on so many fronts: through the EEOC, various state agencies, individual civil suits, union grievances and arbitration procedures, and efforts by the AARP through its services to working members.

The *Wall Street Journal* reports that in 1986, "27,000 complaints were lodged with federal and state agencies, more than twice the number filed in 1980" (Freedberg, 1987, p. 37). The EEOC itself had an annual average of 17,000 complaints based on age between 1983 and 1986, a 60 percent increase over the 10,500 annual average for the three previous years. "Age charges are growing at a faster rate than race, sex or national origins cases" (Cooper, 1987, p. 4A), according to Paul Brenner, an EEOC staff lawyer. Once filed in court, "age cases are far more likely to be successful than race or sex cases" (p. 4A). In 1986, "a fourth of the court actions filed by EEOC fell under the age act" (p. 4A).

Christopher Mackaronis, a former EEOC lawyer who now works for the AARP, reports that his organization receives an average of 400 to 500 letters a month from working members who allege job discrimination. As the population ages and as a younger, better-educated, less passive generation of older workers settles in for the long haul, the number of complaints and lawsuits seems to be headed nowhere but up. So far, about one third of the states have passed companion measures restricting mandatory retirement, and many other states are considering such bills. The *Wall Street Jour-*

nal article also reports that the fines ordered in some of these lawsuits and the amounts agreed on in out-of-court settlements are also daunting. For example, in 1974, Standard Oil Company of California settled an age-bias case out of court and paid $2 million to 264 employees. In 1978, Pan American World Airways agreed to a settlement of $900,000 for some 600 older management employees. And in 1979, a federal court jury awarded a Heublein employee $452,000 in back pay, benefits, and damages when it found that the company had unfairly denied him a vice-presidency appointment that had been promised him. Robert Kirk, a Washington-based management lawyer is quoted as saying, "Although many cases never reach court, the occasional blockbuster settlement, 'puts the fear of God in lots of managers' " (Freedberg, 1987, p. 37).

Who Sues?

The Syracuse University School of Management reported on an analysis of 100,000 EEOC complaints closed from 1979 to 1986 that concluded that the average litigant is a white male supervisor in his fifties who was discharged because of corporate personnel cutbacks (Schuster, Kaspin, and Miller, 1987, p. vi). This average litigant perceives a lawsuit as his only option, since he cannot qualify under racial or sexual provisions of the law and has no union to represent him. Freedberg (1987) quotes a Syracuse University study that indicated that a majority of the complaints originated in the so-called right-to-work states outside the Northeast, where employers "may be more aggressive in discharging, or forcing the retirement of older workers" (p. 33).

Syracuse also conducted a detailed analysis of 280 federal court cases involving claims under ADEA. This study, conducted under AARP sponsorship, revealed that 84 percent of the litigants were white males; 68 percent of the cases dealt with an employee's involuntary retirement or dismissal; 54 percent were filed by employees between the ages of fifty and fifty-nine; and 59 percent were filed by managerial and professional employees.

Other factors also influence who takes their employers to court. Lawsuits tend to be expensive, and it has been claimed that "the cost of court cases weeds out all victims except the middle-class manager who's financially capable of filing a lawsuit" (Cooper, 1987, p. 4A). However, with the act providing for doubling of back pay and liquidated damages, more lawyers are willing to take the more solid cases on the basis of speculation. Even so, the cases of older managers and professionals are most appealing, because older workers with more seniority are usually better paid, so that back-pay awards to them would be correspondingly higher. Mark deBernardo, a labor lawyer for the U.S. Chamber of Commerce, has been quoted as saying that the prospect of double damages has created "a lotto mentality" among older workers and some lawyers who seek "astronomical awards" (Cooper, 1987, p. 4A). He cited a $2.4 million judgment against the I. Magnin clothing stores for dismissing three older workers in California.

The rise in discrimination complaints has also been attributed to greater public awareness of the law and the growing number of workers covered by it. Cooper (1987) claims that in recent years, "the major forces behind the increasing challenges to age discrimination are a national economy undergoing structural changes and a growing number of older workers protected by the law. The shift from an industrial to a service economy—accompanied by mergers, buyouts and cutbacks—has put many older employees out of work, prematurely and unfairly, in the view of [many] people" (p. 4A). These structural changes have affected an unprecedented proportion of managerial and professional people, the very people most able and likely to file an ADEA suit.

Who Wins?

The Syracuse University study of 280 federal court cases found that "on a national basis employers have been victorious in ADEA actions 67.7 percent of the time" (Schuster, Kaspin, and Miller, 1987, p. v). However, "it may be that employees have a more favorable prelitigation success rate, with employers only litigating cases they believe they can win" (p. v). The study also indicated that while among the more than 100,000 EEOC complaints closed between July 1, 1979, and May 16, 1986, most (67.6 percent) had been filed by men, women experienced greater success than men in pursuing age-discrimination complaints, and the complainants experiencing the greatest success were between the ages of sixty and seventy.

Evidence introduced in a hearing before the Special Committee on Aging of the U.S. Senate on June 19, 1988 (Fay, 1986), indicated that of 383 federal cases in which there had been a final resolution by court action, the defendant (employer) had won 74.2 percent, and the plaintiff (employee) had won 25.8 percent. However, the Syracuse University study indicated that judges rule in favor of employers about two-thirds of the time, whereas juries side with workers about two-thirds of the time. Consequently, employers would rather go before a judge, whereas workers would rather have their case go to a jury trial.

An interesting note on performance appraisal from a 1984 Syracuse University study is that while employers have not been required to have formal performance evaluation procedures to win, and the courts have permitted some less reliable sources of employee performance information to be used as conclusive evidence in substantiating an employer's claim of nondiscriminatory decision making, a good performance appraisal system and good use of it help. The study points out that "Among federal cases studied, where validity of the performance appraisal was a critical issue, employers taken as a whole, were successful in defending against ADEA claims 73 percent of the time. However, those employers which had used only informal methods of performance evaluation were successful defendants only 40 percent of the time" (Schuster and Miller, 1984, p. 3).

Another aspect of who wins or loses is the issue of credible testimony and the quality of the "proof" on each side. Freedberg (1987, p. 37) points out that "companies sometimes lose suits because they can't establish that an employee's work justified dismissal. But even with good personnel records, cases often boil down to credibility contests." He cites as an example a case involving Miles, Inc. (which makes Alka Seltzer), in which a jury awarded $1.63 million to nine older workers dismissed in a companywide layoff. Miles, which inherited the age-bias charges when it merged with Cutter Laboratories in 1983, claimed that $60 million in losses had forced Cutter to lay off 1,200 workers in 1982 and "that it picked the least productive employees with the worst sales records" (p. 37). The plaintiffs claimed that the company's performance standards were biased against people over forty. The clincher in their case was that "their lawyers produced records showing that they had received glowing performance evaluations over the years" (p. 37). So who wins or loses is often a matter of who is most believable.

"While some areas of the law are still being mapped, enough cases have moved through the courts to give lawyers and personnel specialists a good idea of what constitutes age discrimination—and what does and doesn't work in pursuing or fighting such charges" (Freedberg, 1987, p. 33). This would indicate that fewer questionable cases would actually reach the courts, but that does not necessarily mean fewer cases. By the year 2010, half the workforce will be people age forty and over who will be protected by the law.

Lawyers claim that the current interest in age-discrimination suits may be nothing compared to what lies ahead. They expect that more older people with medical handicaps are likely to file suits under handicap as well as age provisions of the law. In addition, more older blacks and women will be contending for jobs held by older white men. An insurance industry group predicted in 1987 that age-bias suits will be among the five hottest liabilities facing business in the next five years (Cooper, 1987, p. 4A). And new questions are likely to arise as the workforce and supporting organizations become more sophisticated. For instance, "When does a voluntary early retirement plan become subtly coercive—and is the fast-track method of management—in which younger 'bright stars' are transferred from department to department, to broaden their experience, legal?" (Freedberg, 1987, p. 37).

The final Syracuse University report to the AARP Andrus Foundation (Schuster, Kaspin, and Miller, 1987, p. iv), concluded that "Older workers may tolerate less severe forms of age-based employment discrimination and are generally willing to engage in litigation only when separation occurs"—that is, when they have little else to lose. But the 1986 study report by Syracuse University (Schuster and Miller, 1986) ended on a tragic note. In a survey analysis of discrimination complaints in the state of Wisconsin, the authors reported numerous cases of retaliation on complainants by their employers. Their findings included the following:

- The vast majority of respondents (88 percent) reported that they were the target of retaliatory action by the employer.
- Twenty percent of the respondents were discharged after filing some form of age-discrimination complaint.
- Few complainants (15 percent) remain with employers against whom they have filed.
- Co-workers who were hostile to the filers were reported to be predominantly younger than the complainants.
- Almost half (47 percent) of the respondents felt that the ADEA remedy provided *no* overall benefits.

These findings raise a fundamental question: Does anyone really *win* in a lawsuit? Americans, in particular, are so narrowly focused on winning and losing that they carry the sports analogy into parts of their lives where it has questionable validity. Perhaps when an age-discrimination suit is fought, everyone loses.

A Cooperative Approach

The job of management and workers is to produce, not to fight. There are more than 100 major American firms that have never been the target of an ADEA complaint, let alone involved in such a lawsuit. This is because they train their supervisors well in resolving conflicts in a truly win-win fashion. Obviously, they also train their supervisors not to discriminate, but if they are challenged in a specific case, they have a host of sophisticated, nonmanipulative ways to work out their differences so that the relationship strengthens rather than deteriorates.

By contrast, many employees, managers, and their organizations are stuck with a focus on confrontational, adversarial approaches to getting their own way or proving that they are right, rather than on cooperative ways of respecting others and dealing with conflict. Managers who provoke or engage in combat rather than using their energies, resources, and time to produce lessen the efficiency and general competitiveness of their organizations. Employees who slack off or are passive when they experience discrimination and then "go for the gold" when they do confront the organization with a lawsuit are playing the same game.

Though there are always two sides to any conflict, the organization has the primary responsibility for ensuring age-neutral employment actions. When employees are treated unfairly, the quality of life for them and everyone around them is degraded. If that happens often, the quality of life in our society is equally degraded. A company can no longer discriminate on the basis of age (or any other legally prohibited factor) without consequence. The other employees are watching and will respond negatively—you can count on that. Reprisals against employees no longer keep the others in line as they might have at one time. While that tactic might have worked at the turn of the century, when management efforts were directed toward turning employees into machine components, in this age of knowledge workers, where productivity is in the mind of the employee, such action is self-defeating and outdated.

The proliferation of ADEA cases is not likely to subside in the near future. The provision of the 1978 amendments for jury trials has been an enormous boost to the employee's probability of victory. As George P. Sape, vice-president of Organization Resource Counselors, Inc., noted, "When you put a large corporation against an employee in front of a jury on an issue like this, there is rarely any question as to the outcome" (Freedberg, 1987, p. 37). According to Snyder and Brandon (1983, p. 42), the loss of an ADEA case can also damage the organization's public image. For example, when I. Magnin was ruled against in such a case, "300 irate customers returned their store credit cards. Although 97 percent of these customers were eventually convinced to re-open their accounts, the cost of this persuasion process was not inconsiderable."

Jackson (1978, p. 53) states that the act has an obvious impact on the organization's younger workers. If it is not clear that the organization's practices are fair, not only may companies find that their younger workers seek their fortunes elsewhere, but affirmative action programs for women and minorities may be stalled. Developing optimum policies for all employees may take considerable imagination.

Without the age cap of seventy, workers are likely to become accustomed to the notion that *any* age-based personnel action affecting a person over age forty is subject to serious challenge. Effective, age-neutral management behaviors and policies are likely to be increasingly important to organizational success.

REFERENCES

Ahammer, I. M., and Baltes, P. B. "Objective Versus Perceived Age Differences in Personality: How Do Adolescents, Adults, and Older People View Themselves and Each Other?" *Journal of Gerontology,* 1972, *27* (1), 46–51.

Alpaugh, P. K., Renner, V. J., and Birren, J. E. "Age and Creativity: Implications for Education and Teachers." *Educational Gerontology,* 1976, *1* (1), 17–40.

Anderson, C. M. "Death to Computerphobia: The Older Generation Meets Computers—and Triumphs." *NABW Journal* (National Association of Bank Women), 1983, *59* (6), 21–22.

Bakaly, C. G., and Grossman, J. M. "How to Avoid Wrongful Discharge Suits." *Management Review,* Aug. 1984, pp. 41–46.

"Benefits Important in Costs of Employing Elderly." *Employee Benefit Plan Review,* 1985, *39* (9), 13–16.

Benson, H., and Klipper, M. Z. *The Relaxation Response.* New York: Morrow, 1975.

Bernstein, A., Anderson, R. W., and Zellner, W. "Help Wanted: America Faces an Era of Worker Scarcity That May Last to the Year 2000." *Business Week,* Aug. 10, 1987, pp. 48–53.

Bishop, J. E., and Waldholz, M. *GENOME: The Story of the Most Astonishing Scientific Adventure of Our Time—The Attempt to Map All the Genes in the Human Body.* New York: Simon & Schuster, 1990.

Blocklyn, P. L. "The Aging Workforce." *Personnel,* Aug. 1987, pp. 16–19.

Bolles, R. N. *What Color Is Your Parachute?* Berkeley, Calif.: Ten Speed, 1988.

Bolles, R. N. "The Decade of Decisions." *Modern Maturity,* Feb.–Mar. 1990, pp. 36–46.

Borgatta, E. F., and McCluskey, N. G. (eds). *Aging and Society.* Beverly Hills, Calif.: Sage, 1980.

Brinley, J. F., Jovick, T. J., and McLaughlin, L. M. "Age, Reasoning, and Memory in Adults." *Journal of Gerontology,* 1974, *29* (2), 182–189.

Burkhauser, R. V., and Turner, J. A. "Labor-Market Experience of the Almost Old and the Implications for Income Support." *American Economic Review,* 1982, *72* (2), 304–308.

Canestrari, R. E. "Paced and Self-Paced Learning in Young and Elderly Adults." *Journal of Gerontology,* 1963, *18* (2), 165–168.

Causey, M. "U.S. Offers Big Early Out." *The Washington Post,* April 3, 1988, D2.

Cherrington, D. J., Condie, S. J., and England, J. L. "Age and Work Values." *Academy of Management Journal,* 1979, *22* (3), 617–623.

Churchill, G., Ford, N., and Walker, O. "Personal Characteristics of Salespeople and the Attractiveness of Alternative Rewards." *Journal of Business Research,* 1979, 7 (1), 25–50.

Colburn, D. "Retirement Redefined." *Washington Post,* Mar. 6, 1985, pp. 12–14.

Constandse, W. J. "Neglected Personnel Problem." *Personnel Journal,* 1972, *51* (2), 129–133.

Cook, D. D. "Older Workers: A Resource We'll Need." *Industry Week,* 1980, *206* (1), 42–48.

Cooper, C. L., and Torrington, D. P. (eds.). *After Forty: The Time for Achievement?* New York: Wiley, 1981.

Cooper, K. J. "Age Bias—Workers' Complaints Increase." *Philadelphia Inquirer,* June 13, 1987, 1A, 4A.

Copperman, L. F., and Keast, F. D. *Adjusting to an Older Work Force*. New York: Van Nostrand Reinhold, 1983.

Copperman, L. F., Keast, F. D., and Montgomery, D. G. "Older Workers and Part-Time Work Schedules." *Personnel Administrator,* 1981, *26* (10), 35-38, 65.

Coser, R. L. "Old Age, Employment, and Social Networks." In S. F. Yolles, L. W. Krinsky, S. N. Kieffer, and P. A. Carone (eds.), *The Aging Employee*. New York: Human Sciences Press, 1984.

Covey, H. C. "An Exploratory Study of the Acquisition of a College Student Role by Older People." *The Gerontologist,* 1980, *20* (2), 173-181.

Dalton, G. W., and Thompson, P. H. "Accelerating Obsolescence of Older Engineers." *Harvard Business Review,* Sept.-Oct. 1971, pp. 57-67.

Dalton, G. W., Thompson, P. H., and Price, R. L. "The Four Stages of Professional Careers: A New Look at Performance by Professionals." *Organizational Dynamics,* Summer 1977, pp. 19-42.

DeMicco, F. J., and Reid, R. D. "A Hiring Resource for the Hospitality Industry." *Cornell H.R.A. Quarterly,* May 1988, pp. 56-61.

Doering, M., Rhodes, S. R., and Schuster, M. *The Aging Worker: Research and Recommendations*. Beverly Hills, Calif.: Sage, 1983.

Drucker, P. F. "The Coming of the New Organization." *Harvard Business Review,* Jan.-Feb. 1988, pp. 45-53.

Dubé, L. E. "Removing the Cap: Eliminating Mandatory Retirement Under the ADEA." *Employment Relations Today,* Autumn 1988, pp. 199-201.

Dubin, S., Shelton, H., and McConnell, J. *Maintaining Professional and Technical Competence of the Older Engineer: Engineering and Psychological Aspects*. Washington, D.C.: American Society for Engineering Education, 1974.

Duggan, J. E. "The Labor-Force Participation of Older Workers." *Industrial & Labor Relations Review,* 1984, *37* (3), 416-430.

Dychtwald, K. "The Age Wave." *Business Credit,* January 1988, 38-42.

Dychtwald, K., and Flower, J. *Age Wave: How the Most Important*

Trend of Our Time Will Change Your Future. New York: Bantam Books, 1990.

Dyer, W. G. *Team Building: Issues and Alternatives.* (2nd ed.) Reading, Mass.: Addison-Wesley, 1987.

Eisdorfer, C., and Cohen, D. "The Issue of Biological and Psychological Deficits." In E. F. Borgatta and N. G. McCluskey (eds.), *Aging and Society.* Beverly Hills, Calif.: Sage, 1980.

Elbing, A. O., Gadon, H., and Gordon, J. R. "Flexible Working Hours: It's About Time." *Harvard Business Review,* Jan.-Feb. 1974.

Faley, R. H., Kleiman, L. S., and Lengnick-Hall, M. "Age Discrimination and Personnel Psychology: A Review and Synthesis of the Legal Literature with Implications for Future Research." *Personnel Psychology,* 1984, *37* (2), 327-350.

Fallcreek, S., and Mettler, M. *A Healthy Old Age: A Sourcebook for Health Promotion with Older Adults.* (Rev. ed.) New York: Haworth Press, 1984.

Fay, R. C. Testimony before the Special Committee On Aging. 99th Cong., 2d sess., 1986. Serial 99-21.

Fields, J. "Does Life Exist for Copywriters over 45? You're Only as Old as You Think You Are." *Advertising Age,* 1978, *49* (27), 26-27.

Floyd, H. A. "Why Some Men Sour After 40." *Administrative Management,* Apr. 1969, pp. 22-23.

Freedberg, S. P. "Forced Exits? Companies Confront Wave of Age-Discrimination Suits." *Wall Street Journal,* Oct. 13, 1987, 33, 37.

French, J. *Aging and the Work Force: Human Resource Strategies.* Washington, D.C.: American Society for Training and Development, 1982.

Friend, W. "Turning Thumbs Down on Retirement." *Association Management,* 1983, *35* (6), 67-73.

Giniger, S., Dispenzieri, A., and Eisenberg, J. "Age, Experience, and Performance on Speed and Skill Jobs in an Applied Setting." *Journal of Applied Psychology,* 1983, *68* (3), 469-475.

Ginsburg, H. "Flexible and Partial Retirement for Norwegian and Swedish Workers." *Monthly Labor Review,* 1985, *108* (10), 33-34.

Gist, M., Rosen, B., and Schwoerer, C. "The Influence of Training

Method and Trainee Age on the Acquisition of Computer Skills." *Personnel Psychology,* 1988, *41,* 255–265.

Goddard, R. W. "How to Harness America's Gray Power." *Personnel Journal,* May 1987, pp. 33–40.

Goldstein, M. L. "Tomorrow's Workforce Today." *Industry Week,* Aug. 15, 1988, pp. 41–43.

Goodrow, B. A. "Limiting Factors in Reducing Participation in Older Adult Learning Opportunities." *Gerontologist,* Oct. 1975, *15* (5), 418-422.

Gordon, T. *Leader Effectiveness Training: L.E.T.: The No-Lose Way to Release the Productive Potential of People.* Ridgefield, Conn.: Wyden Books, 1977.

Greene, M. R. "The Effect of Pension Provisions on Employment of Older Persons." *CLU Journal,* 1980, *34*(3), 63–69.

Gustman, A. L., and Steinmeier, T. L. "The Effect of Partial Retirement on the Wage Profiles of Older Workers." *Industrial Relations,* 1985, *24* (2), 257-265.

Haber, L. D. "Age and Capacity Devaluation." *Journal of Health and Social Behavior,* 1970, *11* (3), 167–182.

Haberlandt, K. F. "Learning, Memory and Age." *Industrial Gerontology,* Fall 1973, pp. 20–37.

Haefner, J. E. "Race, Age, Sex, and Competence as Factors in Employer Selection of the Disadvantaged." *Journal of Applied Psychology,* 1977, *62* (2), 199-202.

Hagen, R. P. "Older Workers: How to Utilize This Valuable Resource." *Supervisory Management,* Nov. 1983, pp. 2–9.

Hedaa, L. " . . . or De-escalation? (That's a Euphemism for Demotion)." *Across the Board,* 1979, *16* (4), 23–25.

Heneman, H. G. "The Relationship Between Age and Motivation to Perform on the Job." *Industrial Gerontology,* Winter 1973, pp. 30–36.

Herzberg, F. "One More Time: How Do You Motivate Employees?" *Harvard Business Review,* Sept.-Oct. 1987, pp. 109–120.

Hoerr, J. "Go Team! The Payoff from Worker Participation." *Business Week,* July 10, 1989, pp. 56–59.

Humple, C. S., and Lyons, M. *Management and the Older Workforce: Policies and Programs.* New York: American Management Association, 1983.

Jackson, D. P. "The Management of Age in the Workforce." *Management Review,* Dec. 1978, pp. 50–56.

Jacobs, B. A. "Motivating the 'Plateaued' Manager." *Industry Week,* 1982, *215* (1), 21–22.

Jacobs, S. "Beyond the Twilight Years in the Executive Suite." *New England Business,* 1984, *6* (7), 24–26.

Kaminski, V. "Designing a Seminar for Managers of Older Workers." *Training and Development Journal,* July 1983a, pp. 36–39.

Kaminski, V. "New Personnel Specialty." *Personnel Administrator,* 1983b, *28* (8), 21–23.

Keane, J. G. "Our Aging Populace: Advertising Implications." *Journal of Advertising Research,* 1985, *24* (6), 10–12.

Kenny, T. "Getting the Best Out of the over Forties: From a Personnel Perspective." In C. L. Cooper and D. P. Torrington (eds.), *After Forty: The Time for Achievement?* New York: Wiley, 1981.

Keyfitz, N. "Technology, Employment, and the Succession of Generations." *Insurance: Mathematics & Economics* (Netherlands), 1984, *3* (4), 219–230.

Knowles, D. E. "Middle-Aged and Older Workers: An Industry Perspective." In S. F. Yolles, L. W. Krinsky, S. N. Kieffer, and P. A. Carone (eds.), *The Aging Employee.* New York: Human Sciences Press, 1984.

Knowles, M. *The Adult Learner: A Neglected Species.* (2nd ed.) Houston: Gulf Publishing, 1981.

Knox, A. B. *Adult Development and Learning: A Handbook on Individual Growth and Competence in the Adult Years.* San Francisco: Jossey-Bass, 1977.

Knox, A. B., and Sjogren, D. "Research on Adult Learning." *Adult Education,* 1965, *15* (3), 133–137.

LaBerge, R. "Unemployed and over Forty: The New Minority." *Labour Gazette* (Canada), 1977, *77* (2), 54–58.

Lipton, M. "An Unmentionable Personnel Problem of the 1980s." *Personnel,* 1979, *56* (5), 58–65.

Litwin, G. H. "Achievement Motivation and the Older Worker." In H. L. Sheppard (ed.), *Towards an Industrial Gerontology.* Cambridge, Mass.: Schenkman, 1970.

Maas, H. S., and Kuypers, J. A. *From Thirty to Seventy: A Forty-*

Year Longitudinal Study of Adult Life Styles and Personality. San Francisco: Jossey-Bass, 1974.

McCann, J. P. "Control Data's 'Staywell' Program." *Training and Development Journal,* Oct. 1981, pp. 39-43.

McClelland, D. C., and Winter, D. *Motivating Economic Achievement.* New York: Free Press, 1969.

McGregor, D. M. *The Human Side of Enterprise.* New York: McGraw-Hill, 1960.

Macleod, J. S. "Facing the Issue of Age Discrimination." *Employment Relations Today,* 1983, *10* (1), 57-62.

Macleod, J. S. "The Older Blue-Collar Worker in a White-Collar Environment." *Employment Relations Today,* Fall 1987, pp. 233-236.

McNeely, R. L., and Colen, J. N. (eds.). *Aging in Minority Groups.* Newbury Park, Calif.: Sage, 1983.

Miller, W. R. "Pharmaceuticals for the Elderly." *Vital Speeches,* 1986, *52* (13), 396-398.

"Millions of Older Workers Ready, Willing and Able." *AARP Bulletin,* 1990, *31* (3), 6.

Mogensen, A. H. "Work Simplification: A Program of Continuous Improvement." In H. B. Maynard (ed.), *Industrial Engineering Handbook.* (2nd ed.). New York: McGraw-Hill, 1963.

"More Firms Aid Workers Who Care for Older Relatives." *AARP Bulletin,* 1987, *28* (8), 1, 13.

Murray, J. R., Powers, E. A., and Havighurst, R. J. "Personal and Situational Factors Producing Flexible Careers." *The Gerontologist,* 1971, *11* (4), 4-12.

"Older Students: Quick Studies." *Modern Maturity.* Dec. 1989-Jan. 1990, *32* (6), 97.

Parnes, H. S. "Middle-Aged and Older Men in the Labor Force." *Aging,* Nov.-Dec. 1980, pp. 25-29.

Perham, J. "Big Surge in Age Bias Suits." *Dun's Business Month,* 1982, *120* (3), 56-62.

Peterson, D. A. *Facilitating Education for Older Learners.* San Francisco: Jossey-Bass, 1983.

Ramirez, A. "Making Better Use of Older Workers." *Fortune,* Jan. 30, 1989, pp. 179-187.

Rayburn, L. G. "Relationship Between Corporate Financial Performance and Executive Age." *Mid-South Business Journal,* 1983, *3* (1), 12-16.

Rhodes, S. R., Schuster, M., and Doering, M. "The Implications of an Aging Workforce." *Personnel Administrator,* 1981, *26* (10), 19-22.

Rix, S. E. "Rethinking Retirement-Age Policy in the United States and Canada." *Personnel Journal,* 1979, *58* (11), 780-788.

Rones, P. L. "Older Men: The Choice Between Work and Retirement." *Monthly Labor Review,* 1978, *101* (11), 3-10.

Rones, P. L.. and Herz, D. E. *Labor Market Problems of Older Workers.* Report of the Secretary of Labor. Washington, D.C.: U.S. Government Printing Office, 1989.

Root, N. "Injuries at Work Are Fewer Among Older Employees." *Monthly Labor Review,* 1981, *104* (3), 30-34.

Rosen, B. "Management Perceptions of Older Employees." *Monthly Labor Review,* 1978, *101* (5), 33-35.

Rosen, B., and Jerdee, T. H. "Too Old or Not Too Old." *Harvard Business Review,* Nov.-Dec. 1977, pp. 97-106.

Rosen, B., and Jerdee, T. H. "Influence of Employee Age, Sex, and Job Status on Managerial Recommendations for Retirement." *Academy of Management Journal,* 1979, *22* (1), 169-173.

Rosen, B., and Jerdee, T. H. "Helping Young Managers Bridge the Generation Gap." *Training,* Mar. 1985, pp. 43-51.

Rosen, B., Jerdee, T. H., and Lunn, R. O. "Effects of Performance Appraisal Format, Age, and Performance Level on Retirement Decisions." *Journal of Applied Psychology,* 1981, *66* (4), 515-519.

Rosow, J. M., and Zager, R. *The Future of Older Workers in America: New Options for an Extended Working Life.* Scarsdale, N.Y.: Work in America Institute, 1980.

Ross, E., "Effects of Challenging and Supportive Instructions on Verbal Learning in Older Persons." *Journal of Educational Psychology,* 1968, *59*(4), 261-266.

Rubenstein, C. "Wellness Is All." *Psychology Today,* Oct. 1982, pp. 29-37.

Schuster, M. H., Kaspin, J. A., and Miller, C. S. "The Age Discrimination in Employment Act: An Evaluation of Federal and State Enforcement, Employer Compliance, and Employee Characteristics." *A Final Report to the NRTA-AARP Andrus Foundation.*

Syracuse, N.Y.: Employment Studies Institute, School of Management, Syracuse University, 1987.

Schuster, M. H., and Miller, C. S. "Performance Evaluations as Evidence in ADEA Cases." *Employee Relations Law Journal,* 1981, *6*(4), 561–583.

Schuster, M. H., and Miller, C. S. "An Evaluation of the Impact of Age Discrimination in Employment Legislation." *A Final Report to the AARP Andrus Foundation.* Syracuse, N.Y. School of Management, Syracuse University, 1984.

Schuster, M. H., and Miller, C. S. "An Evaluation of the Impact of Age Discrimination in Employment Legislation." *Employment Studies Institute: A Final Report to the AARP Andrus Foundation.* Syracuse, N.Y.: School of Management, Syracuse University, 1986.

Sekiguchi, S. "How Japanese Business Treats Its Older Workers." *Management Review,* Oct. 1980, pp. 15–18.

Senge, P. M. "The Leader's New Work: Building Learning Organizations." *Sloan Management Review,* Fall 1990, pp. 7–23.

Shea, G. F. "Profiting From Wellness Training." *Training & Development Journal,* Oct. 1981, pp. 32–37.

Shea, G. F. "Payoffs from Self-Directed Work Teams." *Industry Forum,* Nov. 1989, pp. 1–3.

Shea, G. F. "What Is It Really Like to Work for a Japanese-Owned Company in America?" *Industry Forum,* Mar. 1991, pp. 1–4.

Sheppard, C. S., and Carroll, D. C. (eds.). *Working in the Twenty-First Century.* New York: Wiley, 1980.

Sheppard, H. L. (ed.). *Towards an Industrial Gerontology.* Cambridge, Mass.: Schenkman, 1970.

Sheppard, H. L. *New Perspectives on Older Workers: Studies in Employment and Unemployment.* Kalamazoo, Mich.: W. E. Upjohn Institute for Employment Research, 1971.

Sheppard, H. L. "The Relevance of Age to Worker Behavior in the Labor Market." *Industrial Gerontology.* Summer 1972, pp. 1-11.

Sherman, S. P. "The Mind of Jack Welch." *Fortune,* Mar. 27, 1989, 39–50.

Smith, J. M. "Age Differences in Achievement Motivation." *Social and Clinical Psychology,* 1970, *9* (2), 175–176.

Snyder, R. A., and Brandon, B. "Riding the Third Wave: Staying on Top of ADEA Complaints." *Personnel Administrator,* 1983, *28* (2), 41-47.

Sonnenfeld, J. "Dealing with the Aging Workforce." *Harvard Business Review,* 1978, *56* (6), 81-92.

Stackel, L. "Employment Relations Programs." *Employment Relations Today,* Spring, 1988, 72-76.

Stephens, R. "New Hurdles at Work: Technology, Rising Health Costs Hurt Older Workers." *AARP Bulletin,* 1989, *30* (11), 1, 4-5.

Stephens, R. "Turning Back the Clock?" *AARP Bulletin,* 1990, *31* (8), 10-11.

Taub, H. A., and Long, M. K. "The Effects of Practice on Short-Term Memory of Young and Old Subjects." *Journal of Gerontology,* 1972, *27* (4), 494-499.

Tavernier, G. "Decruitment: A Solution for Burned-Out Executives." *International Management* (United Kingdom), 1978, *33* (4), 44-47.

U.S. Department of Health and Human Services, National Institute on Aging. *Special Report on Aging 1982.* Washington, D.C.: U.S. Government Printing Office, 1982.

U.S. Department of Health, Education, and Welfare. *Readings in Psychotherapy with Older People.* Washington, D.C.: U.S. Government Printing Office, 1978.

U.S. Department of Labor. *Dictionary of Occupational Titles.* Washington, D.C.: U.S. Government Printing Office, 1991.

U.S. Senate Special Committee on Aging. *Aging America: Trends and Projections.* Washington, D.C.: U.S. Government Printing Office, 1984.

Verespej, M. A. "Senior Managers: Making Age an Asset." *Industry Week,* Feb. 1975, pp. 31-35.

Walker, J. W., and Lupton, D. E. "Performance Appraisal Programs and Age Discrimination Law." *Aging and Work,* Spring 1978, pp. 73-83.

Wall, J. L., and Shatshat, H. M. "Controversy over the Issue of Mandatory Retirement." *Personnel Administrator,* 1981, *26* (10), 25-28, 30, 45.

Walsh, D., and Lloyd, A. D. "Personnel Planning's New Agenda." *American Demographics,* 1984, *6*(9), 34-37, 51.

Watts, P. "Preretirement Planning: Making the Golden Years Rosy." *Personnel,* Mar. 1987, 32-39.

Weatherbee, H. Y. "The Older Employee: A Neglected Manpower Resource." *Personnel,* Jan.-Feb. 1969, pp. 31-36.

Webber, R. A. "Homogeneous Groups," *Academy of Management Journal,* 1974, *17* (3), 570-573.

Weiss, A. L. "Employing an Aging Work Force." *Business Age,* Aug. 1989, p. 38.

"When Retirement Doesn't Happen." *Business Week,* June 19, 1978, 72-89.

Winston, P. D. "Aging Workforce Presents Benefits Challenge: Study." *Business Insurance,* 1986, *20* (38), 68.

Yolles, S. F., Krinsky, L. W., Kieffer, S. N., and Carone, P. A. (eds.). *The Aging Employee.* New York: Human Sciences Press, 1984.

Youry, M. "GULHEMP: What Workers Can Do." *Manpower,* June 1975, pp. 4-9.

INDEX

A

Accidents, and older workers, 62, 131-133
Achievement: age for, 42-43; motivation for, 106-108, 111, 136
Adaptability, and obsolescence, 109-110
Adenauer, C., 43
Administrative Services Society, 40
Aerospace Corporation, casual employment at, 182
Aetna Life and Casualty, alternative work options at, 189
Age: and motivation, 104-105; as process, not disease, 37-38; and work teams, 140-143
Age discrimination: elements in, 117, 118-119; guidelines for avoiding, 121-124; legal aspects of, 207-219; reducing, and workforce changes, 191-192, 202; responses to, 155-158; study of, 134-135; survey on, 28-29
Age Discrimination in Employment Act (ADEA): and affirmative action, 145; aims of, 208; cooperative approach for, 218-219; coverage of, 10, 177; exceptions to, and defense, 209, 211-212; impact of, 34, 48-49; implications of, 212-214; litigants under, 214-215; and performance appraisal, 115, 117, 119, 121, 122, 123-124, 216; and productivity, 158, 166; provisions of, 210-211; winning cases under, 215-218
Age distortions, in workforce, 24-25
Ageism, and myths, 28-43
Ahammer, I. M., 143
Alpaugh, P. K., 110
Alternative work programs: aspects of, 180-189; examples of, 180-183; flexible, 187; sources of help for, 183-185; win-win options in, 185-189

American Association of Retired Persons (AARP), 43; Business Partnerships/Worker Equity department of, 184; and legal issues, 212–213, 214, 217; National Older Workers Information System (NOWIS) of, 184; surveys by, 15, 71, 87; Workforce Education Center at, 183–184
American Cancer Society, 83, 145–146
American Management Association, 117
Anderson, C. M., 99–100
Anderson, R. W., 103
Andrus Foundation, 87, 217
A. O. Smith, work teams at, 171
Arbitration, for age discrimination charges, 123
Arco, retiree relations at, 186
Arkansas, age discrimination case in, 117
Asset counseling, for motivation, 110–111
AT&T, giving up at, 155–156
Austria, discovery learning in, 98
Authority, structural and expert, 173. *See also* Leadership

B

Bakaly, C. G., 123, 211–212
Baltes, P. B., 143
Bankers Life: attendance records at, 63; voluntary retirement at, 156
Belbin, M., 89–90, 91, 97, 98
Benson, H., 75
Berlin, I., 43
Bernstein, A., 103
Birren, J. E., 110
Blocklyn, P. L., 65
Body parts replacement, 194
Boeing, work teams at, 171
Bolles, R. N., 161–163
Bona fide occupational qualification (BFOQ), 208, 209, 210
Brandon, B., 121, 122, 209, 213, 219
Brenner, P., 213
Brinley, J. F., 95
Bristol Myers Company, and gene replacement, 194
Buckholz v. *Symons Manufacturing Co.,* 119–120
Builders Emporium, job redesign at, 181
Burkhauser, R. V., 26
Bush administration, 212

C

California: age bias cases in, 214, 215; life-styles studied in, 34–35
Canestrari, R. E., 90
Capacity, devaluation of, and health, 47–49
Carone, P. A., 62, 130
Carter, J., 18
Catalyst, 187
Caterpillar, work teams at, 171
Causey, M., 20
Champion International, work teams at, 171
Change: coping with, 37; and learning, 91, 99–100; in workforce, 190–205
Cherrington, D. J., 36, 136
Chicago Title Insurance Company, job-sharing teams at, 181
Churchill, G., 136
Cognitive styles, and learning, 94–95
Cohen, D., 38, 73
Cohen, W., 75
Colburn, D., 9, 73, 75
Colen, J. N., 23
Combustion Engineering, retiree job bank of, 182
Commitment: by older workers, 69–70; and self-directed work teams, 172
Commonwealth Fund, 5, 15
Competitiveness, and workforce changes, 191, 197–198
Condie, S. J., 36, 136
Conference Board, 103, 180
Confrontation, for productivity, 157–158, 159, 167

Consistency and fairness defense, 212
Constandse, W. J., 137
Continental Illinois Bank and Trust, retirees employed at, 182
Contributions: by older workers, 67-69; public, 13
Control Data Corporation, and wellness program, 78, 80, 81
Cook, D. D., 104
Cooper, C. L., 9
Cooper, K. J., 213, 215, 217
Copperman, L. F., 23, 85
Corning Glass Works: discovery learning and, 98; Senior Associates at, 181
Coser, R. L., 31
Costa, P., 76-77
Counseling: on assets, 110-111; on health, 55; for productivity, 159; by supervisors, 112
Court decisions, on age discrimination, 117, 119-120, 122, 209, 212. *See also* Legal issues
Covey, H. C., 95
Creativity, in older workers, 68-69, 110, 120
Credibility, in legal cases, 216-217
Crooks, H., 43
Cummins Engine, work teams at, 171
Curtailment, reversing personal, 13
Cutter Laboratories, and age bias case, 216

D

Dalton, G. W., 88-89, 105-106, 109-110, 157
Days Inn: and older workers, 107; Senior Power National Job Fairs of, 184
Deadwood, and productivity, 162
deBernardo, M., 215
Decline, expectations of, 64-67
Decremental theory of aging, 65
de Gaulle, C., 43
DeMicco, F. J., 69-70, 107
Demographic trends: aspects of, 16-27; background on, 16-18; and early retirement and workplace conflict, 18-22; implications of, 27; and labor market changes, 22-25; and workforce changes, 18-19; and workplace participation, 25-26
Denmark: ageism internalized in, 30-31; demotion in, 160-161
Detouring response, 156-157
Deutsch, Shea and Evans, 63
Digital Equipment, work teams at, 171
Disability: and health, 47-48, 49-51; and retirement, 49
Discovery Method, for living, 91, 97-100
Discrimination. *See* Age discrimination
Diseases, chronic: impact of, 38, 49, 72-73; and work teams, 145-146
Disparate treatment and impact, proving, 208
Dispenzieri, A., 65, 104
Doering, M., 87, 104
Drucker, P. F., 12
Drugs, psychotherapeutic, 57, 194-195
Dubé, L. E., 118
Dubin, S., 64, 106, 108
Duggan, J. E., 196
Duke University, longitudinal study by, 73
Dychtwald, K., 41, 186
Dyer, W. G., 139

E

Early-retirement incentive plans (ERIPs), impact of, 21
Education. *See* Learning
EEOC v. *Commissioner of Pennsylvania,* 209
EEOC v. *Home Insurance Co.,* 212
EEOC v. *KDM School Bus Co.,* 209
Einstein, A., 204
Eisdorfer, C., 38, 73
Eisenberg, J., 65, 104
Elbing, A. O., 145

Elder care, issue of, 78
England, J. L., 36, 136
Enna, S., 182
Equal Employment Opportunity Commission (EEOC), and legal issues, 209-215
Ethnic differences, in learning, 96
Expectancy theory, and motivation, 106, 108
Exxon, and discovery learning, 98

F

Fairness and consistency defense, 212
Faley, R. H., 208
Fallcreek, S., 38
Fay, R. C., 216
Fear of success, 121
Feedback, in supervision, 138
Fields, J., 66
Fifty, as turning point, 10-11
Flower, J., 41, 186
Floyd, H. A., 156, 158
Fonda, J., 9
Ford, H., 175
Ford, N., 136
Ford Motor Company, work teams at, 171
Freedberg, S. P., 213, 214, 216-217, 219
French, J., 119

G

Gadon, H., 145
Gender differences, in learning, 95-96
Gene replacement therapy, 194
General Electric (GE), self-directed work teams at, 170-172
General Foods, wellness program of, 80
General Motors: performance appraisal at, 119; work teams at, 171
Generational differences: and early retirement, 18-22; in learning, 94; recognizing, 135; and work teams, 143-144
Genetic code, cracking, 193
George Washington University, study at, 21
Getting even response, 157
Gill v. *Union Carbide, Inc.*, 119
Giniger, S., 65, 104
Ginsburg, H., 15, 185, 186
Gist, M., 108
Giving up response, 155-156
Goddard, R. W., 112-113, 153, 166-167, 181-182
Goldstein, M. L., 16, 205
Good cause exception, 209, 211
Goodrow, B. A., 88
Gordon, J. R., 145
Gordon, T., 159
Gramm-Rudman policies, 22
Greene, M. R., 25
Grossman, J. M., 123, 211-212
Growth hormone uses, 193-194
Grumman Corporation: age of workforce at, 42; and motivation, 104; retiree job bank of, 182, 183
GULHEMP, applying, 53-56
Gustman, A. L., 25

H

Haber, L. D., 47-48
Haberlandt, K. F., 90
Haefner, J. E., 134
Hagen, R. P., 67, 133-134
Hall, J., 81
Handicapped employees: issue of, 78; and work teams, 145-146
Havighurst, R. J., 95
Health and wellness: addressing issues of, 44-57; background on, 44-45; and capacity devaluation, 47-49; and disability, 47-48, 49-51; future of, 57; and heredity, 52-53; and intellectual decline, 51-52; perceptions of, 72-74; and retirement, 50-51; testing, 53-56; work as contribution to, 45-47,

56, 192, 202–204. *See also* Wellness programs
Health risk profiles, developing, 81
Hedaa, L., 160
Heneman, H. G., 106
Heredity: impact of, 52–53; understanding, 193
Herz, D. E., 7, 17, 19*n*
Herzberg, F., 159
Heublein, and age-bias case, 214
Hoerr, J., 171
Holographic approach, to learning, 175–176
Human genome project, 193
Humple, C. S., 117, 121, 123

I

I. Magnin, and age-bias case, 215, 219
Illinois, age discrimination study in, 134–135
Industrial Health Counseling Service, 55
Information management, 12
Instron, coaching at, 181
Intellectual capacity, and health, 51–52

J

Jackson, D. P., 219
Jacobs, B. A., 155–156, 164
Jacobs, S., 63–64
Japan: and learning organization, 176; work teams in, 140
Jerdee, T. H., 29, 131, 137–138
Jobs: attitudes toward, myths on, 40–42; descriptions of, and performance appraisals, 118; fitness requirements of, 54–55; sharing, 181–182, 188. *See also* Work
John Deere Corporation, partial retirement from, 185
Johnson & Johnson: and motivation, 104; wellness program of, 80
Jovick, T. J., 95
Jung, C., 120

K

Kaminski, V., 26, 149
Kaspin, J. A., 214, 215, 217
Keane, J. G., 23
Keast, F. D., 23, 85
Kelly Services, Encore program of, 182
Kenny, T., 147
Kentucky Fried Chicken Corporation, older workers at, 107
Keyfitz, N., 86, 197–198
Kieffer, S. N., 62, 130
Kimberly-Clark, wellness program at, 80
Kirk, R., 214
Kleiman, L. S., 208
Klipper, M. Z., 75
Knowledge workers, 11
Knowles, D. E., 29, 183
Knowles, M., 93
Knox, A. B., 32, 92
Koyl, L., 53
Krinsky, L. W., 62, 130
Kuypers, J. A., 35

L

LaBerge, R., 31
Labor force. *See* Workforce
Lawrence Livermore National Laboratory, training at, 149
Leadership: by older workers, 63–64; situational, 172, 174–175; techniques for, 177–178. *See also* Supervision
Learning: aspects of, 85–100; background on, 85–86; contributions to, 95; design issues for, 94–96; Discovery Method for, 91, 97–100; generational differences in, 94; holographic approach to, 175–176; lifelong, 12, 87–88, 111; as management issues, 86–87; obstacles to, 87–89; by older people, 89–90; on-the-job, 111; organizational, 175–177; participative techniques for, 93–94; and relevancy, 91; self-paced, 90–91;

styles of, and productivity, 90–94; teaching principles for, 93–94, 96–97
Learning curve, and productivity, 11–12
Leaving response, 156
Legal issues: aspects of, 207–219; background on, 207–209; cooperative approach for, 218–219; of exceptions and their defense, 209, 211–212; implications of, 212–214; and litigants, 214–215; winning cases on, 215–218
Leisure classes, public contribution by, 13
Lengnick-Hall, M., 208
Life-span, increasing, 22–23, 192–193
Lifelong learning: interest in, 12, 87–88; and obsolescence, 111
Lindberg, E., 183
Lipton, M., 145
Litwin, G. H., 111
Lloyd, A. D., 24, 187
Loft, D., 183
Long, M. K., 89, 92
LTV Electronics, and discovery learning, 98
LTV Steel, work teams at, 171
Lupton, D. E., 117
Lyons, M., 117, 121, 123

M

Maas, H. S., 35
McCann, J. P., 80, 81
McClelland, D. C., 108
McClintock, B., 43
McConnell, J., 64, 106, 108
McCrae, R. R., 76–77
McDonald's Corporation, McMasters Program of, 182
McFarland, R., 66–67
McGregor, D. M., 168
Mackaronis, C., 213
McLaughlin, A., 7
McLaughlin, L. M., 95
Macleod, J. S., 31, 163, 164–165
McNeely, R. L., 23
Maguire, G. L., 63
Maine Employment Security Commission, 55
Managers: challenge of older workers to, 7–9; learning issues for, 86–87; learning program role of, 96; and performance appraisals, 114–116, 121–122; and supervisory leadership, 125–205. *See also* Supervisors
Manpower Administration, 55
Manpower, Inc., and senior workers, 182–183
Massachusetts Institute of Technology (MIT), auto plants study by, 171
Maturity, in older workers, 67–68
Medical College of Wisconsin, and growth hormone study, 193
Medical revolution, and workforce changes, 190–191, 192–195
Medicare, 26
Memorization, for older learners, 92
Men, older, in workforce, 23
Mentoring: in boundaryless organizations, 174–175; by older workers, 67
Mettler, M., 38
Mid-career crisis: and organizational rigidity, 200–201; and supervision, 136–137
Miles, Inc., and age-bias case, 216–217
Miller, C. S., 117, 119, 214, 215, 216, 217
Miller, W. R., 83–84, 193, 194, 195
Minority groups: aging of, 23; and work teams, 145
Mogensen, A. H., 199
Morale, concept of, 101. *See also* Motivation
Morrison, M., 21
Motivation: for achievement, 106–108, 111, 136; and age, 104–105; aspects of, 101–113; background on, 101–102; concept of, 101; keys to, 102–103; negative spiral of, 105–106; and obsolescence, 108–110, 111; paradox of, 103–

104; as personal, 102–103, 112–113; and productivity, 159; stimulating, 110–112; supervision for, 135–137
MS International, and older workers, 183
Murray, J. R., 95
Myths about older employees: aspects of, 28–43; background on, 28–29; cultural, 29–40; implications of, 30–32; on job attitudes and performance, 40–42

N

National Center for Health Statistics, 74
National Commission on Aging, 121
National Council on Aging, 30, 55, 183
National Health Interview Survey, 74
National Institute on Aging, 66, 76
New York, age discrimination cases in, 209, 212
Nimodipine, 57
Nissan USA: as learning organization, 176; wellness program of, 82
Norway, gradual retirement in, 185

O

Obsolescence, and motivation, 108–110, 111
Occupational Safety and Health Act, 55
Old-old group: increasing, 23; leadership by, 63–64
Older employees: and accidents, 62, 131–133; biases internalized by, 30–31, 47–48; in boundaryless organizations, 174; calm and stability for, 38–39; as challenge to management, 7–9; changing views of, 3–15; concept of, 9–11; contributions by, 67–69; cost of underutilizing, 26; crossovers for, 201–202; and demographic trends, 16–27; as different, 8, 34–35; and expectation of decline, 64–67; importance of, 9; leadership by, 63–64; legal aspects of working with, 207–219; loss and disengagement for, 32; myths about, 28–43; needs of, 35–36, 104–105, 135–136; new views needed for, 11–13; and organizational success, 59–124; participation and self-actualization by, 32; plight of, 6–7; potential of, 61–70; problem of, 4–7; productivity of, 61–63, 69–70, 153, 167; as resource, 5–7, 14–15; revolution regarding, 13–15; self-devaluation by, 30–31, 47–48; and supervisory leadership, 125–205; work team contributions of, 146–147
Organic brain syndrome (OBS), chronic and acute, 52
Organization for Economic Cooperation and Development, 98
Organization Resource Counselors, 219
Organizations: aspects of success in, 59–124; boundaryless, 172–175; changing structures of, 12; encouragement from, and workforce changes, 191, 199–202; health and wellness programs in, 71–84; learning by, 175–177; motivation and morale in, 101–113; performance appraisals in, 114–124; and potential of older workers, 61–70; supervisory leadership for, 125–205; training and education by, 85–100

P

Pan American World Airways, and age-bias case, 214
Pareto principle, 134
Parnes, H. S., 77
Participation: in learning, techniques for, 93–94; and self-

actualization, 32; in workforce, and demographic trends, 23, 24, 25-26
Past, attention to, 36-37
Peer support, and wellness programs, 83
Pennsylvania: age discrimination case in, 209; group work research at, 140
Pepper, C., 43
Performance: achieving maximum, 169-179; background on, 169-170; leadership for, 177-179; myths on, 40-42; and workplace developments, 170-177
Performance appraisals: age-fair, 114-124; creating climate for, 124; guidelines for, 115-116, 121-124; and legal issues, 216; by managers and supervisors, 114-116, 118, 120-122; for motivation, 112; systems for, 117-120
Perham, J., 119
Personality traits, development of, 39-40
Peterson, D. A., 32
Polaris missile program, task forces and networking for, 173
Polaroid: flexible work alternatives at, 182; and older workers, 104; voluntary retirement at, 156
Portland, Maine, health counseling at, 55
Portland Unemployment Security Office, 55
Powers, E. A., 95
Practice, in learning, 92
Price, R. L., 105-106, 109-110
Problem solving, for productivity, 160
Procter & Gamble, work teams at, 171
Productivity: aspects of increasing, 152-168; background on, 152-154; concept of, 61; crisis of, 17; escaping crunch of, 163-165; guidelines for, 165-166, 167; individual responsibility for, 161-163; joint venture for, 158-161; and learning curve, 11-12; and learning styles, 90-94; of older workers, 61-63, 69-70, 153, 167; problem of, 154-155; and responses to discrimination, 155-158; supervisory actions for, 165-168
Promotions, and ageism, 31
Protirement, view of, 17
Prudential Insurance, wellness program of, 80
Public policy, and workforce changes, 191, 195-197

R

Ramirez, A., 21, 180-181, 182
Rayburn, L. G., 40
Reid, R. D., 69-70, 107
Relaxation response, 75, 81-82
Renner, V. J., 110
Responsibility, by older workers, 13
Retirement: costs of, by ages, 21-22; and disability, 49; and educational level, 31; early, to make way for youth, 32-34; early, and workplace conflict, 18-22; extent of, 5; gradual, 184-185, 187; and health, 50-51; interest in, 40-41
Retirement-on-the-job (ROTJ) syndrome, and productivity, 152, 154, 155, 157, 159, 163-167
Rhodes, S. R., 87, 104
Right-sizing, 173
Rix, S. E., 66
Robbins, L., 81
Rones, P. L., 7, 17, 19*n*, 50, 184-185
Root, N., 62, 131-133
Rosen, B., 28-29, 108, 131, 137-138
Rosow, J. M., 39-40, 86, 92, 199-200
Ross, E., 89
Rubenstein, C., 72, 73, 74
Rudman, D., 193

S

Sabbaticals, for motivation, 111-112

SAGA Corporation, and motivation, 104
Sanders, H., 107
Sape, G. P., 219
Schuster, M., 87, 104
Schuster, M. H., 117, 119, 214, 215, 216, 217
Schwoerer, C., 108
Sekiguchi, S., 146
Self-actualization, and participation, 32
Self-investment, and workforce changes, 12, 191, 198-199
Self-management, 13
Senge, P. M., 175-176
Senility, extent of, 51-52
Seniority, and work teams, 144
Seniority system defense, 212
Sentry Insurance, wellness program at, 80
Shatshat, H. M., 63
Shea, G. F., 80-81, 136, 170, 172, 176
Shelton, H., 64, 106, 108
Sheppard, H. L., 56, 89-90, 91, 156
Sherman, S. P., 172
Sixty-five, as retirement age, 10
Sjogren, D., 92
Skills, and obsolescence, 108-109
Sloan, A., 175
Small Business Administration, 20
Smith, J. M., 136
Smith, work teams at, 171
Snyder, R. A., 121, 122, 209, 213, 219
Social Security: as call on wealth, 5, 21; changing, impact of, 196; and demographic trends, 17, 18, 19, 23, 25, 26; in life plan, 41, 50, 183
Social Security Act of 1935, 10
Social Security Administration, 18, 47, 49
Sonnenfeld, J., 64
Sprague, R., 43
Stackel, L., 183
Standard Oil Company of California, and age-bias case, 214
Status, and work teams, 145
Steinmeier, T. L., 25
Stephens, R., 15, 26, 43, 71, 193-194
Sterile Design, minishifts at, 182
Stovall, J., 43
Stress: managing, 81-82; and productivity, 163; and wellness programs, 75-77
Stringfellow v. *Monsanto Co.*, 117
Sun Oil, retiree relations at, 186
Supervision: of alternative work programs, 180-189; aspects of, 125-205; and ensuring job success, 127-138; and informal groups, 149; for motivation, 135-137; and paradox of special groups, 128; perception issues in, 133-135; for performance, 169-179; and productivity, 152-168; responsibilities in, 128-129; for safety in workplace, 131-133; of work teams, 139-151; and workforce changes, 190-205
Supervisors: counseling by, for motivation, 112; as critical link, 130-131; learning program role of, 96; and performance appraisals, 118, 120-121; and productivity, 165-168; support from, 160-161; young, 137-138. *See also* Managers
Sweden: discovery learning in, 98; gradual retirement in, 185, 186
Synthesis, by older workers, 36-37, 68
Syracuse University, and study of EEOC complaints, 214-218

T

Taub, H. A., 89, 92
Tavernier, G., 30-31
Teaching, principles of, 93-94, 96-97. *See also* Learning
Teamwork. *See* Work teams
Tektronix, work teams at, 171
Tennessee, age discrimination case in, 119
Terminal illnesses, issue of, 77-78

Testing: for health and wellness, 53–56; for older learners, 92–93
Texas Refinery Corporation, part-time salespeople at, 181–182
Thompson, P. H., 88–89, 105–106, 109–110, 157
3M, and wellness programs, 78
Torrington, D. P., 9
Training, for work teams, 149–151. *See also* Learning
Travelers Insurance: job-sharing at, 182, 188; and older workers, 104; retiree relations at, 186; Unretired Program of, 184
Turner, J. A., 26

U

United Kingdom: disabilities in, 48; discovery learning in, 98
U.S. Bureau of Labor Statistics, 23, 24, 62, 131, 196
U.S. Bureau of the Census, 18, 23
U.S. Chamber of Commerce, 215
U.S. Department of Defense, 20
U.S. Department of Health and Human Services, 66, 76
U.S. Department of Health, Education, and Welfare, 38
U.S. Department of Labor, 54, 55
U.S. House Select Committee on Aging, 123
U.S. Senate: Governmental Affairs Committee of, 20; Special Committee on Aging of, 41, 74, 216

V

Values, work, and age, 36
Varian Associates, retirement transition program of, 180–181
Verespej, M. A., 63

W

Walker, J. W., 117
Walker, O., 136
Wall, J. L., 63
Walsh, D., 24, 187
Walt Disney Company, retired employees at, 184
Watson, T., Sr., 175
Watts, P., 183
Wealth, goods and services as, 5
Weatherbee, H. Y., 120–121, 157
Webber, R. A., 140–141
Weiss, A. L., 184
Wellness programs: aspects of, 71–84; background on, 71–72; comprehensive, 82–83; costs and, 83–84; democratization of, 82; designing, 81–83; issues for, 77–78; premises of, 78–81; and stress, 75–77; and taking charge, 74–75. *See also* Health and wellness
Wells Fargo Bank: retiree job bank of, 182; sabbatical program of, 181
Wichita University, older students at, 88
Winston, P. D., 26
Winter, D., 108
Wisconsin, age discrimination cases in, 120, 217–218
Wisdom, need for, 12–13
Women: labor force participation by, 24; and work teams, 145
Wood, G., 9
Work: alternative programs for, 180–189; concept of, 45; as healthy force, 45–47, 56, 192, 202–204; views of, 203–204. *See also* Jobs
Work in America Institute, 39
Work-out approach, 173
Work teams: and age, 140–143; aspects of, 139–151; background on, 139–140; balanced, 147; conflict sources for, 143–146; contributions of older workers to, 146–147; informal, 148–149; obstacles to, 142–143; processing of behavior in, 151; self-directed, 170–172; training for, 149–151
Workforce: age discrimination reduction in, 191–192, 202; changes in, 190–205; competitiveness in, 191, 197–198; demo-

graphic changes in, 18–19; increasing, 24; and labor market changes, 22–25; and medical revolution, 190–191, 192–195; new realities in, 204–205; and organizational encouragement, 191, 199–202; and public policy, 191, 195–197; and self-investment, 12, 191, 198–199; themes of, 190–192; and work as healthy force, 192, 202–204
Workplace: aspects of revolution in, 1–57; changing views in, 3–15; conflict in, and early retirement, 18–22; and demographic trends, 16–27; health and wellness issues in, 44–57; myths in, 28–43; participation in, 25–26; and performance, 170–177; safety in, 131–133

X

Xerox, wellness program of, 80

Y

Yolles, S. F., 62, 130
Youry, M., 53, 54, 55
Youth: bias for, 109; blocking advancement of, 144–145; decreasing numbers of, 24; and early retirement issues, 18–22, 32–34; focus on, 3–4; and productivity problems, 154; as supervisors, 137–138; in work groups, 141–142

Z

Zager, R., 39–40, 86, 92, 199–200
Zellner, W., 103

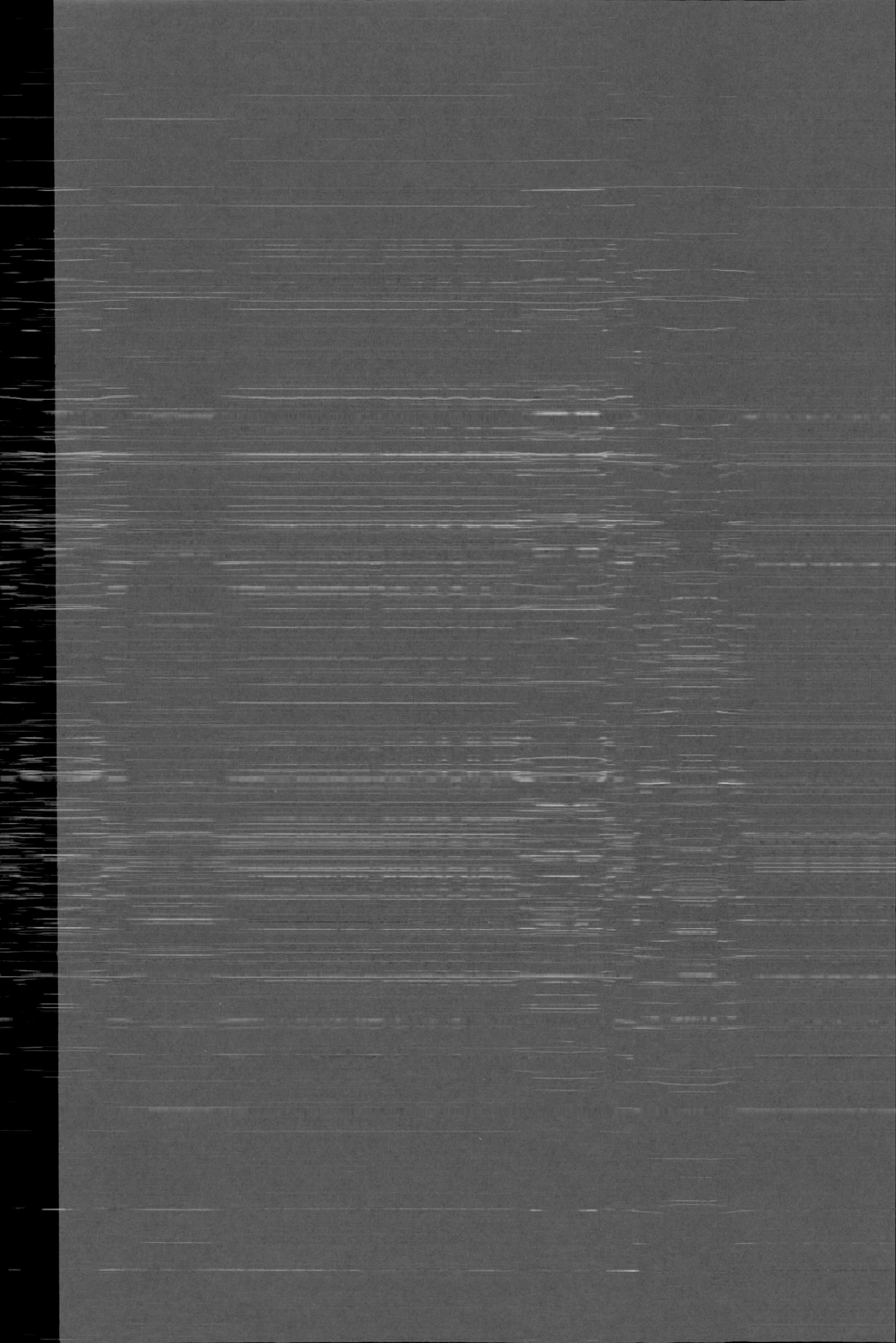